CW00348308

ENDURING PASSION

The Mercedes Simplex 40PS from 1902

Published in 2005 by
John Wiley & Sons, Ltd,
The Atrium, Southern Gate
Chichester, West Sussex,
PO19 8SQ, England
Phone (+44) 1243 779777

Email (for orders and customer service enquires):
cs-books@wiley.co.uk
Visit our Home Page on www.wiley.co.uk or
www.wiley.com

Other Wiley Editorial Offices

John Wiley & Sons, Inc. 111 River Street, Hoboken,
NJ 07030, USA

Jossey-Bass, 989 Market Street, San Francisco,
CA 94103-1741, USA

Wiley-VCH Verlag GmbH, Boschstr. 12, D-69469
Weinheim, Germany

John Wiley & Sons Australia, Ltd, 42 McDougall
Street, Milton, Queensland 4064, Australia

John Wiley & Sons (Asia) Pte Ltd, 2 Clementi Loop
#02-01, Jin Xing Distripark, Singapore 129809

John Wiley & Sons Canada Ltd, 22 Worcester Road,
Etobicoke, Ontario, Canada, M9W 1L1

Wiley also publishes its books in a variety of electronic formats. Some content that appears in print
may not be available in electronic books.

ISBN-10 0-470-01802-X
ISBN-13 978-0-470-01802-6

Cover and book design: Warren Dean Bonett
Printed and bound in Italy by Conti Tipocolor

ENDURING PASSION

THE STORY OF THE MERCEDES-BENZ BRAND LESLIE BUTTERFIELD

John Wiley & Sons, Ltd

Leslie Butterfield and his father, Southampton Water, 1961

Leslie John Butterfield renovating his 1929 Austin Seven Mulliner coupé

To my father, Leslie John Butterfield (1900–1983), an engineer who loved cars. He would have been proud of this story.

CONTENTS

Writing this book has been a voyage of discovery — one that has lasted over two years. My own involvement with the Mercedes-Benz brand goes back some years before that — to 1996. But if I thought I knew the brand before setting out on this journey, I know better now.

It's a journey that has taken me and my colleagues around the world and through the doors of 30 different offices in 10 different cities.

It all began with a phone call in December 2002. In my role as consultant to DaimlerChrysler, I had completed an extensive and provocative review of the Mercedes-Benz brand. J Justus Schneider, Director of Global Marketing Communications for Mercedes-Benz, called me to discuss some of the issues I had raised in my presentation, and his own reflections about the unique strengths of the brand. He wondered whether we should create a permanent record of the Mercedes-Benz brand at this crucial point in its history. As we discussed the idea, the concept grew and the idea became a reality.

Thus it is to J Justus Schneider that I owe my first and perhaps greatest debt of gratitude. It was his insight and inspiration that started this voyage. have valued his support, input and contribution throughout and it is thanks to him, and to DaimlerChrysler, that I have been afforded unique access to the highest echelons of the company and its friends around the world.

ACKNOWLEDGEMENTS

On our voyage, there has been a third person who has helped us navigate the world of Mercedes-Benz. Sarah Heard has been my colleague for many years — but never have her skills been more appreciated than in this particular venture. Whether in terms of developing the thinking about the brand, or in managing the process of producing the book, or in sharing the workload of interviews, her input has been invaluable.

So where did our interview journey take us? These are the key people to whom I am most indebted: Dr Eckhard Cordes, Professor Jürgen Hubbert, Dr Joachim Schmidt, Dr Hans-Joachim Schöpf, Dr Dieter Zetsche and Helmut Petri — all current or recent board members of DaimlerChrysler and generous with their time and insights. Special thanks to Hilmar Kopper and Professor Werner Breitschwerdt for their unique perspectives on the brand and the company over the last two decades. For their insights from the world of design I am particularly grateful to Bruno Sacco, Peter Pfeiffer and Stefan Sielaff.

For their support with all aspects of company history, I am most grateful to Dr Harry Niemann, Dieter Landenberger, Max-Gerrit von Pein, Wolfgang Rabus and Stanislav Peschel. For research background and insights I want to thank Rainer Valentin and Mathias Töpel. Valuable additional perspectives on the brand today — and the company historically — came from Wolfgang Presinger and Helmut Werner.

Thanks are also due to Erich Klemm for his important perspective from the 'shop floor', and to Hans-Georg Brehm, guardian of the brand for many years until his retirement in October 2004.

From outside the company, but giving their unique perspectives on the brand, I am especially indebted to Wolfgang Reitzle (former head of R & D at BMW), Konstantin Jacoby (Springer & Jacoby advertising), Andre Kemper (ex Springer & Jacoby), Ron Dennis (McLaren) and Alex Gellert (Merkley Newman Harty advertising). Hans-Georg Appenzeller, Otto Emil Daul and Manfred Merkel (Automobilgesellschaft Schoemperlen & Gast) gave me a terrific insight into dealer views of the Mercedes-Benz brand.

David E Davis, Fritz B Busch and Beverley Rae Kimes all gave me a powerful journalistic perspective. For their help in giving me a global picture of the Mercedes-Benz brand, I want to thank Marco Colnaghi (Colnaghi Manciani), James Moffatt (Sonnenberg Murphy Leo Burnett), Glan Ryan (Clemenger BBDO), Shinji Kanno (Dentsu) and Rod Pullen (Batey). For their support with sourcing photographic material: Maria Feifel, Norbert Herrlinger, Stefan Schuster and Jasmin Schwarzinger.

A whole host of people have worked hard behind the scenes to bring this book to fruition. Particularly, I want to thank Annette Maier, Tanja Hinner and Simone Lacher for their project management support in Stuttgart and Lorna Fray for her similar support in London. Special thanks to all the

team at John Wiley & Sons in the UK, and also to Ellen Alpsten, Amy Cohen and Roz Elwes.

In the UK I want particularly to thank Nicola Jackson and Hannah Adcock who typed and retyped the innumerable drafts of the manuscript. Also my colleagues at the Ingram Partnership, who supported me in this venture in every way. A personal thank you to all the staff at the Rising Sun Hotel in Lynmouth, where I spent many weeks in 2003 compiling the early drafts, and to my partner Penny Harris for her unstinting support during the many long months of writing and rewriting. Her patience was extraordinary.

Finally, my thanks go to Giorgio Armani, whom I had the privilege of interviewing, and who then agreed to write the foreword to this book.

Leslie Butterfield
London, June 2005

As a young man growing up in Italy, there were many beautiful cars that we admired: Porsche, Jaguar, Alfa Romeo and Bentley all come to mind. But for me Mercedes-Benz was always the one that stood slightly above the others; in many ways it was *the* car.

Although I'm a patriot at heart, when it came to choosing a car for myself, I chose a Mercedes-Benz. That was a long time ago, but I still own a Mercedes-Benz today. And I still have some of the same feelings about the brand now as I did then. The cars have a certain solidity about them, but it's matched with attention to detail and a lack of extravagance in their design. In this respect there

are parallels with my own brand: glamorous but elegant, without going to extremes.

And there are parallels too, I think, in our *attitude* to our brands. It has always been important to me not to over-inflate or overexpose my brand. It's essential to know what people want, of course — but it's also important to know when not to do something that might be at odds with the brand. To sacrifice, in other words, for the sake of the long term.

I see the Mercedes-Benz brand facing up to some of these challenges too — and learning from its past experience how to tackle them.

That's why a book such as this is important: to capture and record some of the lessons of the

past, to clarify some of the opportunities that face the brand today and to suggest a way forward in the future. This book does all of this: it tells an honest story of a remarkable brand with vigour, intelligence and insight. I commend it to you.

Giorgio Armani
Giorgio Armani
Milan, May 2005

Cars by Andy Warhol. Commissioned by Mercedes-Benz for the centennial celebrations in 1986 and featuring the W125 Grand Prix car

Brands have fascinated me since I was a child, although I didn't use the expression 'brand' then, nor did I realise the source of that fascination until much later in life. It was my grandfather who told me about the original Fabergé jewellery made in Moscow during Tsar Alexander III's reign. I had asked him about his tiepin — a dark shimmering owl head with burning red eyes. It was the way he spoke about its specialness and uniqueness that promised much more than just the ability to hold a tie in place. Everything he said seemed to set Fabergé apart from any other purveyor of jewellery.

Years later, when I developed a professional interest in brands, I realised what I had experienced as a boy was in fact the power of a brand: the aura of absolute specialness, something that nobody could copy and something that made you want to own it, for reasons way beyond its physical properties. Brands intertwine with our everyday existence,

giving meaning to events, moments or periods in our lives. They have deep roots, getting passed on from generation to generation. Many brands we use or admire today have such long histories, yet the chances are they will be used or admired by our children too.

This book tells the story of just such a brand: Mercedes-Benz. It has deep roots, having been passed down through the generations for about 120 years. But it has something else: ubiquity. This is a brand that is present in almost every country in the world and — uniquely — in just about every form of motorised transport, from road sweepers to limousines. Yet Mercedes-Benz somehow manages to marry this ubiquity to an extraordinary reputation for prestige. It brings together scale and intimacy in a way that few other brands can.

The Mercedes-Benz brand is also an enigma. It combines authenticity — Daimler and Benz invented the car — with leadership. A kind of leadership that

is broader and more holistic than just technological leadership. This duality, sometimes even contradiction, has characterised the brand since its early days. And this book sets out to get to the heart of that duality, understanding its origins, how it has evolved, where that enigmatic quality has come from and what it means today.

Of course, there have been many books written about Mercedes-Benz: stories about key individuals, racing successes, famous models and company histories. This book is none of these. It is a book about the Mercedes-Benz *brand*: the living, evolving, total character that we all interact with. Interestingly, very few books have been written about *any* brand covering such a broad remit. In telling this story, it may offer new ways of thinking about brands, new ways of understanding how brands evolve and respond to changing circumstances. So this book has broader relevance, to the business world as well as to aficionados of the global car industry.

The 300SL coupé Gullwing,
produced from 1954–1957

It was a natural choice to embark on this book with Leslie Butterfield, my sparring partner on Mercedes-Benz strategy, and critical advisor. He has worked with my colleagues in Stuttgart for many years, and with Mercedes-Benz in the UK, as well as in the international Mercedes-Benz arena. Whatever the project or task, we would always return to discussing the brand: the combination of product, values and associations, and this was the reason for a book about the brand.

It's a book that should appeal to anybody who is working for Mercedes-Benz, aspiring to own a 'Merc' or 'Benz', already driving one, or simply interested in great brands. It analyses how the brand

that we perceive today as one integral brand was actually forged out of two quite different, even competing, car companies. It covers an intriguing and rich brand history with highs and lows and highs again. It explains the different values of the brand brought to the fore by key individuals and which of those values truly govern today's thinking. It looks at the internal and external forces that have shaped the brand over some 120 years.

But it is not simply trying to glorify Mercedes-Benz. As was brilliantly expressed by the former Wimbledon Champion Boris Becker (also a long-time friend of Mercedes-Benz): 'I have learnt more from my failings than from my successes.' It is with this

attitude that people responsible for the business in Stuttgart have over many years analysed and addressed the brand's strengths, as well as its weaknesses, to stay true to their ambition of defining the future of the automobile. Hence this book also looks at events or periods of the brand's history that have been less successful or which eventually led to significant changes in strategy. It tries to learn from the mistakes lesser brands would have been eager to forget.

It is in the nature of reflecting upon decisive moments that this book will either find wholehearted support or generate intensive debate. Leslie Butterfield has not shied away from pointing out these moments nor from asking difficult questions.

In my view it is this ability to constantly question and subsequently adjust our strategies, while at the same time trying to understand what makes a Mercedes-Benz a true Mercedes-Benz, that enables us, the people working for and with this unique brand, to stay true to what we are best at *and* what customers can rightfully expect from us.

In essence, I see the Mercedes-Benz brand today as having arrived at a critical juncture, some would say a watershed. The choices we make over the next few years will be fundamental to determining where the story goes from here. The brand has endured enormous upheavals in its past but none may be as great as the competitive threats it faces today. Mercedes-Benz is poised between the potential for continued growth and competitive eclipse. At such a moment, it is important to capture how the brand got to where it is now, to help today's managers define where it should go tomorrow. For that reason the sometimes controversial conclusions in this book should find our endorsement. I believe where this book is critical it is for good reason and in the best interest of the brand that we all love.

Ultimately the brand will prosper if it keeps learning the lessons of its history. The strength of Mercedes-Benz today is a tribute to the generations of former employees who have forged this remarkable brand. The future may hold challenges, but the brand is resilient. I believe it will not only continue to produce the best cars in the world, but that it will thrive on its enduring passion for many generations to come.

J Justus Schneider
Director of Global Marketing
Communications for Mercedes-Benz
Stuttgart, June 2005

CHAPTER ONE

AMAZING GRACE

THE MERCEDES-BENZ BRAND TODAY

Business hotels are pretty much the same the world over — usually dull, soulless places that inspire neither the guests nor the staff. Just such a hotel sits a few hundred metres from the main entrance to DaimlerChrysler's head office complex in Stuttgart's Möhringen district.

By contrast with the latter's modernist design and landscaped surroundings, the Millennium Hotel is, externally at least, quite brutal. The interior (which became very familiar during the course of writing this book) does little to diminish this first impression. A sea of bars and restaurants, some quite bizarrely decorated, serves only to heighten the sense of other-worldliness.

Yet it was here, in the hotel's Weinstube restaurant, that I observed something early on in my work that began to explain one of the most fundamental and deep-rooted strengths of the Mercedes-Benz brand.

It was the end of a cold, wet Tuesday evening in February 2003. I was almost the last person in the restaurant — just two other guests, and two women serving, or rather standing, behind the deserted bar. Then an extraordinary thing happened. At least, it would have been extraordinary in just about any other hotel in the world. One of the two waitresses produced from beneath the bar a box of cloths and cleaning products and began to spray and wipe and polish the glass-fronted wine and beer refrigerators that lined the wall behind her. And this was no quick wipe-down. She polished every surface, every corner, every hinge, every seal until, 20 minutes later, the refrigerators gleamed and sparkled.

In most other countries, this kind of thoroughness would have been unthinkable. The waitress, after all, was just that: a waitress. She was not the owner, manager, proprietor... nor the cleaning lady. It was not 'her' job — a distinction that in most hotels would have meant this task being left to someone else. As she stood back to admire her work, I called her over to ask for the bill. Curious, I also asked her why she had been so conscientious in her endeavours.

'Because it would be better for the customers' came the reply. Because she had time, because she cared about the way it looked, because it projected a better impression.

'Are you Schwabian?' I asked. 'Yes' she said.

'Are you Schwabian?' I asked. 'Yes' she said

The Mercedes-Benz brand is one of *the* most powerful brands in the world — and almost certainly the most powerful automotive brand. Its symbol (or logo), the 'three-pointed star', though less than a hundred years old is better recognised around the world than the Christian cross. This simple, staggering fact emerged from a worldwide survey conducted by the International Olympic Committee in 1995 and confirms something that even the casual observer might conclude: that Mercedes-Benz is a truly outstanding global brand.[1] The same casual observer might think that that position has been achieved effortlessly — that success came easily. And here they couldn't be further from the truth.

The truth is that the success of the Mercedes-Benz brand has been a struggle. That, in some ways, the brand has survived *despite* itself. It has overcome significant hurdles that might have defeated a lesser company, or destroyed a lesser brand. Of course, that makes the truth of the Mercedes-Benz brand much more interesting, and demonstrates that

today's position of pre-eminence has been hard won. It *is* an amazing brand, but the story of how it got there is even more amazing. If simple awareness is one key measure of a brand's success, then close behind is the extent to which a brand enters popular culture and the degree to which it is valuable financially. On both these measures, Mercedes-Benz scores highly.

A search for lyrics on the internet turned up over 300 songs that feature the brand: from P Diddy to Eminem to the New Radicals to REO Speedwagon to Janis Joplin's fabulous 'Oh Lord, won't you buy me a Mercedes-Benz'. By contrast, the same search turned up 63 references to Lexus, seven for Jaguar and just four for BMW.

In the world of film, too, the brand is constantly referenced. Glamorous saloons and convertibles appear in no less than eight Bond films. Mercedes old and new feature in famous movies old and new: *Donnie Brasco, Raiders of the Lost Ark, Midnight Express, The Firm, Gone in 60 Seconds,*

Ronin, American Gigolo, The Lost World, Bonfire of the Vanities, Men in Black — the list goes on and on.

Mercedes-Benz is much more than a car, or even a conventional brand — it is a cultural and social icon. It comes with meanings and associations that give it a unique place in our world and in our consciousness. By and large, this position is a positive one. The brand is highly regarded and highly valued in the eyes of the consumer. But is it highly valued in the eyes of the business community? The answer is a resounding 'yes'.

For the last 15 years, Interbrand (one of the foremost international branding consultancies) has conducted regular analyses of the strength of the world's leading brands.[2] The key factors in determining a brand's strength include stability, market leadership (share), internationality, and promotional support. On this basis, Mercedes-Benz has consistently featured in the top ten most valuable brands — alongside the likes of Coca-Cola, Microsoft, Gillette, Disney and McDonald's.

Interestingly, it is often the only non-US company to feature in that list. But Interbrand, together with Citigroup and JP Morgan, also analyse the *financial* value of brands — expressed as the net present value of future earnings directly attributed to the brand; in other words, its intangible asset value.

By this definition, in 2004, Mercedes-Benz was valued at over $21 billion worldwide — and again in the company of some of the world's greatest brands, now including Intel, GE, Nokia and Marlboro. Importantly, in the case of Mercedes-Benz, its brand value accounts for over one-third of its total business value — a percentage exceeded by only three others: Coca-Cola, Disney and McDonalds. This valuation puts Mercedes-Benz ahead of any other company in the automotive sector except Toyota. Close behind come Ford, Honda and BMW. Much further behind come Volkswagen, Harley-Davidson and Nissan.

Interbrand's general conclusion about the sources of brand strength identifies three critical characteristics of the world's strongest brands:

clarity, consistency and leadership. Since these will form the template by which the Mercedes-Benz brand will be evaluated over the course of this book, they are worth spelling out in full.

Clarity — of vision, mission and values, which are understood, lived and even loved by the people who need to deliver them. Clarity of what makes those values distinctive and relevant; and clarity of their ownership in both people's minds and trademark law around the world.

Consistency — not simply the old-fashioned consistency of product, and not to be confused with predictability. Strong brands show consistency in who they are, whatever they're doing. Brands also need consistency and alignment of values in all their manifestations — whether in product, in-store environment, in the way people answer the phone, in social responsibility and, of course, consistency of investment.

Leadership — out of some 2,500 Interbrand studies in brand valuation throughout the world,

the most discriminating factor in generating long-term brand value at the highest level is leadership. This is a brand's ability to lead and exceed expectations, to take people into new territories and new areas of product, service and even social philosophy at the right time. Leadership is also demonstrated through a brand's ability to be restless about self-renewal.

The story of the Mercedes-Benz brand has not been a smooth ride in any of these three areas. Today's image of success conceals some pretty tough times for the brand over the last 120 years. And while this book is not a history of the cars or of the company — it is the story of the Mercedes-Benz brand — an understanding of those tough times is essential to fully appreciate how the brand got to where it is today.

That 120-year perspective is also crucial because, in my view, *authenticity* is a 'fourth factor' that should be added to the Interbrand criteria, particularly for premium or luxury brands. Karl

Benz and Gottlieb Daimler created the car, and that unique claim still affects the fortunes and the thinking of the company today. It also gives owners, however unwittingly, the sense of owning something truly original. It is an authenticity that cannot be matched or claimed by any other automotive brand and it supports the brand's leadership position even today.

Over the years since 1886, as we will explore in much greater detail later, the Mercedes-Benz brand has built, consolidated and extended this leadership position in all senses. The cars it makes, the price premium they command, the status they confer upon owners, the innovations that have been a consistent feature of the brand's life — all of these have generated a strong sense of pride within the company and an inimitable prominence in the eyes of customers, and potential customers, around the world.

As part of the research for this book I have looked in detail at the brand and user image of Mercedes-Benz worldwide. And while there are obviously differences in the way the brand is viewed in different countries, what is really striking is how many similarities there are. What unites the brand globally today, in image terms, is most definitely stronger than what divides it.

Whether in Japan, South-East Asia, Europe, Australia, the Americas or South Africa, three key strands are consistently played back by those responsible for the custodianship of the brand in its key markets. Firstly, and most fundamentally, are the core virtues of the brand, understood by owners throughout the world: quality, engineering, luxury, comfort, elegance and solidity.

Secondly come the brand's prestige and status connotations — the sense, again worldwide,

that this is a brand clearly associated with success and a feeling of power.

Thirdly, and more recently, is the strong hint that across the world the brand today is less intimidating than it was, say, ten years ago. Through new models, more competitive pricing and more accessible supply, the brand has reached out to new groups of owners — younger people and women in particular — and has become as a result perhaps a little less exclusive (in the true sense of that word) than it was.

In Germany, of course, the brand's original home, Mercedes-Benz has a special place in the hearts and minds of the population. Here the brand is more than just a business success — it was a beacon of hope within the German economic miracle, a symbol of national renewal, and is still today an icon for national pride on the world stage. Germans

are proud of the company and of the brand. Even non-owners and those uninterested in cars will concede this — and that makes Mercedes-Benz unlike most other brands in any category.

Authenticity has resonance here too. Germany, at least as one nation, is a young country — only coming into being 16 years before the car itself.

Cars are close to the heart of the nation — not surprising when one remembers that one in five of the German workforce is in one way or another associated with the automotive industry. For many, Mercedes-Benz epitomises that link between Germany and the car — it is the car that many Germans aspire to own one day. More importantly, here and now as a premium brand, it commands an 11% share of its domestic market. Again, parallels to this kind of performance

are hard to come by for other premium brands.

The Mercedes-Benz brand therefore commands respect worldwide and particularly in Germany. Its luxury and prestige mean that people look up to it, yet its ubiquity means that it has a presence (and awareness) around the world that is disproportionate to its *actual* size as a business. It is a brand, in other words, that has both breadth *and* height — a rare combination, and one worth exploring a little further.

For a start, it's interesting that we've come this far in our story of the brand and yet not mentioned the fact that the three-pointed star doesn't just exist on passenger cars. In fact, Mercedes-Benz is the world's leading truck manufacturer and, as those who live in major cities around the world will know only too

well, is often the brand of choice for metropolitan bus companies. The parent company, DaimlerChrysler AG, is across all its businesses the world's largest manufacturer of commercial vehicles, selling about 400,000 trucks, buses and vans that carry the Mercedes-Benz logo every year.

In Germany in particular (but in many other countries too), Mercedes-Benz is also the predominant manufacturer of taxis. In the domestic market about 70% of all taxis come out of Stuttgart — and again anyone alighting from plane or train in one of Germany's cities can't help but notice the sea of usually beige-coloured C-, E- and occasionally S-Classes of all ages that assemble there. Given that German taxis can cover well over 50,000 miles per year (and some older Mercedes-Benz models are said

to have over half a million miles on their clock), it's easy to see how this is a very positive testimony to the durability of the cars.

But it is odd. Turn the situation on its head and think of Jaguar, Lexus or BMW producing trucks, buses and taxis and it would seem, in brand terms, at best tangential, at worst downright dangerous. And not only that, but even within its passenger car range, the spread of Mercedes-Benz models is far greater than for any other equivalent marque. In the UK, for example, in October 2004 prices ranged from under £14,000 for an A140 Classic to over £90,000 for a top of the range S-Class. By contrast, the Jaguar range runs from £20,000 to £72,000, Lexus from £19,000 to £57,000 and BMW from £16,000 to £80,000.[3]

The most expensive Mercedes-Benz, in other words, is over six times as expensive as the cheapest — for the other brands this multiple is only between three and five. Yet somehow Mercedes-Benz seems able to carry off this extraordinary diversity of product and price and at the same time produce cars that are the preferred transport of the rich and famous.

The answer to this paradox lies partly in the origins of the company — diversity has been a characteristic since the beginning — and partly in the values that unite all of these disparate manufacturing activities. The truth is that the company has made commercial vehicles since its very early days. Indeed, Gottlieb Daimler was in some ways more interested initially in engines and their multiple applications than in cars.

The first Benz 'Patent Motor Bus' went into service in 1895, and in 1896 Daimler delivered the first motorised truck to a customer in London. Today's varied model line-up across vehicles of all shapes and sizes can in part be traced back to Daimler's vision of 'all-encompassing motorisation', a concept of which we'll hear a lot more later in this book.

From a brand point of view, all of this again sets Mercedes-Benz apart from others in the category. For decades Rolls Royce carried the epithet of 'the best car in the world', but that was in part because it produced cars only at the very pinnacle of the market, and in tiny numbers. Harley-Davidson, a fantastic and highly admired brand, commands loyalty among owners that is unparalleled — but in part because it is the quintessential American motorbike and

This page: 5-ton Daimler-Lastwagen, 1899
Opposite: Benz-Hotelwagen-Omnibus for eight passengers, 1895

nothing else. (Indeed, it has been heavily punished by consumers and competitors when it has moved outside this core territory.) And even BMW (perhaps Mercedes-Benz most emotionally charged competitor), with the exception of motorcycles, has until very recently never strayed far from its heartland of performance saloons, coupés and convertibles.

But Mercedes-Benz can and does diversify, and continues to do so. It's almost as though the brand gains strength from its breadth, with each area of activity contributing important but complementary meanings to the whole. Taxis bring reliability, buses durability, trucks robustness. And together they make up a visible and ever-present part of today's cityscape.

In a marketing world often overly obsessed with brand extension or 'stretch', here is a truly original example of beneficial synergy between different parts of an enterprise. (It's worth saying, though, that some of the holding company's later forays into other sorts of businesses — consumer electronics and aerospace to name but two — were conspicuously *less* successful, and more will be said about the implications of this in chapter 8.)

Even more interesting than the absolute diversity of the Mercedes-Benz brand is the fact that the consumer doesn't seem to have a problem with these apparently disparate activities. What one sees time and again in research with customers is that they have an extraordinary ability to hold a kind of

'personal image' of the brand that is limited to their particular frame of reference. Of course, rationally they know that the company makes trucks, buses and taxis, but it is as if for each of them there is a selective and delineated perception of only those models that are personally relevant to them.

It's hard to think of examples of other brands that are able to achieve this. It would be akin to Nike producing gardening boots or Armani producing industrial overalls. Virgin, Caterpillar and Rolls Royce (in aero engines) are the only ones that come close... but not that close.

As well as breadth though, the brand today also has 'height'. It has stature as a brand, of course, but also a degree of prominence that is ahead of its *actual* scale in the global context.

Worldwide, Mercedes-Benz can count up to 7 million customers who own some 10 million vehicles. Annually the company produces over 1.1 million passenger cars and about 400,000 commercial vehicles.

But put this in the context of over 600 million cars on the road worldwide and a global population of over 6 billion and it quickly becomes clear that Mercedes-Benz is not by any means a huge, populist brand. Toyota, for example, produces four times as many cars per year — and, for a true measure of global scale, consider the fact that over a billion servings of Coca-Cola are sold in the world every day.

Part of the Mercedes-Benz brand's disproportionate prominence comes from the fact that not only are cars themselves highly visible, but Mercedes-Benz owners are quite keen to display their cars even more prominently.

A fascinating insight into this phenomenon of visibility came out of research conducted in the UK, where drivers of Mercedes-Benz and competitive marques were asked to bring a photo of their cars outside their homes to research groups. All were happy to oblige, but what was noticeable was that while owners of competitive marques parked their cars facing into the house (ie pointing away from the road), the Mercedes-Benz owners, almost to a man, parked their cars facing out — with the star facing the pavement for all to see.[4]

To confirm these findings, a year later I commissioned a different researcher to go out and just take photos of cars in driveways — and got exactly the same result.

This desire to display, of course, is something most of us can relate to — if not in relation to cars, then in some other aspect of our lives. For a brand like Mercedes-Benz it is part of what owning the brand is about to many people — a visible signal of a long-awaited ambition.

For some, this ambition is extremely long-awaited. During the research for this book, I was told by Mercedes-Benz South Africa of a customer, a rather aged gentleman, who came into one of the showrooms to buy his first car. Amazingly, it turned out that this customer had always dreamt of

This page: a Mercedes-Benz-style coffin is presented to a Ghanaian man on his deathbed

owning a Mercedes-Benz — and had taken out an investment policy when he was in his twenties. At age 80, after nearly 60 years of diligent saving, his dream came true. This is brand loyalty on the grand scale — on a par with the Harley-Davidson owners who tattoo their brand's logo on to their arms — and is a powerful example of the degree of commitment that a brand like Mercedes-Benz can generate.

For pure display value, though verging on the distasteful, the Ghanaian practice of building wooden coffins in the shape of a Mercedes-Benz saloon takes some beating, particularly since the future occupant stores the car-shaped coffin in his house until the day arrives when he is united in death with the car of his dreams.

These are extraordinary tales, but the fact remains that Mercedes-Benz is a brand that commands not only high levels of loyalty but also of reverence. Hence its disproportionate prominence in the eyes of the world. What is interesting from the brand perspective is the fact that that appeal seems to be quite universal. Talk to car buyers about Mercedes-Benz and you find a degree of admiration that often holds true for non-owners too, and seems to transcend 'brand partisanship'.

Maybe authenticity has something to do with this — being the 'original' perhaps earns universal admiration. Or might it be today that Formula One, and genuine breakthrough cars like the Mercedes-Benz SLR McLaren, have a part to play in generating this attitude? Either way, it does seem as though the brand achieves a significantly broader respect than many of its competitors.

In Europe, we're used to seeing lottery winners choose a Mercedes-Benz as their first purchase, and we're used to seeing famous actors and rock stars stepping out of them. But we're also familiar with Mercedes-Benz in the world of the powerful. Politicians drive them (or rather are driven in them). From Third World dictators to popes, people of influence in all quarters are routinely pictured with Mercedes-Benz as part of the backdrop. Whether it's an elegant long-wheel-base saloon or a stunning sports car, a gangster 'getaway car' in a movie or part of a politician's plumage, Mercedes-Benz has become part of our world, and of our lives.

Opposite: Pope John Paul II
This page: film star Morgan Freeman

The big mistake is to assume that this prominence has been achieved effortlessly. Just as with success in any other walk of life, it's easy to look at people or companies, perhaps enviously, and assume that their achievements somehow just 'fell into place', maybe through luck. It's particularly easy (but also particularly wrong) to think this way about the Mercedes-Benz brand. The truth is in fact a lot less linear than this, a lot more ragged. An obvious reason for this is that the story of the Mercedes-Benz brand is, at least in part, the story of Germany itself.

Of course, 'German-ness' has some powerful upsides: precision, reliability, engineering skills, focus on quality to name but a few. But as anyone will realise, the course of German history over the last hundred years in particular has been anything but smooth. Being the 'original' may have stood the founders in good stead for the first 30 years of their respective histories, but two world wars, hyper-inflation and the Great Depression turned all the old certainties upside-down in the next 30.

The merger of the two companies, Benz & Cie and Daimler-Motoren-Gesellschaft (DMG), in 1926 was born of necessity, and it was really only after 1945 that any kind of stability for the new business, Daimler-Benz AG, was established. Then came the golden years — the only period of sustained growth in the company's history — from 1945 to the mid-1980s, before the company was once again plunged into what has been described by some as a 'deep crisis'.

All of these we will explore. And along the way we will discover some of the more fascinating aspects of this most resilient of brands. In particular, I'll try and get to the truth of the brand's first name: Mercedes. A Spanish word meaning 'grace', it aptly sums up an enduring aspect of the brand's character: the ability to hold one's nerve and carry oneself with dignity, when all around is in turmoil.

This is the story of a brand that has been remarkably adaptive, that has had 'the ability to be restless about self-renewal' and that now more than ever before thinks about itself in a structured and receptive way. The story that this book will tell is more complicated, but infinitely more interesting than the self-congratulatory corporate histories that so many companies seem to prefer. It is also more honest — even when the tale does not have a happy ending.

The character of Schwabia, the area of Germany from which the company hails, plays a big part. Attention to detail, fastidiousness, concern for quality and a fascination for how things work have been key drivers — but, as we shall see, they have also presented the company with some unique problems in its later years.

Above all, this book will paint a picture that is not one of effortless success, as so many seem to perceive it. The brand has had to fight vigorously to succeed at almost every stage — despite the fact that the word 'brand' didn't really enter the language of the company until the 1990s.

I used the word 'amazing' at the outset too. Perhaps it seemed like an over-statement then. I believe it was a well-chosen word because, for the Mercedes-Benz brand, truth is most definitely stranger than fiction. This *is* an amazing story.

CHAPTER TWO

MYTHS AND REALITIES

Brands are powerful in our culture because they help us make choices. Those choices may be rational or emotional, but few of us can afford the time to critically assess all of the available product options in a market. Brands simplify that process — we know what they stand for and what they promise.

Strong brands, particularly in premium sectors, go further. They give meaning to categories that are impossible to assess rationally (think of perfumes) and they confer certain associations on to the purchaser. Brands say things about us, as well as about the product we've just bought.

Nowhere is this 'conferral of associations' stronger than in categories that are highly visible: the newspaper we hold up for all to see, the packet of cigarettes (or, these days, more likely the mobile phone) that sits next to us at a restaurant table, the watch we wear every day and, perhaps above all, the car we drive. Brands here become a universally understood common language — we know what someone means when they refer to a 'BMW driver' or a 'Volvo owner'. And just like other aspects of our lives — our jobs, relationships, hobbies — stories

emerge and evolve around the things we consume. Sometimes they begin as rumours or misunderstandings; sometimes they are based on little bits of knowledge. In the age of the internet, these stories can travel very fast and create fashions within days.

For older brands, the stories accumulate over time — adding layers of meaning on top of the facts, to the point where the facts are no longer visible — and may not even have been wholly true in the first place. But no matter, the story becomes more interesting than the facts — and few really care what the original truth was. Brand owners, indeed, often encourage these kinds of stories because they know the power of dreams — and brands, after all, are one way in which we can package and purchase a dream.

Think of Chanel, and all the associations of glamour and beauty that flood the senses when you picture that brand. Few women can afford a Chanel dress. Many more can afford the No. 5 perfume, and with it gain access to a little of the Chanel dream. Chanel, in fact, is managed in a careful and disciplined way, around five key brand values. But the stories associated with Chanel No. 5 are an important part of that management. The name itself, it is

said, came from the fifth sample of a new perfume tested and ultimately selected by Coco Chanel herself. The company is happy also to remind us of the story of Marilyn Monroe who, when asked what she most liked to wear in bed, replied simply: 'Chanel No. 5'. From stories such as these, dreams indeed are made.

But who knows any more whether these stories are true or not? Sadly, neither Coco Chanel nor Marilyn Monroe is still around to ask — and would they even remember, or want to change the story, if they were?

Levi's are the original jeans — a truly authentic brand, and one that still commands a premium position today. The stories here are legendary: the name 'denim', it is said, was derived from a strong French cotton called *serge de Nîmes*; the word 'jeans' apparently arose from the 'fact' that it was Genoese sailors who first wore them.

The first story sounds plausible enough, but the second? Are there any Genoan sailors from that time to ask? How did 'Genoese' become 'jean' — or was it someone's name, then post-rationalised to a more romantic origin? It is doubtful we'll ever know.

This page: Santa Claus in a 1930s Coca-Cola advertisement
Opposite: Daimler-Benz share certificate featuring Gottlieb Daimler and Karl Benz

Perhaps most extraordinary of all is when a brand creates a story around itself that then enters our culture completely. There can be no better example of this than Coca-Cola. Not just because it is the ultimate ubiquitous worldwide brand, but because it is also said to have changed our picture of one of our most important institutions: Christmas.

If the story is to be believed, then apparently up until the early 1930s Father Christmas was usually portrayed wearing either black and white or green and white. In 1931, Haddon Sundblom, the artist commissioned to work on that year's Christmas advertising campaign, came up with the idea of an exhausted Santa drinking Coca-Cola. To make the image fit more closely with the brand, he pictured the aged gentleman wearing Coke's red and white colours. This image, we are constantly told, has redefined our picture of Father Christmas ever since.

It's a brilliant story, but is it true? Well, it seems not. Despite the plausible claim, the truth appears to be that the Santa Claus figure dressed in red was pretty much the standardised image by the late 1920s, several years before the Coca-Cola advertisement.

The real point of this tale though is that such stories do arise, can gain credence in a relatively short time, and then become cemented through repetition to the point where the true story is lost. That indeed is the nature of a myth: plausible but hazy, powerful but false.

Coca-Cola was created in Atlanta, Georgia in 1886, the year that Karl Benz and Gottlieb Daimler created the car. And the stories that have built up around the Mercedes-Benz brand are just as legendary. So much so that truths or facts have sometimes become lost in history, because the myths have become more interesting, or simply easier to assimilate.

The word 'myth' is used carefully — in the English language it means 'a commonly held belief that is either untrue or without foundation'.[1] Many of the stories around the Mercedes-Benz brand, and its predecessors Benz and Daimler, have assumed this status. These myths are routinely recycled — but rarely examined for their factual accuracy. In a recent book published in the UK, *Cool Brandleaders*, three myths are reported on the same page: that in 1898 Karl Benz designed a car for a Mr Emil Jellinek which was then named after his daughter; that the logo came from a postcard sent by Karl Benz to his wife; and, more controversially, that 'racing has always been in the brand's blood'.[2] As we shall see, the first two are plain wrong, the third an over-generalised assertion that conceals a much richer truth.

Between 2003 and 2005, I interviewed over 40 people who have either shaped the recent history of the brand or could provide unique insights into its development. In the course of even those interviews, I found many examples of uncertainty about the factual basis of some of the Mercedes-Benz myths.

And more generally, there are many cases of confusion, mixed messages and just simple inaccuracies in the way people talk (and write) about this most famous of brands.

This book seeks to set the record straight by exploring some of the commonly held myths — and uncovering the realities that lie behind them. And often the true story is more interesting than the myth.

Myth number one is probably the most common among those circulating outside Germany. It is that Karl Benz and Gottlieb Daimler were partners in a shared enterprise that invented the car in 1886. It's a myth that, albeit unwittingly, the company has given credence to over the years. The car was, after all, invented in that year — but by the two men acting independently. The company is (or rather was) called Daimler-Benz AG. Even its earlier share certificates (sold as souvenirs today in the Mercedes-Benz Museum) showed the two men as though they were partners. No surprise then that to many it looks like a joint venture. But the truth is: nothing could be further from the truth.

In fact, not only did the two work entirely independently, but Karl Benz in his autobiography stated: 'I have not in all my life spoken to Daimler. Once I saw him in Berlin from a distance. When I tried to catch up with him, he had disappeared'[3]. The two men, in other words, never met.

The truth is that by the time the two enterprises merged in 1926 (to form Daimler-Benz AG), they had been operating not only as separate companies but as fierce competitors for 40 years. The timing of their original separate inventions

happened to coincide in 1886 primarily because they were both responding simultaneously to the imminent end of the patent on the four-stroke engine, invented by Nikolaus August Otto in August 1876.

Not only were the two men from very different backgrounds, they also took very different approaches to their separate but shared goal. Daimler's focus was on engines in whatever form they could be applied, static or vehicular. Frau Irmgard Schmidt-Maybach, the granddaughter of Daimler's partner, Wilhelm Maybach, spoke of Daimler as 'a visionary who wanted to motorise anything and everything', and indeed Daimler didn't build a vehicle from scratch until 1889, three years after Benz.[4] Benz's fascination was with the holistic concept of the automobile — to compete with the railways. In his own words: 'I wanted to free the railway from its straitjacket.' His dream was to build a vehicle which, again in his own words, 'runs under its own power, like a locomotive, but not on tracks, but like a wagon — simple on any streets'.

These are important differences of emphasis in the two men, and thereafter in their respective companies. The result, far from being any kind of shared enterprise, was that Daimler and Benz took quite different roads in fulfilling their ambitions. For the brand Mercedes-Benz this is highly significant.

What derives directly from this myth is the false assumption that, somehow, the path of the company was steered to some kind of plan or predefined set of objectives. Again, nothing could be further from the truth. Sadly (but like most companies it has to be said), there was no such vision or guiding hand for either Benz & Cie or Daimler-Motoren-Gesellschaft (DMG). In fact, both companies were more remarkable for the chaotic nature of their progress in the early years and the seeming lack of any clear management control or direction.

Gottlieb Daimler was alive only for the first ten years of DMG's life and spent most of those years either in dispute with his partners, or suffering from ill health ahead of his death in 1900. Benz too argued with his co-directors and fought doggedly to protect the simplicity of his original invention. He was not a visionary and, disenchanted with the direction in which others were pulling him, effectively left the company in 1903.

Although there are literally dozens of statements from both men about their personal beliefs (and in Benz's case an autobiography), there seems to be no evidence of any kind of plan, set of objectives, or what today one would call a mission statement for either company. That was not unusual at the time. What is unusual is that this lack of planning seems to have filtered down through the years and been a feature of the operation until relatively recently.

Benz spoke of his pursuit of 'the best of the good', while Daimler spoke of his belief in 'the best or nothing'

As one interviewee from within the company today put it: 'The brand is not the result of a strategy, it is the result of working in little steps... a happy accident'. In fact, according to the same individual, it was only in the 1980s that the company 'had its first serious strategic discussions'. The origins of this lack of planning can be traced back a hundred years.

But if there was no plan, and no guiding hand, and indeed no single company until 1926, what was it that kept the two businesses afloat, and ultimately welded them together into the brand we see today?

The answer is some powerful guiding ideas and a shared belief in quality. Two quotes, one from Benz, one from Daimler, did themselves achieve a kind of legendary status within their respective companies, and since 1926 within Mercedes-Benz. Benz spoke of his pursuit of 'the best of the good', while Daimler spoke of his belief in 'the best or nothing'. The latter in particular shaped the company's philosophy and business practices until quite recently — not always to the brand's advantage. But notice, for now, how close the two quotes are. Both have an almost naïvely idealistic quality. Both betray a determination to excel. And unlike most of today's mission statements, neither mentions the customer or, incidentally, the cost of being 'the best'.

They do though draw attention to quality as an absolutely fundamental touchstone for both companies. Daimler, in a letter to a co-director, talked of the company 'having to stick very strictly to the principle that [we] only build the best engines, even if it gets a little more expensive'. Benz's quote is more inner-directed: 'I worked restlessly on the perfection of my vehicles — flaws disappeared and perfection appeared'.

In this obsession, clearly the two men did share a common vision — even if it did not take the shape of a plan. The desire for quality has been at the heart of the brand since its inception. But quality is a moving target — what defines quality today may not be as important tomorrow. When quality has been definitive and relevant, the brand has prospered. When the company has lost touch with what quality means for the customer, the brand has suffered. We will see evidence of both situations in the recent history of Mercedes-Benz.

The second myth is also pretty pervasive among many I have spoken to. Probably because people vaguely know that Daimler and Benz invented the car, and see the brand Mercedes-Benz as being hugely successful today, they simply 'join up the dots' between those two points and assume that the progress between, in sales terms, has been a kind of relentlessly smooth progression.

Opposite: the four-stroke engine patented by Nikolaus August Otto in August 1876

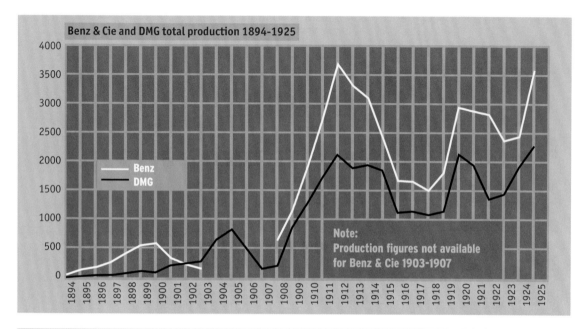

Benz & Cie and DMG total production 1894-1925

Benz
DMG

Note:
Production figures not available
for Benz & Cie 1903-1907

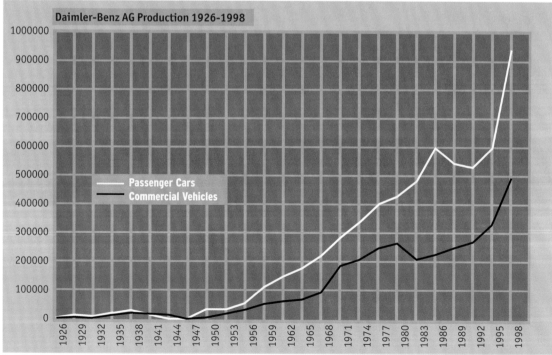

Daimler-Benz AG Production 1926-1998

Passenger Cars
Commercial Vehicles

Again, not so. Take a look at the two graphs to the left. One shows Daimler and Benz sales separately up to the merger in 1926, the other shows the combined sales for Mercedes-Benz from 1926 to recent times. Neither is smooth, nor relentless. Both have blips and hiccups that relate to major upheavals either in the companies' fortunes or in the world around them. Indeed, the only period of truly sustained growth in the last 120 years was the period from 1953 to 1986. For the other two thirds of the companies' lives, it has been a bit of a rollercoaster!

Some of the reasons for this will be explored shortly, and the final chapters look in more detail at the last 20 years in particular. Suffice to say here, though, that a number of things stand out from this 'big picture' look at sales performance, some of which might come as a surprise. For example, Benz & Cie sold far more cars in the ten years after Karl's departure in 1903 than in the ten years before. In fact, Benz outsold Daimler in almost every year up to the merger in 1926 — even though it was at that moment deemed to be the weaker party.

Notice too just how few cars DMG was producing up to the point of Daimler's death in 1900, but then how production accelerated after Emil Jellinek's involvement from about the same time. Interestingly, observe how production for both companies continued throughout the First World War. By contrast, Mercedes-Benz sales disappeared during the Second World War. See also the absolute volumes that Mercedes-Benz was producing in the 1920s and 1930s. By today's standards, car manufacturing was almost a cottage industry in those decades — a best seller might sell only 10,000 cars.

Above all, look at how quickly the company rebuilt volume after the Second World War and really

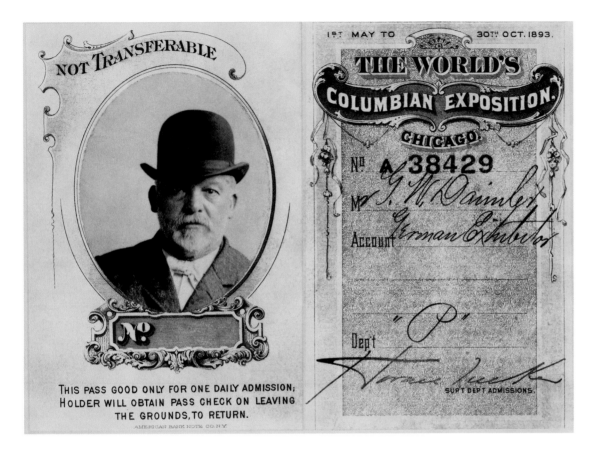

NOT TRANSFERABLE

THE WORLD'S
COLUMBIAN EXPOSITION.
CHICAGO.

N° A 38429

M__ G. W. Daimler

Account German Exhibitor

"P"

Dep't

SUP'T DEP'T ADMISSIONS.

THIS PASS GOOD ONLY FOR ONE DAILY ADMISSION;
HOLDER WILL OBTAIN PASS CHECK ON LEAVING
THE GROUNDS, TO RETURN.

AMERICAN BANK NOTE CO. N.Y.

This page: Gottlieb Daimler's entry pass for the 1893 Chicago World Fair

did maintain that momentum for the next 30 years. But then also look at the period of the late 1980s and early 1990s. The plateauing doesn't look too severe, but this was a critical time for the company — a 'deep crisis' that took the business into the red for the first time since the war.

Only in the last few years was growth restored — almost exponentially. But of course this too brought its own unique pressures. So it is not a smooth progression. This is a brand that has had more than its fair share of highs and lows.

Myth number three is that the company and the brand are German through and through. Of

course it's true of the origins and nationality of the founders, but in fact the company (and especially the brand) has had international leanings from its earliest days. As early as 1893, Gottlieb Daimler was at the Chicago World Fair exhibiting his engines — and the only car in the entire exhibition. Among the visitors to his lonely display was one Henry Ford — who knows what inspiration he took from this brief encounter?

Benz too was active internationally from the outset. By 1900 his cars were the first to be sold in South Africa, the first to climb the mountains of New South Wales in Australia, and Benz cars had been sold

as far afield as India, Singapore and Java (Indonesia). Europe, though, was the principal market for both companies in these early years — in fact, consistently well over half of their volumes was going to owners outside Germany. France, being the first country in the world to truly embrace the motorcar and especially motor racing, was the key market for most of the period up to the turn of the 20th century. The UK, the Benelux countries, Austria and Italy followed and from 1901, so did the USA.

More recently, of course, production too has had an international flavour. Today, in addition to the six plants in Germany, the company has car-

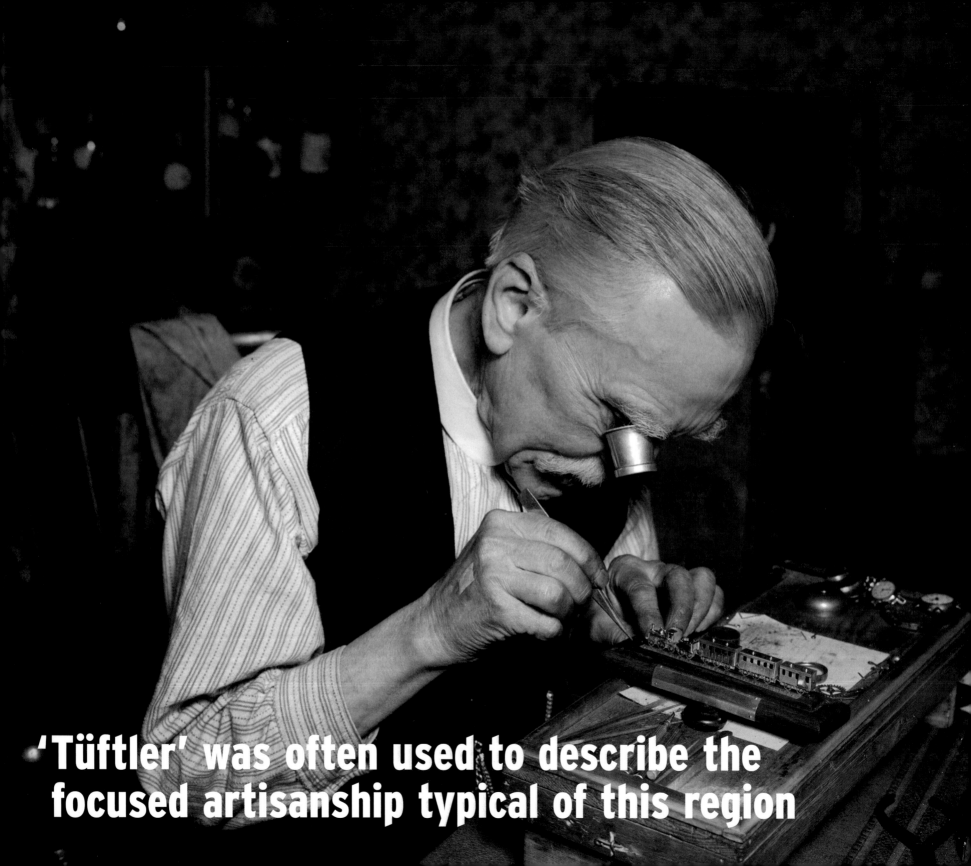

'Tüftler' was often used to describe the
focused artisanship typical of this region

This page, from left: the 1930 770 'Grosser Mercedes'; the 170V cabriolet (the first 170 was launched in 1931)

production facilities in South Africa (Port Elizabeth), the USA (Tuscaloosa) and Brazil (Juiz de Fora).

In another sense too, the Mercedes-Benz brand is not 'just' a German company. For Daimler in particular, the Schwabian origins have been especially important in defining Mercedes' place *within* the boundaries of Germany.

'Schwabian-ness', as alluded to earlier, is the particular characteristic of those who hail from the area of Germany that lies in the southern part of Baden-Württemberg, to the northwest of Bavaria. But it is distinct from both: not so much geographically or politically, but rather attitudinally. Typically, Schwabians are associated with frugality, modesty, a strong sense of ethics and decency of behaviour, with undertones of piety. Practically, this translates into commitment to one's employer, attention to detail (the word *tüftler* was often used to describe the focused artisanship typical of this region), a strong work ethic and, above all from the brand point of view, a focus on quality. It is these characteristics that, even today in some respects, mark the

brand out from its competitors — internationally, but also inside the home country. To think of the brand as 'just German' is a long way from the reality.

The fourth myth (and the one that perhaps exasperates me the most) probably runs something like this: 'Don't Mercedes-Benz always makes big, luxurious cars for rich people?' Even leaving aside the long history of commercial vehicles — trucks, buses and even fire engines manufactured from the earliest days of the company — this is still a grossly misleading view. Of course, from the beginning and right up until the 1930s, all cars were expensive relative to the living standards of most people. Almost by definition therefore they were, certainly up to the First World War, the preserve of the rich. But both Daimler and (especially) Benz took steps early on in their companies' lives to broaden the appeal. The Benz Velo, launched in 1894, was arguably the world's first 'compact' car — carrying two people and with half the horsepower of its bigger sister, the Victoria. And it's true that even as late as the Great

Depression in the 1930s, Mercedes-Benz cars were typically twice the price of their closest competitors. But from about that time everything started to change — and the Mercedes-Benz brand was no island. Ford's work on mass-production techniques in America was quickly emulated by his competitors, particularly General Motors (GM). In Germany the Opel company (part of GM from 1929) was one of the first of the major European manufacturers to pick up the gauntlet. Retail prices began to tumble, particularly since the Depression was dramatically reducing real incomes. Mercedes-Benz had to respond... and did. And what followed was one of the most interesting if least well-known chapters in the brand's life — one that scotches the rumour that Mercedes-Benz only builds big and expensive cars.

By 1930, Mercedes-Benz prices ranged from 6,000 to 20,000 marks, and the company had just topped this with the 7.7-litre 'Grosser Mercedes' — a huge car, out of step with the times, but immensely beautiful. Whereas, in the late 1920s, 60% of all cars sold in Germany cost less than 5,000 marks, by the

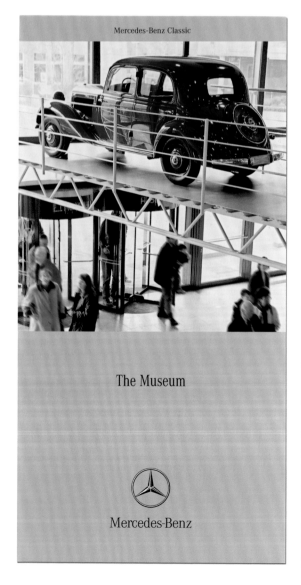

Mercedes-Benz Classic

The Museum

Mercedes-Benz

After the Second World War ended, the company turned to the 170 once again in its quest to rebuild

early 1930s that percentage had dropped to nearer 10. And then, in 1931, Mercedes-Benz launched the 170, and priced the four-door saloon version at 4,400 marks. But this was no stripped-down economy model. Certainly it was smaller, but with independent swing-axle suspension, hydraulic brakes, pressed-steel wheels and even a sunroof on later models it was a remarkably advanced family car. And people loved it. Nearly 14,000 were produced by 1935 and, in 170V guise, a further 67,000 were sold by the outbreak of war.

This *small* car from Mercedes-Benz was critically important for the brand. In fact Mercedes-Benz ultimately sold almost as many 170s in the years 1931 to 1939 as *all* the previous production of both companies, separately and together, since their inceptions. For the first time, the 170 provided an accessible, affordable Mercedes-Benz — but still one with all the quality and brand values of the three-pointed star on its bonnet.

But this is not the only reason to admire this car. Remarkably, after the Second World War ended, the company once again turned to the 170 in its quest to rebuild. Machine tools and dies had been spared the widespread destruction and they formed the beginning of the new company after 1945.

Basically, production of the 170V picked up where it had left off in 1939. And by 1953 a further 45,000 170s had been built *since* the war. New variants were added in 1949, the 170S and D (diesel was becoming increasingly important at this time), and it was not until the mid-1950s that annual sales of other models, notably the 220, overtook that of the 170, by now over 20 years old. For me, therefore, the 170 was in some respects the car that saved the company, not once, but twice.

Its role in terms of the Mercedes-Benz brand is hard to overstate. While it didn't exactly bring cars to the masses (that role fell to the original Volkswagen), the 170 most certainly did extend a

hand to the German middle classes and tradespeople and, for the first time, made the brand accessible, not just desirable.

So if people think that the A-Class was the brand's first foray into small cars, remember the 170. Better still, go and see it in the Mercedes-Benz Museum in Stuttgart — it gets deserved pride of place as an exhibit, and on the cover of the museum's guide.

The next myth is a more controversial one. As mentioned, it's not uncommon to read commentators saying things like 'racing has always been in the company's blood' or 'racing has been part of the brand's heritage since the beginning'. There is some truth in both of these statements, but neither is completely accurate. In fact, the involvement of Benz, Daimler and Mercedes-Benz in motor racing has been intermittent, often overstated and was most definitely not in the blood of at least one of the founders.

What people remember, of course, are the periods when the brand was heavily involved in racing. The 'glory years' of the original Mercedes at the beginning of the 20th century, the Silver Arrows of the 1930s, the Gullwing SL sports cars of the early 1950s, Formula One in the 1950s and again, since 1994, with McLaren right up to the present day.

Less well recalled are the years when Mercedes-Benz either withdrew or was excluded from motor sport. In fact, in the last century in total, Mercedes-Benz was out of Formula One for more years than it was in. The brand, in other words, has survived and prospered both with and without involvement in motor sport. Clearly racing adds an important credential to the brand's armoury, and it was a valuable marketing tool right from the beginning, but it is less fundamental than some observers (and most writers) have suggested.

The reasons behind this are not so hard to fathom. Gottlieb Daimler (partly through the prompting of his son Paul) did take an interest in the early days of motor racing, but it was only after his death that the company's involvement really took off. Remember too that Daimler either couldn't drive, or didn't like to drive a car himself — another myth, perhaps, dispensed with.

This page, from left: the 40 PS Mercedes at the first Herkomer Rally in 1905; the W25 racing car driven by Rudolf Caracciola at the Klausen International hill climb in 1934; Kimi Raikkonen driving an MP 4/20 in the San Marino Grand Prix, Imola, 2005

This page: early on-car badging before consistent branding was introduced. Left to right: a Benz & Cie plate on the Victoria, 1893; the DMG hubcap on the Simplex, 1903; Mercedes script on the front of the Simplex, 1904
Opposite: detail of Gottlieb Daimler's postcard to his wife featuring the 'inspiration' for the three-pointed star

Benz was more actively and negatively disposed. He counselled his workforce and his customers against excessive speed. His view was that cars should not be designed to go above 25 mph since they shared the roads with horse-drawn vehicles and children. He did drive, but wanted nothing to do with the racing fashion at the turn of the 20th century.

Motor racing may well have been 'in the blood' of many of the brand's subsequent managers, workers and customers — but it was not there from the outset.

Myth number six goes right to the heart of one of the brand's key symbols: the three-pointed star. To this day, many believe that it is a symbol that goes back to the very beginning of the company — usually because they are unaware of the 'separate lives' of the two companies, Benz and Daimler, until 1926. In fact, not only did Gottlieb Daimler never live to see a car called a 'Mercedes' (the first one to be thus badged was in 1900, after Daimler's death), but the famous three-pointed star didn't emerge until nine years later.

Benz, likewise, was never associated with this symbol either. His cars simply carried the word 'Benz', garlanded with laurel leaves, as their badge. And only in 1926 did the two come together to form today's full logo, a three-pointed star set within laurels.

The origins of the laurels are lost in history. The origins of the star are better known, but the deeper one digs the more curious the story becomes. I've heard tales of the star being painted on the side of Daimler's house in Cologne (Köln), stories of it being a corruption of the pyramidal Deutz logo (the company in Cologne at which Daimler first worked). Both, I believe, are untrue.

But the real story is far from crystal clear either. According to the 'official' version, it was Alfred von Kaulla, who had recently become chairman of DMG, who decided in 1909 that the Mercedes brand needed a trademark. (Before that, like Benz, DMG's cars had simply carried the word 'Mercedes' in a variety of styles and positions.) Von

Kaulla discussed various ideas with Gottlieb's son Paul. And, so the story goes, Paul showed him a postcard that his father had sent home to his wife at the start of his time at Deutz in 1872. On the reverse Gottlieb is said to have written: 'A star shall rise from here and I hope it will bring blessings to us and to our children', and on the front, indicating the location of his current and their future home, he'd drawn a three-pointed star.

There are a number of odd things about this official story. Firstly, there is no reference in any archive to the back of the postcard, only to the front, the photographic side. Secondly, would Paul really have had such an old (more than 30 years old) postcard just lying around his home? Thirdly, and most significant, the 'star' on the photograph is actually an asterisk (*), roughly drawn, quite small and on closer examination seems to have five points. It must have taken a significant leap of design faith to translate this into the very regular and upright three-pointed star logo.

'A star shall rise from here and I hope it will bring blessings to us and to our children'

 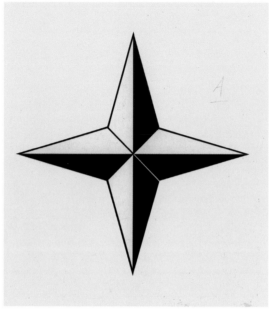

Finally, though much has been written subsequently about the symbolism of the three points, in fact DMG simultaneously registered a four-pointed star, which was used on internal components to maintain it as a trademark, and was re-registered to the company as late as 1921. What's more, this four-pointed version briefly reappears later in our story — as the logo for Deutsche Aerospace (DASA), created by Daimler-Benz in 1989.

Brands are much more than logos. But this particular logo has become so famous, and commands such loyalty that it's a shame that there is not greater clarity about its origins.

The last myth is, from the point of view of anyone interested in brand marketing, the most significant. Later chapters will explore it in much more detail. Suffice to say here that it is the assumption of many commentators and observers that, because Mercedes-Benz is such a powerful brand today, it must have been the case that a brand and marketing ethos would have pervaded the company from early on. Not so. True brand thinking didn't really enter the mindsets of those running the company until very recently. That doesn't mean that a brand as such didn't exist, clearly it did: for Benz, for Daimler and for Mercedes-Benz.

What it means is that there was no conscious concept of brand management for most of the life of the company. Hans-Georg Brehm, former Head of Brand Strategy at DaimlerChrysler, describes his early years at Mercedes-Benz: 'We were not a brand-orientated company. We were a development and production-orientated company. No one would have used the word "brand"'.

Professor Jürgen Hubbert, CEO of Mercedes-Benz Car Group until October 2004, pinpoints the moment even more precisely: 'The first conversations I remember [about brand] were in about 1993. Before that time, the brand was the company and the company was the brand'.

At its heart, and no matter how powerful its brand actually became, Mercedes-Benz has been an engineering business until very recently. Marketing is something of a baby by comparison; 'brand' a relatively recent concept.

It's worth restating though that this does not mean that there wasn't a brand — evidently there was, from the very beginning. Nor does it mean that the company didn't listen to customers, or act on customer market pressures.

What it means is that brand thinking wasn't orchestrated or conscious until recently, a point very much confirmed by Dr Joachim Schmidt, Sales and Marketing Director of Mercedes-Benz until March 2005, who told me: 'Conscious development of the brand started in the 1990s from a marketing and communications point of view. There was a marketing department before that but just in the sense of advertising, not really in terms of strategic direction'.

The two former principals of Mercedes-Benz oldest dealership gave me their unique and telling perspective on this corporate attitude. As Hans-Georg Appenzeller put it: 'In our earlier times, sales were

It was almost as though the company was run by engineers for engineers

not the essential point for the company, construction was. They said: "We build the best cars in the world, you have to sell what we build". We tried to give our input about customers' wishes... but they were not interested. The Head of Sales (at Mercedes-Benz) never had the same influence on the board that the Head of Production had. This remained the case from when we started in the 1950s until the end of the 1980s'.

Tellingly too, one of the company's advertising slogans in the 1950s was 'We build what you need', which (in today's world at least) betrays an extraordinary assumptiveness, even arrogance, on the part of the company. It was almost as though the company was run by engineers for engineers — and customers were somehow seen as 'privileged' to receive their output.

Today, the story is very different. Now, according to Dr Hans-Joachim Schöpf, until 2004 Head of R & D, 'marketing has a top-table position' — as has the brand.

In the German language, the word '*Mythos*' has a very different meaning to the English word 'myth'. While the latter means a falsehood, the German word means a kind of exaggerated belief *rooted in a truth*. This is an important distinction — particularly since, for example, the planned new corporate exhibition centre is going to be built around the eight *Mythos* of Mercedes-Benz.

The challenge here has been to dig beneath some of the commonly held falsehoods, and uncover the real stories. Not only are these realities in some ways more interesting, hopefully they also whet the appetite for what is to follow: the story of a brand that in some respects succeeded against all odds. And, as I've already hinted, it's not the story of just one brand — but rather of the two brands that make up today's name: Mercedes and Benz.

Stories and myths around a brand are very important in perpetuating its appeal, both across and between generations. Some of our earliest childhood impressions of brands emanate from these

stories and become deeply embedded. Indeed, in some respects the number and depth of such stories, true or false, are a measure of the strength of a brand. They suggest a degree of engagement and interest among consumers that more recent brands can only watch with envy. It's the stories that give great brands almost a life of their own — the brand becomes a property shared almost equally by the original owner, the customer and society as a whole.

That might lead some to think that 'brand' is therefore a loose, fluffy, ethereal concept — not given to measurement, quantification or definition. It's true that trying to measure a brand's societal impact is hard. It's not the case that brands can't be defined. The job now is to do just that, and in so doing to create a kind of template for all that is to follow.

CHAPTER THREE
WHAT IS A BRAND?

Brands can fulfil a whole array of our needs as human beings: belonging, recognition, status, even self-esteem

Brands, as we saw in the last chapter, are important to us as consumers — helping us make choices in crowded markets, giving meaning to products in categories that are hard to assess rationally. But that's only a part of the story. Brands also play a powerful part in our lives as human beings and in the complex economic system in which most of us live and work.

As people, we've often grown up with brands that are themselves over a hundred years old. They were part of our parents' legacy to us. The bonds we form with those brands are immensely strong, and are sometimes intrinsically linked with childhood memories.

Originally brands may have been chosen to meet simple physiological needs — nourishment and shelter, for example — but as we've grown up with them, our relationships have become more complex. Coca-Cola quenches our thirst of course, but drinking Coca-Cola satisfies more than that simple need. It identifies us as having made an authentic choice, as being part of a worldwide community of Coca-Cola drinkers, perhaps even as being a vibrant, energetic,

youthful person. It meets needs that go well beyond the physical, that in fact are about self-expression — and for that reason Coke may have been our brand of choice for decades.

That concept of self-expression is one that others in the drinks market have taken even further. Brands like Perrier, Badoit and, notably, Evian have elevated water to almost a lifestyle statement: they say something about the kind of person we are and the kind of life we lead.

Brands, in other words, can fulfil a whole array of our needs as human beings: for belonging, recognition, status, even self-esteem. They are a new kind of currency in our lives — and we surround ourselves with them precisely for the value that they bring.

But brands are also important because as we use them, as our relationships with them build up over the years, we also begin to develop a kind of trust in them. Like friends, we know where we stand with them, we don't interrogate their motives repeatedly, we take them at their word. And brands reward that trust. They are, by and large, consistent,

predictable, satisfying. They don't let us down — so we keep buying them and using them.

But in one crucial respect our behaviour towards brands is unlike that of a friendship, because it is ultimately a commercial transaction. We pay for the brands we consume — and, critically important, we usually pay a premium.

Because they are familiar and valuable to us, we don't mind paying a little bit more for 'our' brand than, say, a cheaper supermarket own-label alternative. We may even recognise that the alternative is functionally equal to our preferred brand — but still we choose the latter, and pay over the odds for it. This is the essential 'contract' that brands strike with their users — and it's a relationship that business-people appreciate only too well.

Some years ago, the chief executive of a major European food manufacturer was quoted as saying: 'Buildings age and become dilapidated. Machines wear out. People die. But what lives on are the brands.'[1] And in this quote we start to see why brands are so vital — they are often the most significant, long-lasting and valuable asset that a business possesses. John Stuart, former Chairman of the US food giant Quaker, was even more direct. He said, 'if this business were split up, I would be glad to take the brands, goodwill and trademarks, and you could have all the bricks and mortar — and I would fare better than you'.

It's precisely because of this belief in the durability of brands that companies devote so much effort to the management of them. And successful brand management is no simple matter. Juggling the different priorities of all the stakeholders is only the beginning: the needs and wants of the consumer, the demands of shareholders, the security of employees, the ambitions of management — all of these need to be taken into account. Then add to these the inherent lifecycle of brands, the activities of competitors, the changing political, legal and environmental issues that surround the brand. Finally, for good measure, add in the various strategic opportunities that the brand itself presents to its owner: how it should be packaged, priced, promoted,

distributed; whether it can be extended into other categories or other geographic markets. All of these factors, all of the time, are what the brand owner needs to consider and manage. It's neither simple nor easy, in fact it's a kind of 'soft rocket science' to those involved, but one that nevertheless retains its intrigue and fascination for practitioners.

To understand why all of this often unseen activity surrounds the brands we use, it's important to remind ourselves of some simple first principles — exactly why it is that brands are so important to their owners, the companies behind the brands.

First and foremost it is because brands create preference and, ultimately, loyalty. Yes, they help us choose, but having chosen (and provided the brand doesn't let us down in any way), they reward us for that choice and hence increase the likelihood that we will choose them again. And when that same brand introduces a new product (or new model) to us, then our propensity to choose that too increases.

Over time, partly out of familiarity, partly out of this constant cycle of choice and reward, our

purchasing in whatever category becomes habituated. And that is the first step toward loyalty: the sense that this is 'my' brand, one that I'm happy to use and happy to be seen to be using.

This feeling, multiplied millions of times over by consumers across the world, is immensely valuable to brand owners. It means that they can charge a premium, but it also means that they can literally 'count' on the loyalty of the consumer — and hence generate predictable, and hopefully growing, cash flows from that brand.

It is those cash flows, specifically the proportion of them directly attributable to the brand (rather than to the tangible assets that the company employs), that generate the $21 billion figure of brand value for Mercedes-Benz. This is the true quantitative measure of the power of the brand, and of its immense worth to its owners.

But what happens when something goes wrong? What happens when our brand does 'let us down'? Surely this is the greatest test of any brand, and of the loyalty of its customers?

It is, but it's a testimony to the strength and resilience of great brands that they often can withstand even the most damaging of problems. Perrier's ability to survive the contamination of its source, Nike's ability to overcome the hugely negative stories about its sweatshop manufacturing locations, Coca-Cola's ability to sidestep critical PR in India, where the company has been criticised for over-exploitation and pollution of water as a result of its operations — all of these are examples of brands that are so strong that they earn the benefit of the doubt.

Like a friend who lets us down once or twice (but probably no more than once or twice), they are forgiven. We give them another chance, because we see it as a one-off — something to be viewed in the context of a long-standing relationship. So too with brands. Provided we've had a generally positive long-term relationship, we give them the benefit of the doubt. For Mercedes-Benz, just such a moment arrived

in 1997 with the famous 'Elk test'. Later, in chapter 10, we'll see how the brand coped with this. Did it achieve the benefit of the doubt? Or did it, as Dr Wolfgang Reitzle, formerly of BMW, suggests, mean that the Mercedes-Benz brand 'lost forever its mantle of infallibility'?

Strong brands are strong because they can command this kind of loyalty, but what is equally clear is that there is no single route to reaching this exalted position. Different brands achieve it in different ways, using different strategies.

Most branded businesses (according to Constantinos Markides, Professor of Strategic and International Management at London Business School), have two basic strategic choices: to be better or to be different. In his view, the former is the tougher route, constantly battling it out with your competitors for the next product advantage. He believes being different is the easier — finding

a place in the market, or a route to market, that others have not.[2]

'Being better' is a tough act to put on day after day. And when companies enjoy near-monopolies, as IBM did in the 1970s, the incentive to improve may not be that strong in the first place. This leaves them vulnerable to brands that actively choose to be different. Apple chose just such a route — to revolutionise the technology, liberate the user and create, effectively, a lifestyle difference around its brand.

Constantly striving to be better characterises many of the world's great brands — and they fight hard to maintain this leadership position. Nike is one outstanding example: driven by the passion of its founders, always customer-focused, committed to product excellence — all these set it apart from its competitors and give it a pre-eminent position in the world of sport. But make no mistake, this is hard work and the rewards are hard won.

This page: Auto Bild article showing the A-Class tipping during a repeat of the Elk test, 30 October 1997

Though phrases like 'living the brand' have become clichés, the fact remains that a strong internal sense of vision and values (what might be called the 'internal brand') has been crucial to the success of many organisations. Again, Nike is a classic example. The company talks openly about how employees derive their mission from their founder Bill Bowerman, how 'through his eyes we see our future'. They talk about how Nike 'pursues its destiny', how theirs 'is a language of sports, a universally understood lexicon of passion and competition'. They talk about 'legends' and how the founders left an 'indelible mark' upon the company.[3]

These words, these sentiments are the clear hallmarks of a company with a very powerful internal culture — one that has played a crucial role (alongside quality product) in making Nike the brand it is today. What they also tell us is that if you really want to understand a brand, you have to go right back to the beginning — right back to what was in the heads and hearts of the founders — the authentic origins of the business.

Companies (and hence brands) usually start with an idea and then come to life in the first instance as a new product or service offer. Ideas can take one of two forms. Invention, the rarest, is a genuinely new idea — arising perhaps through serendipity (like Wrigley's chewing gum) or through the concerted efforts of an individual to solve a problem or a need (Hoover and the original Kodak camera might be examples). Innovation is much more common, and distinct from invention because it implies building on an already existing idea. (Sony's Walkman would be a good example here: tape recorder technology already existed; the brilliance of this innovation was to miniaturise that technology and turn the speakers into earphones.) Importantly, we can find evidence of both of these sources of ideas within the origins of the Mercedes-Benz brand.

The idea, and the person who had it, may well leave an indelible mark on the company that emerges. That indelible mark will take the form of a core thought, philosophy or what we in the world of brands would call 'essence'. This essence then stays with the company, and hence its brand, perhaps unchanged, forever.

First and foremost, this 'essence' will impact upon the product that the company starts selling — and it will probably define the heart of that company's offer well into the future. For Nivea this core thought might be 'care', for Rolex 'reliability'. But as well as defining something important about the product, that original thought — or brand essence — will also give birth to a set of values within the company, the beginnings of its internal brand.

This page: 'No substitute... for breast milk'. Protest graffiti on a Nestlé poster, UK, 2001
Opposite: brand associations for Burberry have changed in recent years

Values are what the brand owners (the founders at the outset, but not necessarily later) believe about their company and their brand from within. They are probably, at least in part, what they also want to communicate to the outside world. The product itself may encapsulate some of these values, but others may be less visible. For the brand, it is the combination of the two, product and values (both drawing upon the original 'essence') that the owners will, in all likelihood, wish to convey.

But though they will see both in a positive light, others may not. Just as with the human char- acter, many traits or values that seem positive to us appear less so to others. We may consider punctuality a virtue, others may see it as 'predictable', even dull. We may be proud of being fair, others may see this as naïvety. And so it goes on. There is, in other words, always a flip side to a brand's product virtues and company values that means it will never be to

everyone's taste. But this is to be expected — strong brands, like strong individuals, produce strong reac- tions. Very few brands seek to appeal to everyone. Most have a clear view about who will and will not buy into what they make and stand for.

In parallel with this evolution of product and values, but much less within the control of the brand owners, a set of consumer associations will also develop around the brand — effectively defining its external personality. Brand owners will try to manage these associations — addressing the nega- tives, reminding about the positives — but in large part these associations are beyond their short-term influence. That's because they arise simply as a func- tion of what the product is, how the brand is posi- tioned, its history, its price and distribution and, most importantly of all, from who else uses it.

Levi's in its Scandinavian markets in the 1980s deliberately would not stock men's jeans in sizes above

a 34-inch waist — it simply didn't want overweight guys to be seen in its brand. The company saw that end of the market as being the preserve of Wrangler, and was happy to leave it to its competitor.

In today's world of regulated markets, anti- competition laws and lack of price maintenance, such strategies are more troublesome. Adidas' attempt not to be stocked (and discounted) in Tesco, the UK's leading supermarket chain, led to a swift rebuke for that brand. Like it or not, brands can no longer 'control' who buys their product. And with buyers go associations, positive and negative.

Burberry is a classic example of this phenom- enon. Starting out as a highly exclusive and distinc- tive range of macs and outerwear, the brand has rocketed in sales terms through the introduction of casual wear, scarves, shoes and personal accessories. So far, so good. But today walk through any shopping centre in the UK and you'll see teenage girls with prams

Brands may be strong and resilient, they may have broad shoulders and thick skins – but they are not impregnable

carrying Burberry handbags and, worse, aggressive young lads sporting Burberry baseball caps. Is this really the audience the brand owners want us to associate with their distinctive check design? Or is the brand being stretched too far — perhaps born of market greed? Could it be that, through associations, the strategy of brand extension (as it was for Pierre Cardin many years ago) will ultimately be the undoing of this elegant and once-exclusive brand?

And therein lies the trick: to retain a sense of being special without being too exclusive. Of course, every brand has the ambition to grow but, as it grows, the brand increasingly becomes the 'property' of not only the brand owner, but also of the customer. They become the brand's ambassadors, for better or for worse. In part they define what the brand's associations are for those who arrive later. Brands may be strong and resilient, they may have broad shoulders and thick skins — but they are not impregnable. The constant task of the owner is to shore up the walls of the brand: to protect in order to survive.

As we have seen, that involves attending to things that are largely within the owner's control — product and values — but also to those that are less easy to steer or manipulate: the brand's associations. Car brands are no exception to this general rule, these general observations. But they do represent a particularly complex example of a branded market-place. Complex because emotions run high in this market — cars bring out the best and worst in both drivers and commentators — and loyalties are fiercely contested. Cars, arguably, are more inter-twined with our society than many other consumer goods — economically and, again, emotionally. They are powerful symbols of our personality... and of our wealth. They make big visible statements about us. And the part they play in our lives is in a constant state of flux. Let's explore further.

Of the 440,000 cars produced at the Sindelfingen plant in 1998, only three were totally identical

The world today is a very different place from that of Karl Benz and Gottlieb Daimler. The traditional social structures and privileges they would have known have crumbled — still are crumbling — in most of the Western world. People today are more sceptical of fixed notions and settled identities, for themselves and for others, including the brands they buy. This produces a clear tension between the need for new forms of self-expression and at the same time, the ability to anchor these in familiar territories.

Clearly, Henry Ford's world of 'any colour you like as long as it's black' is long gone — and one of the more astonishing statistics to emerge from the interview with Dr Hans-Joachim Schöpf (formerly Director of DaimlerChrysler's Sindelfingen plant) was that of the 440,000 cars produced in that plant in 1998, only three (yes, three) were totally identical.

Flexibility is key: flexibility of supply to meet ever-changing customer needs. But needs are changing in other respects too. Mobility, which was at the heart of the Mercedes-Benz brand in its earliest days, is today being redefined to embrace not only physical mobility but mobility of information, of lifestyle, of home and work. Information technology, not cars, is the 'sexy' industry of the early 21st century.

The car today is less an outward signifier of wealth, as it very much was a hundred years ago, more a lifestyle statement; less a mode of transport, more a mode of self-expression. But it is because this 'expression' and these associations are so visible that cars attract such keen interest. Attitudes to cars *per se* may be changing, their place in society may even be questioned, but still we find them exciting and desirable. And still we treat them almost as

extensions of ourselves: we give them names, call them 'she', build them rooms in our houses (garages), we even talk to them and they (in the era of SatNav) talk back!

Needs may have changed, but cars have adapted to meet our new ones. Originally cars were liberating because they allowed us to explore new places, even just drive for the pure fun of it. Today, in the crowded cities where most of us live, they offer a new kind of liberation — cocooning us in a protected, quiet environment, a personal space that, unlike the outside world, we can control completely.

Opposite: 'Silent Movie' advertisement for the S-Class, 1997

The door shut

with all the reassurance

of a vacuum sealed vault.

Then I sat back in my seat

and watched the world outside

unfold upon the screen,

as if it were a silent movie.

Picture the scene.

Set against the evenings pale and chaotic backdrop, your Mercedes S-class awaits you. Your heart, heavy from the days toll, lifts.

You take your seat. A servo assists you in closing your door by pulling it firmly shut, with the minimum of noise.

Double-layered side windows thankfully cocoon you from the city's clamour.

You take a moment to adjust the lumbar chamber in the backrest. Cradled in comfort, you turn on the engine.

Soundproofed, it immediately responds, whispering to you in hushed tones.

Images, slightly softened in the twilight, flicker across your screen. People, places, lights and faces slowly fade away together with the days arduous events.

For a personal presentation of the Mercedes S-class please call 0171-536 3555 ext 1420.

S-class

Der Käfer läßt sich den Winter nicht versalzen.

Selbst wenn die Temperaturen im tiefsten Keller verschwinden, bleibt der Käfer bei Laune.

Nach einer ganzen Nacht unter der Laterne kommt er sofort in Fahrt. Denn er hat ein 12-Volt-System mit starkem Drehstromgenerator. Und eine reaktionsschnelle Startautomatik.

Sein luftgekühlter Motor erwärmt sich spontan bei klirrender Kälte. Schließlich braucht man Luft nicht erst aufzutauen.

Und weil sich Luft schneller erwärmt als Wasser, hat der Käfer auch schnell eine angenehme Innentemperatur. Für den Fond hat er eine Fondheizung. Und für die frische Luft sorgen eine Belüftungsanlage und eine Zwangsentlüftung im Heck.

Und selbst wenn die Straße bergan geht, weder geräumt noch gestreut ist, marschiert der Käfer fröhlich los. Denn er hat große Räder und belastete Antriebsräder. Die einzeln aufgehängten Räder wiederum haben

ein sportliches Fahrwerk, so daß der Käfer durch keine Straße und keine Kurve aus der Bahn zu bringen ist.

Zu alldem hat er noch eine ebene Bodenplatte, die Kabel und Gestänge vor Beschädigungen schützt. Und einen serienmäßigen Unterbodenschutz, der allen gefräßigen Streumitteln das Fressen erschwert.

Wenn doch alles im Leben so gut funktionieren würde wie der Käfer.

And it is in this topsy-turvy world that car brands fight it out for our attention, our loyalty and our money. We want the latest, the newest, the most appropriate to our new kinds of lives — but we also crave the rootedness (just as in other categories) that comes with names we can trust, origins we can still remember and relate to.

Car brands try to offer us both. They seek to carve out emotional territories that they can fill better than any other. They try to create their own space around their marque and then protect it vigorously. And there's plenty of room: the myriad of needs that can potentially be fulfilled means that any one brand can easily create a unique offer. Matching that to a viable (and valuable) customer segment is, however, another matter.

Successful car brands do achieve these unique territories and they do so by a combination of concentration and sacrifice; concentration on the best fit between their product and values and their defined target audience. And being prepared to make sacrifices by not seeking to be all things to all people. That's how brands such as Volvo created a powerful niche around the territory of 'safety', or how VW has come almost to own the territory of 'dependability'. But it is customers' associations that are hardest to manage. And, unlike almost any other market one cares to think of, cars have a unique challenge in this area: people buy them second hand.

It's one of the paradoxes of the car market that the longer a company's cars last, the more old ones there are on the roads. In fact, at any one time there are more 'old' (say, three years plus) Mercedes-Benz on the road than there are current models.

Yet these, just as much as current models, may shape people's image of the brand — particularly since older models, selling on for a fraction of their original cost, will find their way into the hands of owners a long way from the original target audience that the brand had defined for itself. Nevertheless these

CAGES SAVE LIVES.
VOLVO

drivers too (just as with the Burberry example) will shape our views, our associations with the brand.

Car brands also illustrate a number of the routes to success that were touched upon earlier. Like Nike, Ferrari idolises its founder and seeks to keep his vision of 'to go fast beautifully' alive. That essence comes to life in its product and values, even if it is at the expense of some more basic credentials like practicality or cost. As a brand Ferrari's associations clearly polarise people, but Ferrari only wants to sell 4,000 cars a year.

Jaguar draws heavily on its racing pedigree and authenticity, and marries these to an image of power (the big cat). Its product may have let it down

in the recent past and its associations may not be for everyone, but this is very much a brand on the way back — and up.

Alfa Romeo has always been an innovator, particularly in the areas of performance and styling, but also in more mundane technologies like 'common-rail' diesel engines. Perhaps because of this, though, its flip side is uncertain quality and dubious reliability (innovation can be very much a double-edged sword in this market).

Lexus is a true success story. A relatively new brand (established in 1989) and known to be part of the much more mass-market Toyota company, it has quickly established itself on the world stage. And it

did this not through innovation, great performance credentials or passionate founders, but rather by offering quality of the highest order in an uncontroversial design package at a sensible price point relative to the premium European manufacturers. In the USA particularly this has been a winning combination. Lexus may lack heritage, may even have rather dull associations, but this seems not to have held it back for a large segment of buyers.

Opposite: 'Winter doesn't spoil the fun for the Beetle', 1973
This page: classic Volvo safety poster, 1991

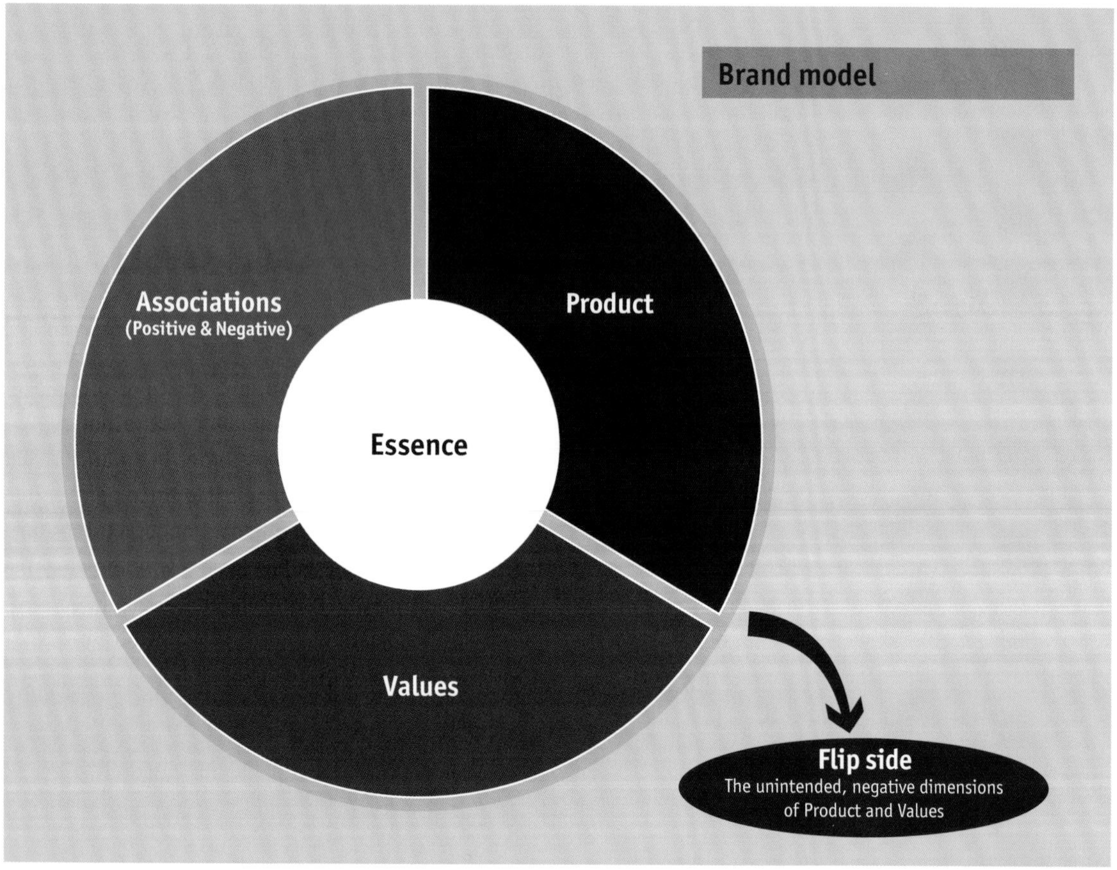

Brand model

Associations
(Positive & Negative)

Product

Essence

Values

Flip side
The unintended, negative dimensions
of Product and Values

All of these examples, from both within and outside the car market, confirm the view that it is the combination of product, values and associations that is the key to understanding a brand in its entirety. And it is these three, with 'essence' still at their heart, that provide the broad shape of a model for 'what a brand is' that will be used for the rest of this book.

To clarify the terms: 'essence' is the original, defining, central idea or thought that is at the very heart of what the company/brand is and represents. It is relatively unchanging — left perhaps as an imprint from the founder or as a constant touchstone to which all can subsequently subscribe.

'Product', of course, is what the organisation actually produces. But, more importantly, it will encapsulate the characteristics of that product which the brand owner will see as particularly important. It will in some senses be the brand owner's definition of what 'quality' is for its product. As such, it may change over time.

'Values' are what the organisation positively believes about itself and about its brand, and what its brand stands for. This may or may not be codified

Essence is the original, defining, central idea or thought that is at the very heart of what the brand is and represents

(today it usually is, though this is a relatively recent phenomenon), but it will be a set of words or statements that will have generally accepted currency within the organisation, and will therefore be seen as admirable.

For both of these last two, as the model opposite indicates, there is a flip side — a less positive adjunct to what the brand does or believes about itself. This flip side will be the unintended or even inevitable negative aspects of product and values that arise simply because what the brand is and does will not be universally admired by those outside.

This brings us finally to 'associations'. These are the actively positive or negative feelings that people (both within and outside the target audience) will have about the brand. Some may be strongly

felt, others more weakly. They may be based on personal experience or the reported experience of others. They may be rooted in truth, myths or just plain inaccuracies. No matter. They are what people believe for better or for worse — and they are very hard to manage, let alone shift. (Look no further than Skoda though to see how such a shift can be achieved.)

To understand the Mercedes-Benz brand today we need to understand the make-up of each of these components — and how they arose and evolved. The journey is going to be meticulous. It will explore the origins of the brand, arriving at a clear view of how the brand started and how it became what it is today. And that means the task is doubly difficult... literally. Because to understand

Mercedes-Benz today, we have to remove that small but symbolically important hyphen, uncouple the two words and examine what both 'Mercedes' and 'Benz' separately were as brands before they became one.

This, then, is the tale of two brands: Mercedes and Benz. Only by unravelling each will we be able to reconstruct this most famous of car names today. And, I would argue, it is only by doing this that the brand's true strength is revealed. Mercedes-Benz today draws on both ancestries. Its essence, products, values and associations include elements of both of its original corporate predecessors, and of their founders. Though welded together in shareholding terms in 1926, this by no means meant that those origins were lost or forgotten. Even today, Mercedes-Benz employees who work at Mannheim

talk of 'working for Benz', and those in Stuttgart of 'working for Daimler'. Thus do the echoes of the founders and of their different companies resonate with today's generations.

Equally interesting, and perhaps more important for today's managers, is the fact that even since the merger these two ancestries haven't always coexisted in perfect harmony. Sometimes one has been to the fore at the expense of the other, and one can

see the results for the company and for the brand at times like these. For management, what that means is that as well as all the other factors that they need to manage within the marketplace, part of their job will also be to manage the balance between these two aspects of the Mercedes-Benz brand.

Again, we will see what has happened historically when past managers have failed to manage that balance. 'Brand' may be a relatively new word in the

language of Mercedes-Benz, but the concept of brand goes right back to the beginning. Karl Benz and Gottlieb Daimler (and some significant other contributors) undoubtedly still leave their indelible mark today.

This page from left: Benz badge on the 1921 6/18 PS; Mercedes script on the 1910 22/40 PS (the three-pointed star would have been added later)

D.R. PATENT.

To understand fully the Mercedes-Benz brand of today requires an understanding of each of its two principal components: Mercedes and Benz. And to get to the heart of what the Benz brand was and stood for means delving a little into the mindset and character of its founder, Karl Benz.

Karl Benz does not fit the popular image of the 'mad inventor'. Far from that erratic, wild-eyed stereotype, Benz was in fact a hugely practical man, interested in the fundamentals rather than the glamour of invention. He cared more for practicalities than for the plaudits of his peers — preferring to be judged by the reliability of his creation than its outright performance. Yet a true inventor he was — and one can see the sources of this inspiration from the earliest years.

Born in Karlsruhe in 1844, the young Karl was only two years old when his father, an engine driver on the railways, died. Yet his father's influence seems to permeate the son's life as much as any other individual in Karl's adulthood. And not just in terms of an interest in things mechanical, but also in his highly principled attitude. As Benz would write later in his autobiography: 'I am proud of my father, even though I never knew him. His life was a shining example of the ideal — man should be worthy, helpful and good'.[1] The use of the present tense in the opening clause is telling — this, after all, was written nearly 80 years after his father died.

Telling too is his account of how, as a child, every game he played, every drawing he made ended up in some way being about the railways. He acknowledged too the debt to his teacher, Professor Ferdinand Redtenbacher, who 'understood the necessity to replace the steam engine', and that though he, Redtenbacher, had no specific ideas, 'the capital invention was still out there to be made'. Perhaps it was from him that the young Karl first sensed that, in the world of transportation, there was something missing.

Certainly, before too long this ambition seemed to take root, and one can detect also a degree of impatience. After technical college, traineeship at a mechanical engineering firm, a scales manufacturer and a bridge construction company, Benz wrote 'years of apprenticeship are not years of mastership'.

But the mastership he sought was a pragmatic one. 'Natural science', he wrote, 'should provide practical solutions to problems, that is its real value'. And later: 'In order to answer future demands, in order to create extraordinary values, one has to start with the foundation, at the bottom'.

At the age of 27 he started his own company, together with a less-than-reliable partner called August Ritter. Though primarily in the business of metal bending, his 'Iron Foundry and Machine Shop' became the vehicle for Benz to begin exploring his dream of 'freeing the railways from their straitjacket'. In this quest, his future wife Bertha was to play a crucial role. It was she who used her dowry to buy out Ritter, she who supported her (by then) husband when the business got into difficulties (at one point Benz had his tools confiscated by bailiffs), and she, famously, who completed the world's first significant journey by motorcar.

Benz's dream was clear though. As he wrote years later: 'I brazenly picked the most ambitious

goal — I wanted to construct a vehicle like my father had driven, but without horses and without rails. A street car that drives itself'. Fundamental to this, of course, was the development of a usable internal combustion engine to create such independent motion, and in the mid 1870s it was to this that Benz turned his attention.

Many internal combustion engines were developed after Otto's breakthrough. Benz observed that they 'all suffered from all sorts of problems, so I had to roll my sleeves up. And I was lucky, but it was not the luck of an invention by chance, it was the luck that rewards steady hard work'. Benz's first

stationary two-stroke engine came to life on New Year's Eve 1879. And despite his quote, serendipity *did* intervene. Benz's early two-stroke engine used coal gas and it wasn't until a freak fire in Mannheim (caused by a local woman cleaning gloves in a bowl of petrol) that Benz recognised the true potential of this new, volatile power source.

Petrol fuelled his four-stroke engines too and, as Otto's patent neared its end, Benz registered his design in 1884. But Benz's ambition, unlike Gottlieb Daimler's, was not to perfect an engine, rather it was to create a complete self-propelled vehicle. The engine, in other words, was a means to an end, not

an end in itself. Fundamentally important, of course, but not the inspiration for Benz's work.

Having left the business he had started in 1871 (and in which he by then had only a 5% stake), Karl, together with Max Rose and Friedrich Esslinger, founded Benz & Cie in Mannheim in 1883. Pursuing his vision of a complete car, rather than an engine mounted in a preconstructed carriage as Daimler was developing, Benz tested various models in the next two years before finally unveiling his first three-wheeled 'Benz Patent Motor Car' in 1886. To say it took the world by storm would be an overstatement. Benz the engineer was no great self-publicist and

even when the car was first exhibited in Paris a year later, Benz merely placed the vehicle on a stand and let visitors draw their own conclusions. This reticence was to be a key feature of the company and of the Benz brand in its later life. Perhaps not surprisingly for, as Karl later reminisced, 'In those days it was unthinkable that anyone would want to swap a stately horse-drawn carriage for an unreliable, ugly, smoky, rattly steel vehicle'.[2]

Looks were not a major concern for Benz then or much thereafter; reliability however was — and from this too one can detect the priorities that came to characterise the emergent 'Benz brand'.

Interestingly though, it fell to Benz's wife Bertha to demonstrate this reliability through her much-celebrated 60 mile journey from Mannheim to Pforzheim, widely acknowledged as the first long-distance trip in a motorcar.

Reliability, above all else, was indeed the priority of the early road user (the inconvenience of multiple breakdowns alone ensured this) and, given the enormous cost of cars in those days, simplicity also helped keep prices at least within the reach of a viable number of buyers. Benz's quote, again from his autobiography, makes clear that these indeed where his goals: 'I opted more for reliability and

economic driving than mere speed'. Here too one gets an early sense of what the Benz brand was going to be about: frugality rather than extravagance were to be its watchwords, simplicity rather than sportiness its character.

Opposite, from left to right: Karl Benz driving the original 1886 Benz car; advertisement for the original Benz Patent-Motorwagen, from an 1888 brochure This page: a depiction of Bertha Benz's long-distance drive from Mannheim to Pforzheim in 1888

This page: Karl Benz
Opposite, clockwise from top left: the Benz Victoria
(1893); Velo (1894) with Karl's daughter Klara; and
Dos-à-dos (1900)

Given this attitude, it's not surprising that Benz's cars did not evolve rapidly. The move to four wheels (in the Victoria) in 1893 followed Daimler's example. The Velo (in 1894) became, effectively, the first large-scale production car. But by the turn of the 20th century, Benz cars were looking all too similar to Karl's original invention of 14 years earlier, and decidedly old-fashioned by contrast with some of the brand's key competitors.

In the United States, an interview with Beverley Rae Kimes (author of the 1986 centennial book *The Star and the Laurel*) threw new light on how Benz was performing *vis-à-vis* Daimler in that market at the end of the 19th century.[3] Benz were bought by budding mechanics — 'tinkerers', perhaps extending their own crafts into this new field — and by country folk. Daimler, by contrast, was less well known, being the preserve mainly of the rich, those who would rather just drive, and were happy to leave the mechanicals for someone else to worry about. Looks and performance, not engineering, were Daimler's main selling point in this market.

Karl Benz truly was the inventor of the car. His was a more complete vision than that of Daimler. He built his car from scratch and then focused on perfecting that invention, not by over-elaboration but rather by making the basic concept as durable

and well engineered as possible. His cars were simpler than Daimler's, ultimately to their detriment, but though simplicity later became a millstone, in the early days it was the key to their success.

In truth, Benz probably stayed with his initial creation too long. He was an inventor, but not an innovator. Coming from behind (in design, if not technology), Daimler at first caught up and then overtook Benz in both the integrity of look and the modernity of engineering in his cars. Benz never really embraced the front-engined designs of others, never really entered into the spirit of competition, specifically on the racetrack, that was reshaping cars on the road. He became, if anything, more dogged in his life-long focus on functionality and fitness-for-purpose.

'I have always been a cautious driver', he wrote. Any one of my employees I caught speeding had to return to bench work again'. And Benz's conservatism applied equally to the company. By 1900, his commercial director Julius Ganss was regularly bringing in large orders. Yet Benz feared these, partly because he believed quality would suffer. Despite all of this, by 1900 Benz & Cie was the biggest car company in the world, producing over 600 cars in that year, from a workforce approaching 500 employees. Over six times as many cars as Daimler, with over half

'Benz refused to have his eyes opened to the fact that his early efforts were but stepping stones towards better things'

of these going to customers abroad. The cars might have changed little but their reliability continued to be a benchmark for the market and this, together with (even then) the sense that Benz were the 'original' had built a strong, loyal customer base.

But with the turn of the century came a turn too in Benz's fortunes. Commenting on this period, motoring author David Scott-Moncrieff is both insightful and critical: 'Benz refused to have his eyes opened to the fact that his early efforts were but stepping stones towards better things. In his view, something approaching finality in motorcar design had been reached by the turn of the century. The slow-running, heavy, unresponsive horizontal engine was the correct design, so he told himself, and for some years he made a desperate effort to swim against the tide of progress — until his own business began to collapse over his head.'[4] Scott-Moncrieff made the crucial point: 'By about 1901 the buying public began to turn away from the reliable, but paralysingly slow Benz cars, which even then had a remarkably antiquated appearance.'[5]

Others were even more damning. The British writer RW Buttemer wrote in 1904 that a discussion on the belt-driven Benz of that time was 'somewhat an excursion in palaeontology'. St John C Nixon, another commentator on the era, claimed that 'the Benz car was becoming the subject of ridicule, and every move made in the direction of designing more powerful cars only served to bring to light the weakness of the original Benz design'.

One can only guess at how Karl would have reacted to this kind of criticism at the time. Events moved rapidly though and, ultimately, his actions spoke loudest. With sales falling after 1900, Ganss brought in two new designers and gave them parallel briefs to build a new road car and to develop a competitive response to the new Mercedes on the racetrack. The internal politics, the tension between these two briefs (and the men responsible for executing them), the pressure from Ganss and, no doubt, the poor publicity the company was receiving at the time — all of these conspired to drive Karl Benz to resign from the management board of the company in 1903. The product of all this upheaval, the Parsifal, was introduced to the market later that same year.

Benz, the genius, the creator of possibly one of the most life-changing inventions of the past 200 years, had been the company's greatest asset in its early years. By 1901, without a doubt, he had become its greatest liability.

From being a leader (and in my mind there is no doubt that the car was his brainchild more than that of Daimler), he became a follower. The basic, simple, durable, original design was, quite simply, out-classed. The cars were seen as heavy, dull and unimaginative, the engineering almost overly sturdy, by comparison with their lighter, faster, sleeker competitors — notably the Mercedes. Benz the inventor ultimately could not convert himself into Benz the innovator. And yet one is left feeling a huge fondness and respect for the man. His commitment was total, his motives genuinely those of the professional engineer. He was not a salesperson at heart (his wife again took responsibility for much of that role), nor was he an avaricious man. Wealth, for him, was counted in achievements and ideas, not in status or cash. Above all, though, he left his mark on the company, and the brand, to this day.

With Benz's departure (although he continued to serve on the advisory board) and the arrival of the Parsifal, the company's fortunes began to recover. From a low point of 172 vehicles in 1903, the business was rebuilt, although it wasn't until 1908 that sales

success. Just as today, brand perception often lags behind the reality — even though the new Benz was, undeniably, a step-change in both design and technology, the company could not just shake off the image it had developed over the previous years. As Beverley Rae Kimes pointed out in her book *The Star and the Laurel*, 'because the Benz name was so identified with out-moded belt-drive motor carriages the new model was promoted in Europe with emphasis on the name Parsifal, not Benz'. Unlike Daimler's change of brand name to Mercedes however, the same trick didn't seem to work for Benz.

Worse still, the Parsifal itself, though a quantum improvement, was still only catching up with some of the newer Mercedes models, of which no less than four had been launched in the years 1901 to 1903. As Scott-Moncrieff noted: 'Ganss had fallen between two stools. No-one wanted to buy either the antiquated Benz cars, now almost a joke, or the new Parsifal Benz models which were poor motor cars'.

exceeded the high water mark of 1900, at 646 cars. Thereafter progress was rapid: 1,700 vehicles in 1910, 2,700 in 1911 and over 3,000 in each of the three years leading up to the First World War. In any one of these years, therefore, the company was producing more cars than it had in total under Benz's stewardship in the last ten years of his involvement. What accounted for this dramatic turnaround in fortunes?

In the Benz & Cie annual report for 1903/4, the commentary speaks of looking forward to 'our new models', describing them as 'outstanding both in construction and making, and universally admired'. Even at the time this was something of an optimistic statement. The 'new model' in question was the Parsifal but it hardly proved to be an overnight

This page: the Benz Parsifal, 1903

This page: the 1906 Herkomer race. Prince Heinrich of Prussia with his Benz 40 PS
Opposite: the 'Blitzen Benz', launched in 1909, was capable of more than 125 mph

Despite encompassing the recently developed shaft-drive system, the original two-cylinder Parsifal sold just 24 cars. It was only after the new vertical four-cylinder engine (developed by Benz himself) was installed in the car that sales picked up. But it was clear that yet more fundamental change was required. New sources of inspiration needed to be found if the company was to fully reinvent itself in the post-Karl years. It was to motor racing that the company turned for just such inspiration.

We've already touched upon Karl Benz's antipathy to motor racing. True to character he saw far more value in long-distance endurance testing in proving the real qualities of the car. Even as recently as 1900/01, the company's annual report had criticised 'the recently emerging obsession for competitive racing at ever greater speeds'. And in the same

year Karl had personally scratched his son Eugen's entry from the Gordon Bennett race. Racing was most certainly not in his blood.

Benz cars had been entered privately of course in a number of tournaments, and Scott-Moncrieff reported that 'the racing record of the privately entered cars was good. They did not score many wins, but they nearly always finished'. Karl would probably have approved of this outcome. Indeed, in the last two years of his involvement Benz was persuaded to sanction his cars being entered as works models in competitive events, driven by his sons Richard and Eugen. But they left when Karl resigned in 1903 (later to form Carl Benz Söhne, and focus on small commercial vehicle production), so the company really did face a fresh start in this competitive arena.

The years 1904 and 1905 were lean ones, with Benz scoring only minor successes in competitions in which the all-conquering Mercedes were not entered. The breakthrough came in 1906 and particularly 1907. The Herkomer Trophy (effectively a 1,000-mile reliability competition) had started in 1905 and Benz had performed well in the first two years. But in 1907 the company swept the board, winning six of the thirteen prizes on offer, including the overall trophy. In 1908, Benz won the even stiffer Prince Heinrich tour from Berlin to Frankfurt, beating the Mercedes. But both of these truly were endurance tests, and it wasn't until later that same year that Benz entered Grand Prix. They didn't win (that prize, naturally, went to Mercedes) but all three of their cars finished and in recognition the team was awarded the 'dependability' team prize.

Again, Karl must have smiled at this. The very facet that he had most prized was still underpinning the brand's success, even though Benz & Cie's new managers had moved heaven and earth to create fast, desirable racers.

The Benz brand, in other words, was still about endurance and reliability. The founder's hallmark of 'fitness for purpose' was still more deeply embedded than the embryonic racing credentials, for which his successors continued to strive. But their moment was about to arrive.

Paradoxically, at the very moment that 'racing fever' was reaching its peak, an economic downturn was making its way steadily across the Atlantic from the USA to Europe. No matter what plaudits were being won on the racetrack, domestic car production in

Germany was being hard hit, especially for the luxury manufacturers.

Daimler cut its workforce by over 1,000 between 1906 and 1908 and its production by two-thirds. Benz fared better, turning as it had before to stationary engines, but was still forced to cut car production by half. By 1909, due to the continuing recession, the major manufacturers (including Benz & Cie and DMG) signed a racing boycott to spare themselves the additional expenses of these competitions. This probably benefited Benz since it shifted the focus back to the showroom and away from the racetrack at the very moment when its road-car model range was looking the best it had for many years. In 1908, Scott-Moncrieff noted, 'considerably more interest is being evinced in Benz models this year than in previous years, owing to their smart

performance this season. In design these cars possess no feature of novelty, being modelled entirely on approved lines.' Benz's legacy was still apparent therefore, but the brand's associations were beginning to change.

No car changed them faster than the 'Blitzen Benz' launched the following year. Motor racing may have been shelved for the time being, but the pursuit of ever higher speeds had not. Based on the Grand Prix cars of 1908, the 'Blitzen Benz', designed by Hans Nibel, was capable of speeds of more than 125 mph — extraordinary performance in those days. And it looked the part. Unlike the clumsy, upright, functional Benz cars of old, this car had the swooping lines and aggressive styling of a true racer. Its enormous 21.5 litre engine produced 200 bhp at a relaxed 1600 rpm. In 1911, it set a new world speed record of 143 mph, faster than the fastest train, and twice the speed of the fastest aeroplane of that era.

This new Benz was a far cry from Benz cars of old, and Ganss (still at the helm) wasted no time in capitalising on this 'new dimension' to the Benz brand. Between 1910 and 1914, a quick succession of new models was launched; from the small but highly successful 8/18 to the largest and most powerful Benz ever: the 39/100.

In 1912, 12 different Benz models covered a price range of 7,000 to 40,000 marks. Some clamoured for rationalisation, but while business was booming Ganss was able to overrule them. Only the outbreak of war brought this rapid period of success to a premature end.

Benz & Cie had not been idle on other fronts either though, and two developments that were highly significant in shaping the character of the brand took place in these years too. Firstly, with more truck orders than the Mannheim factory could cope with, the company affiliated and then merged with Süddeutsches Automobilwerk Gaggenau to create Benzwerke Gaggenau as its commercial vehicle division. The plant survives and prospers to this day and is still first and foremost associated with the Benz name, for its workforce at least, even now.

Secondly, and again very much in the spirit of Karl's priorities, from 1908 Benz & Cie began developing diesel engines — the ones that, later in the brand's life, would come to give Mercedes-Benz such dominance in both commercial vehicles and, above all, taxis. Early diesels were already proving themselves robust and long lasting and as such were a natural fit with the Benz brand.

Karl Benz's legacy also filtered through to these years in the shape of his personal ethos, reflecting those aspects he most admired about his father: 'worthy, helpful and good'. Indeed, he himself earned the nickname 'Papa Benz' for his generous, paternalistic oversight of those who worked for him. More importantly, he put some of those values into practice within Benz & Cie — and they continued to shape the internal brand of the company long after the founder's departure.

By 1910, Benz workers enjoyed unparalleled provisions in the workplace even beyond their above-average salaries. There were benefit funds, salaried-staff relief funds, even a foundation to help over-worked or unwell employees to take a holiday. This kind of support is still evident within Mercedes-Benz today — but how many of today's workers know that they have Papa Benz to thank for instilling such attitudes into the company over 100 years ago?

Opposite: Benz & Cie workforce, Mannheim, 1897

Opposite: the emotional `Mein Benz' advertising first ran in black and white in a German magazine called Jugend (Youth) in 1913. The colour advertisements date from 1920 and 1921
This page: the Benz 18/45 PS Runabout, 1914

Just as the internal brand was evolving, so too was the sophistication of external communications about the brand. By today's standards, most car advertising from the 1890s and 1900s looks pretty clumsy and prosaic. Some early advertisements for Benz (as for its competitors) were no more than profile lithographs of the car, together with price lists and technical specifications. If anything Benz & Cie was slightly ahead of the competition in this field. As early as 1888 advertising stressed comfort and practicality and by 1904 (probably in a desperate attempt to find something good to say about its outdated cars) the advertising talked about 'the marque of confidence'.

But *true* confidence in brand communications for Benz didn't emerge until some years later, shortly before (and then again after) the First World War. The '*Mein Benz*' advertisements ran all over Europe and truly broke the mould of brand advertising.

Contrary to the brand's previously stuffy (and generally masculine) image, here we have not only beautiful young women embracing (literally) the car, but even hinting at the joy of ownership: 'My Benz'. This was a far cry from the rational, reliable world of the founder, and one wonders what he made of these images at the time. My view is that they are both beautiful and powerfully relevant. Not only do they attempt to soften the external image of Benz, they also suggest that the car is ownable, personal — a possession to be treasured. This 'pride of ownership' theme is one that is carried down through the years, but these advertisements set the bar very high for those that followed — and the line '*Mein Benz*' is still owned by the company to this day.

But, again as any student of brands will know, the radical changes that Benz & Cie made to their product and its advertising in the last few years

before the First World War would not have been sufficient to overwhelm the deeply rooted associations built up around that brand over the previous quarter of a century.

Yes, the Benz brand was reinventing itself, particularly after 1907, but by no means had these later sporting, even sexy, credentials done much to change fundamentally the popular perception. The Benz brand, even in 1914, was still viewed first and foremost as an 'original' (the company's showroom communications in that year still stressed Benz as the inventor of the car), not as a leader. Authenticity was a value that the brand, after all, could truly claim and be proud of, as it could too with quality.

Benz cars may have been a bit old-fashioned in the public view, but in terms of both design and construction they had maintained the virtues of simplicity and consistency — which delivered the

His cars were designed to fulfil the desire for free motion, not to be rich men's jewellery or overly fast confections

still-important benefit of reliability. This meant that they had earned a large degree of trust from the car-buying public and those who aspired to join it. The cars might be perceived as being a bit heavy, even unimaginative until the later years, but they were sturdy and frugal, at least by the standards of the day.

In truth the product had evolved considerably; the model line up in 1910 bore no resemblance to that of the company at the time of Benz's departure. But memories linger and attitudes shift more slowly than new models in the showroom might suggest. As late as 1910, according to Kimes, Benz owners were still driving nine- or ten-year-old cars and writing eulogies to the company about their love of these earlier models. So while the product reality might have changed by the First World War, the overwhelming perception of Benz cars was still that they were more basic than some of the flashier competitors, well engineered (maybe even *over*-engineered) and above all durable in the extreme. Like their original creator, they might not be the most innovative cars on the market but in terms of functionality and fitness-for-purpose they were second to none.

Now, finally, we can begin to construct our model of the Benz brand, as it stood in 1914. We've seen how Karl Benz's vision was of a 'complete' car, one that would, in his words, 'raise us to a higher degree of evolution — free motion'. And we've seen how his invention brought this vision to reality.

But we've also seen how his focus on perfecting that original invention probably held the company back in the years immediately before and after his departure — and yet how his priorities shaped the product, at least in the minds of the public, even beyond that time.

We've observed how his values became the company's values, and hence the brand's values — both internally and externally. In part these values come from the fact that he was the inventor (notably authenticity); in part they reflect the 'worthiness' that Karl so admired in his father.

We've noted along the way the associations that built up in the public's mind around what the Benz brand stood for. How these associations have gathered around the cars, almost by accretion, laying down new sediments of meaning as the years rolled by. And those meanings clearly have both upsides

and downsides. But as noted in the previous chapter, no brand is or wants to be all things to all people. The Benz brand clearly appealed to many — remember that it consistently outsold DMG throughout this period. It may have been less glamorous than Mercedes, but perhaps its greater depth, authenticity and rootedness appealed to many. Perhaps, though again less romantic, Benz's focus on safety before speed caught the imagination of more timid (but equally prosperous) potential owners. In some ways, the Benz brand reminds one slightly of Volvo — not to everyone's taste, but catering for a careful safety-conscious segment.

Remember that Benz's sturdiness was reinforced, then as now, by its involvement in commercial vehicles. It's no accident that Benz's original factories today produce primarily DaimlerChrysler's commercial vehicles and buses. No surprise either that it was in these same factories that resistance to the 1998 corporate name change (from Daimler-Benz AG to DaimlerChrysler) was most vocally expressed. The Benz name as part of the holding company title was, it is true, sacrificed by Jürgen Schrempp in order to keep 'Daimler' at the front of the new

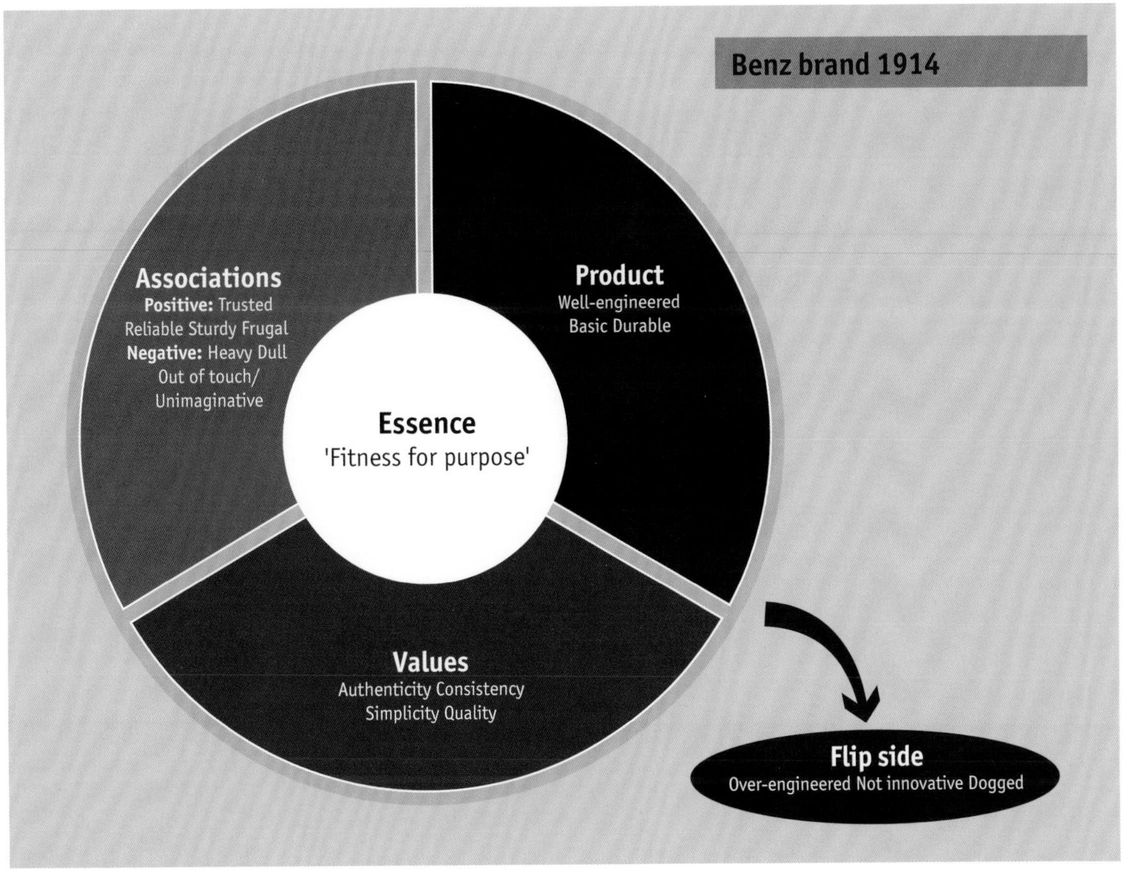

Benz brand 1914

Associations
Positive: Trusted
Reliable Sturdy Frugal
Negative: Heavy Dull
Out of touch/
Unimaginative

Product
Well-engineered
Basic Durable

Essence
'Fitness for purpose'

Values
Authenticity Consistency
Simplicity Quality

Flip side
Over-engineered Not innovative Dogged

organisation's corporate brand. Symbolically though, it was hard for the workforce at Mannheim to accept — and remains a sore point in that city to this day.

And at the centre of all of this, what do we have? What is the essence that is at the heart of the Benz brand? In my view it is quite simply Karl Benz's original focus on function before form, on fitness-for-purpose. He himself described his earlier cars as ugly — looks, styling, glamour were not what drove him. What was important was functionality; that his treasured idea should actually work. His cars were designed to fulfil the desire for 'free motion', not to be rich men's jewellery or overly fast confections. What mattered was that they did the job they were intended to do — and kept on doing it. It is these beliefs that form the essence of the Benz brand.

Karl Benz *was* a genius and his invention lives with us to this day. But so too does his brand, and what it stood for, as part of today's Mercedes-Benz brand. It is truly an enduring legacy.

CHAPTER FIVE

THE BIRTH OF MERCEDES

Daimler-Motoren-Gesellschaft
CANNSTATT

Auszeichnungen:

Cassel 1889
Silberne Medaille.
Bremen 1890
Silberne Medaille.
Leipzig 1892
Ehrenpreis
der deutschen Kaiserin und
Goldene Medaille.
Halle 1892
Diplom.
Moskau 1892
Broncene Medaille.
Eger 1892
Goldene Medaille.
Scheveningen 1892
Goldene Medaille.
Troppau 1893
Silberne Medaille.
Essen 1893
Diplom.
Mainz 1893
Goldene Medaille.
Hannover 1893
Silberne Medaille.
Aussig 1893
Goldene Medaille.
Bolsward 1893
Diplom.
Metz 1893
Goldene Medaille.

Auszeichnungen:

Nymwegen 1893
Silberne Medaille.
Chicago 1893
5 Diplome mit Medaillen.
Uithuizen 1894
Grosse silberne Medaille,
Ehrenpreis d. Königin-Regentin
und 300 fl. Prämie.
Norden 1894
Goldene Medaille.
Erfurt 1894
Broncene Medaille.
Stuttgart 1894
Goldene Medaille.
Lauenburg a. E. 1894
Diplom.
Ulm a. D. 1895
Broncene Medaille.
Turin 1895
Goldene Medaille.
Lübeck 1895
Goldene Medaille.
Düsseldorf 1896
Broncene Medaille.
Aberdeen 1896
Goldene Medaille.
Banff 1896
Goldene Medaille.
Perth 1896
Goldene Medaille.
Baden-Baden 1896.
Goldene Medaille.

2pferd. Daimler-Boot auf dem Neckar.

Daimler-Kajütboot mit 20 pferd. Motor.

Station. Daimler-Motor.

12 HP. Daimler-Bo

Daimler-Victo

Daimler-Beleuchtungswagen.

Daimler-Geschäftswagen.

Daimler-Locomotive.

DAIMLER-MOTOREN-GESELLSCHAFT
CANNSTATT

Daimler-Lastwagen.

Daimler-Omnibus.

Daimler-Draisine.

Daimler-Wagen.

Daimler-Waggonet.

otor.

gall-Maschine
Motor.

Opposite: Gottlieb Daimler's vision extended beyond the automobile to the all-encompassing motorisation of land, sea and air
This page, from left to right: Gottlieb Daimler, 1898; Wilhelm Maybach, c 1920; Emil Jellinek, 1905

'Papa Benz' may have been clearly the father of the Benz brand, but for Mercedes the lineage was much less singular. The latter, as we will see, was not the offspring of one parent, or even two. Mercedes was, in fact, the child of many parents.

Most significant of these was Gottlieb Daimler, but it's worth remembering that he never saw a car called a Mercedes, never knew the girl after whom the car was named, and would not have recognised the three-pointed star that was to become the symbol of his legacy. As with Benz & Cie, the turn of the 20th century proved to be a turning point in the life of Daimler-Motoren-Gesellschaft (DMG) too — because with Daimler's death in 1900 the baton of progress, in innovation at least, was effectively handed on to Wilhelm Maybach and Emil Jellinek. As the former was to say to the latter some years later: 'You and I are the inventors of the Mercedes car'. This was an uncharacteristically immodest quote from the usually humble Maybach and belies the fact that, without Daimler, neither man would have been able to make that claim. Maybach may well have been Daimler's 'bridge to the future', but the foundations for that bridge were laid much earlier — by Daimler himself.

Today one often associates innovation with youth — one's thirties often seem to be the peak years, particularly in the more creative or high technology industries of Europe and North America. Career progress in the 19th century was much slower, even though life expectancy was considerably shorter. Gottlieb Daimler was no exception, though it may surprise some to know that he was already in his late thirties when he joined Deutz, in his forties when he moved to Cannstatt with Maybach, and 52 by the time of the unveiling of his first vehicle in 1886. Indeed, it was only in the last quarter of his life that the achievements for which he is most remembered were forthcoming.

Having lost his first wife in 1889, he remarried four years later — to a woman 22 years his junior — and to the five children by his first marriage added another two. This, together with failing health in the last few years of his life, perhaps explains why his impatience for innovation was matched only by his determination to secure a strong financial position for himself and his family, over that last decade in particular. From this we can perhaps trace some of the seemingly insatiable appetite for improvement that we find in the company today. But Daimler's innovative engineering skills outstripped his business acumen in large measure. His genius, importantly very different from Karl Benz's, stemmed from a vision of 'motorisation': the potential role for engines in all areas of life, not just transport. This ambition, as we shall see, has also created a powerful vein of diversity within the brand today.

And so it was to the business of engines and engine production that the not-so-young Gottlieb

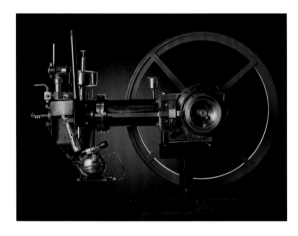

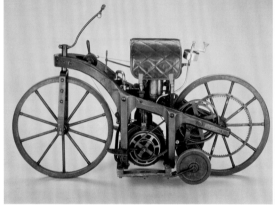

This page, from left to right: Daimler's original four-stroke engine; Daimler Reitwagen, the world's first motorcycle, 1885
Opposite, from left to right: Max Duttenhofer and Wilhelm Lorenz, partners in DMG

Daimler turned his attention when he joined Gasmotorenfabrik Deutz (near Cologne in Germany's Rheinland) in 1872. Maybach, whom Daimler had met seven years earlier, soon followed in his patron's footsteps and the two of them familiarised themselves with the workings of the four-stroke engine (developed by Otto) over the next few years.

As for Benz, but for different reasons, the shortcomings of the railway were a prompt for Daimler's interest in independent travel. In 1881, during a visit to Russia, he wrote in his diary: 'The overcrowding on the trains in summer and the constraints of the railroads were abhorrent to me, and led to the idea of self-propelled driving'[1].

Though trained as an engineer and having served a long apprenticeship both in his home town of Stuttgart and a number of cities abroad, Daimler was an ambitious man too. His interest in the constant testing and trialling of prototypes often waned faster

than Maybach's, and when the opportunity to start his own business closer to home, in Cannstatt, arose, he took it. Having bought a new house with a greenhouse in the grounds that would serve as a workshop, he and Maybach (who again followed his master) set about building their new venture. Daimler's focus was engines and with Maybach's help he built on Otto's core technology. Together they developed a new design of ignition system that allowed the engine to run at much higher speeds than had previously been achieved. Daimler and Maybach then turned their attention to reducing the size and weight of the complete engine — such that, initially, it could be fitted to a bicycle-like frame. The patent for this was granted in 1885.

What happened next illustrates perfectly the different approaches of Daimler and Benz. Whereas the latter produced his complete car in the following year — truly an *invention* — Daimler's next step was to order a carriage to which he planned to fit his and

Maybach's engine. Theirs, in other words, in respect of the car at least, was an innovation. Carriages, clearly, had existed for centuries and over the previous 50 years a number of modes of self-propelling power had been tried — steam, coal and gas in particular.

What Daimler and Maybach were developing was a better sort of self-propulsion: smaller, lighter and more powerful than anything that had gone before, but an innovation nonetheless. Their *invention* was the compact, high-revving, four-stroke engine, not the car. That distinction went to Benz. This difference of focus is one that Daimler too would have acknowledged. According to Kimes: 'Daimler believed that acceptance of the gasoline powered automobile would follow, not precede, acceptance of the gasoline engine in other modes of transport'[2].

Thus we find (again unlike Benz — and remember that each was unaware of the other's work), Daimler next experimenting with engines for

motorboats. Despite this, to Gottlieb Daimler goes the credit for the world's first *four-wheel* automobile at the end of 1886. This distinction, between the contributions of Daimler and Maybach on the one hand and Benz on the other, is important because of what it later tells us about the two companies, the two brands and Mercedes-Benz today.

Benz was the true inventor, arguably staying with that invention too long. His concept was the complete car, engines being a means to that end. Daimler (with Maybach) by contrast invented the modern petrol engine, but in respect of the automobile they were innovators. That spirit of innovation ultimately led them to overtake Benz for a period commercially (and certainly on the racetrack). And it has also shaped the innovative spirit and reality of the brand and the cars today. To some this may be a controversial distinction, to me it earns the two men equal plaudits.

But if Gottlieb Daimler's vision of 'all-encompassing motorisation' was beginning to become a reality, his business ambitions most certainly were not.

As Maybach's need for testing grew, and with it the workforce (primarily in the late 1880s producing boat engines), Daimler found he was ploughing more and more of his personal money into the business, and profits were thin or non-existent. His principles may have been (according to Scott-Moncrieff) fine and lasting workmanship, and constant research and development, but these weren't saleable in their own right.[3]

Daimler sought partners and, with them, capital — and in 1890 found them in the shape of Max Duttenhofer and Wilhelm Lorenz, each of whom invested 200,000 marks in the new company. The matchmaker in fact was Kilian Steiner, Head of Württembergisches Vereinsbank and what today we would call a venture capitalist. Through an earlier

deal, he had brought together Duttenhofer and Lorenz; now he introduced the pair to Daimler. Perhaps because of their earlier relationship, or maybe just their greater commercial nous, the two men soon outmanoeuvred Daimler in the running of the newly founded Daimler-Motoren-Gesellschaft (DMG). Maybach, unhappy with the terms of his contract, left a year later and, now without his partner, Daimler's position *vis-à-vis* the two new directors worsened further. The key to their dispute was the latter's insistence on producing the more lucrative stationary engines while Daimler was by now more interested in vehicle production.

Though technically in breach of their contracts, vehicle development was henceforth carried out covertly by Maybach, with Daimler's financial backing, in separate premises — initially in Maybach's home, later at the famous Hotel Hermann. Relationships between Gottlieb and his partners did not improve,

however, and in 1894 the by now unwell Daimler was threatened with either paying off historic debts or turning his shareholding over to them. He was forced to agree to the latter course of action and effectively left the company at this time to work with Maybach.

Gottlieb Daimler, in his diaries, was certainly embittered about this period. In 1893 he wrote: 'Trusting the promises of friends, I signed and left the power to them. Now I see that I was deceived.' And later: 'In my whole life I have never been judged so badly as by this pack of wolves in sheep's clothing.'

'Wolves' Duttenhofer and Lorenz may have been, but stupid they were not. When, just a year later (1895), the company was approached by a group of British industrialists to buy the rights to the Daimler engine for the huge sum of 350,000 marks, but only on the condition that Daimler (and hence Maybach) returned to the company, they quickly agreed.

(This, incidentally, is how the Daimler name came to be used in the UK independently of its German parent. And while no car in Germany has carried that badge since 1901, the Daimler name and brand continue to exist in the UK, albeit within the Jaguar stable, right up to the present day.)

Daimler and Maybach's return to the company in 1895 coincided with an almost immediate turnaround in DMG's fortunes. By now cars were becoming significantly more popular and, though the company's volumes were trivial (less than 70 cars produced in the six years since DMG started), Maybach's work at the Hotel Hermann had produced some strong new designs. He at least was looking forward to rebuilding the business.

For Daimler though, time was running out. Although he had reinstated a healthy financial position, his own health was failing. Tragically, after spending six years fighting his partners, he spent the next four fighting heart disease. In truth, his earlier innovative genius played little part in the first decade of DMG's life — that contribution was already passing to Maybach. And while he took a keen interest in the performance of his cars, both in the market and on the track, his influence was waning. Gottlieb Daimler, the man later described as 'unquestionably the father of modern automobilism', died in March 1900.[4] He may in fact have shared that paternity with others, but there is no doubt that he has left a lasting impression on the company to this day.

Like Benz, Daimler was committed to quality. But through his company's product (even in his lifetime) performance was higher up the agenda than it was for his Mannheim competitor. Through his innovative genius he placed performance — and the leadership position it subsequently delivered — at the heart of the Mercedes brand.

Gottlieb Daimler's death in 1900 did not portend the end of the company. In a remarkable parallel with Benz & Cie after Karl's departure, DMG actually performed better in the early years of the 20th century than it had at any previous time. The key to this was Wilhelm Maybach, and his new-found partnership with Emil Jellinek, the man whose daughter would famously lend her name to the car that changed the company's fortunes.

It's almost as though, with Daimler's death, Maybach emerged from the shadow of his patron. Born 12 years after Daimler, in 1846, the young Wilhelm had been taken under Daimler's wing at the age of 19, after a childhood largely spent in an orphanage. He followed Daimler's career at every stage and as DMG's chief engineer he was the natural successor to his former benefactor.

But between 1870 and 1900, Maybach very much worked under the great man. As Maybach's granddaughter recalled later: 'Gottlieb Daimler had the ideas and Wilhelm Maybach implemented them.' Maybach himself wrote that 'Daimler presented himself as the supreme authority whose decisions must never be questioned' — and this hint of arrogance also finds its way through to the brand in its later years.

Opposite: DMG's 1886 motor coach, with Adolf Daimler driving his father Gottlieb

Two of Wilhelm Maybach's innovations
This page: four-cylinder petrol engine (1898)
Opposite: the honeycomb radiator that was
invented in 1900

It must have been hard for Maybach to work in such a shadow, particularly since the corporate environment of DMG was pretty bloody throughout its early years. Perhaps the move to the Hotel Hermann was a breath of fresh air after the politics of the Cannstatt offices, perhaps indeed it was in some way liberating to be able to 'fly solo' after Daimler's death.

Maybach's diligence and patience in those early years are legendary, perhaps deriving from his experience in the orphanage where, according to his biographer Dr Harry Niemann, sermons and lessons taught Maybach that 'there is no such thing as individual success, only the collective good which the work and toil of each individual strives for'.[5] His humility too was a constant feature of his life at DMG — I was left with the strong sense that he always put someone else's interests ahead of his own and hence was often disadvantaged financially relative to others. But if his outward spirit was quiet, his inner drive for constant technical advance rang out. Crucial in assisting Daimler in the original invention of the engine, Maybach, often single-handedly, not only took this work forward but also began increasingly to turn his attention to innovations in fields related to the car as a whole, not just its powerplant. In quick succession came the sliding pinion gearbox and the spray-nozzle carburettor, the honeycomb radiator and, in 1898, the world's first four-cylinder petrol engine.

Though a friend is said to have remarked 'Maybach seems to have gone mad — he wants to build carriages that run without horses!', Wilhelm's extraordinary energy and talent earned him from the French the title '*Roi des Constructeurs*' — King of the Designers.

But for the king to truly earn his crown, for the prolific innovator to amalgamate all of his individual achievements into a single vehicle, Maybach had to team up again with another strong personality — one whose demands, however unreasonable, drove Maybach to new heights. And this new partner, Emil Jellinek, could not have been more different from Maybach. As Niemann, in his biography of Maybach, observes: 'The Mercedes car was a synthesis of the ideas of an open-minded businessman and *bon vivant* and those of a meticulous technician with all the exaggerated piety of his native Schwabia'.

What a combination! Maybe, though, Maybach did enjoy this unlikely relationship — the attraction of opposites is a well-established theory. Certainly the two together seemed to achieve things that Daimler, Lorenz and Duttenhofer could only have dreamed of a few years earlier.

Jellinek's involvement with DMG (and it was with the company rather than with the founder, whom he probably never met) began in 1897. Having seen an advertisement the previous year, he travelled to Cannstatt from his home in Nice to purchase a 6 hp belt-driven car capable of just 15 mph. Already

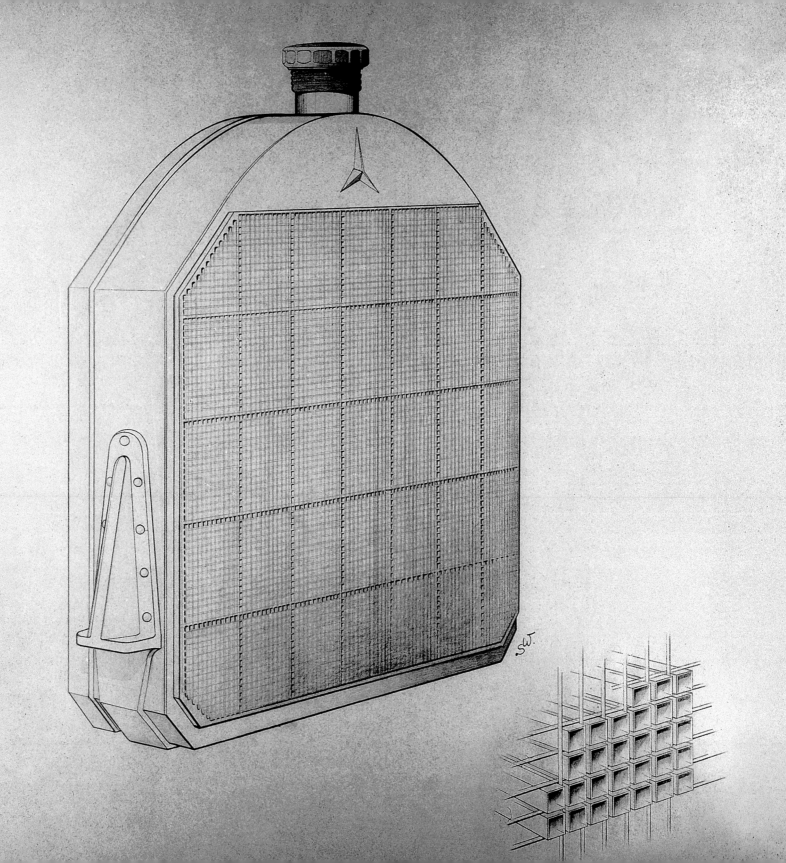

This page: the four-cylinder, front-engined Daimler
Phoenix of 1900
Opposite: Emil Jellinek with his daughter Mercedes,
c 1895, and his yacht of the same name

interested in competition (the first true 'race', the 80-mile Paris to Rouen race, organised by the newspaper *Le Petit Journal*, had been held in 1894), Jellinek wrote back the following year to order four further cars, provided that they were capable of 25 mph.

The order of four cars was 'to get the company's attention' and the strategy seemed to work. But only after the directors had agonised over whether such a speed could be attained. Jellinek reassured them that the speed was 'his business' not theirs, and the company duly complied. Shortly after delivery, according to Jellinek's biographer (his son Guy), this demanding customer wrote again to say that the

speed had been safely achieved but that 'I do not like the position of the engine... the engine replaces the horse, therefore it should be in the front'. Suggesting they save their objections for the next point, Jellinek continued: 'I want a four cylinder engine — I know you will say it is impossible... But look into it and don't put it on the side'[6]. Demanding indeed was Mr Jellinek, but since his demands came with an order for a further six cars to that specification, the company again, and specifically Maybach, pondered its response.

Clearly Jellinek was no ordinary customer, clearly too he was selling the cars on to others

among his wealthy friends on the Côte d'Azur. They in turn were already enjoying the thrills of racing the cars in the hills above Nice while Maybach was toiling away in Cannstatt.

The 28 hp Daimler Phoenix, developed by Maybach in response to Jellinek's brief, was certainly no looker. Though front-engined and embracing Maybach's four-cylinder design, the car had a high centre of gravity and heavy lines. The first outing in Nice in March 1900 (the month of Daimler's death) ended in tragedy — DMG's factory foreman, Wilhelm Bauer, was killed at the first corner of a hill climb and fingers of blame were pointed in all directions.

DMG announced it was withdrawing from competition... and Jellinek hit the roof.

Racing and competition were increasingly seizing the public imagination at this time and, though still the preserve of the rich, Jellinek was well aware of their commercial value. Having joined the board of DMG in 1900, he managed to persuade the company that it would be 'commercial suicide' to withdraw — and to back up this assertion told Maybach that what was needed was a totally new car: lighter, lower, wider and longer than the ungainly Phoenix, and with at least 35 bhp. His argument was that such a car would not only win races, but sell itself,

and to back *that* up, he said he would order 36 such cars at a total value of over half a million marks.

The company really could not refuse such an offer, even when it came with two significant strings attached. The first was that Jellinek should have exclusive sales rights in France, Austria, Belgium and the USA (another early hint at the company's internationality), the second was that the cars should be badged 'Mercedes'. This name, meaning 'grace' in Spanish, was that of his daughter — and cars were not the first possession to which Jellinek had applied it. Both his home and his yacht were similarly named and he had also used it as a pseudonym for his racing entries.

Bizarrely, with hindsight, the company did not put up more than a token resistance. Certainly, had Gottlieb still been alive, it might have caused more consternation. But Gottlieb's son Paul Daimler was there and was involved in the development of the new car, and even he did not seem to demur from this most radical of rebranding proposals. Though unthinkable today, after over 15 years of proudly displaying the Daimler name, the company seems almost immediately to have been prepared to acquiesce to Jellinek's strange request, and the name Mercedes was finally registered in June 1902.

The new Mercedes, having won its debut race at Nice in 1901, was fitted with a comfortable body and driven quietly around the city

Perhaps it was the fact that 36 cars would make up roughly a quarter of a full year's production for the factory — or maybe it really was that a 'wind of change' was blowing through the business after the founder's death. (It is hard to think of a significant analogy in another business for such a radical name-change — certainly not one prompted by a single buyer.) Either way, the change that occurred as a result of these further demands by Jellinek was truly amazing. The new car that emerged was genuinely revolutionary and literally redefined the shape of cars for years to come.

The contrast with its predecessor was acute: the new Mercedes really was 'lighter, lower, wider and longer' — it looked not just technically more advanced than anything else on the road, but was also beautifully shaped in its own right. In less than a year Maybach, working with Paul Daimler, had created something truly special, a car that pulled together all his previous innovations — right down to the honeycomb radiator that remains a feature of Mercedes-Benz saloons today.

Unlike Benz's original invention of 1886, the new Mercedes really did take the world by storm. Commentators in Europe and the USA spoke of its speed and 'noiseless running', as well as its elegance of design. Even at the time it was recognised as having redefined the concept of the car. As Paul Meyan, Secretary of the French Automobile Club, wrote at year-end: 'We have entered the Mercedes era'[7].

Again, with hindsight, this was a significant moment. Somehow Daimler's concept, Maybach's creativity and Jellinek's persistence as a customer had all been welded together into a brilliant whole. More importantly for what it would say about the brand, the new Mercedes epitomised the founder's values of competition and innovation, Maybach's advanced product technologies, Jellinek's customer-driven requirement for performance, and the quest for quality that united all three.

The car, and the brand, went from strength to strength. In what Scott-Moncrieff called 'a master stroke of salesmanship', the new Mercedes, having won its debut race at Nice in 1901, was 'fitted with a comfortable body and driven quietly around the city'. This then was not just a racer, but a car designed equally to fulfil the needs of the ordinary driver. Orders flocked in: DMG's sales rose from 232 in 1903 to 698 in 1904 and 863 in 1905. New models followed, based heavily on the original 1901 design, notably the 40 and 60 hp 'Simplex' that refined the Mercedes 'look' yet further.

Despite these triumphs, corporate life at DMG became, if anything, even more explosive. Duttenhofer, Maybach's principal supporter on the board, was shot dead in 1903 by the jealous husband of his mistress. Lorenz (now single-handedly running DMG) made no secret of his dislike of Maybach — conveniently failing to remind him of the expiry of his contract in 1900, and using that pretext to hire a replacement technical manager, Friedrich Nallinger, when Maybach was away from work due to illness in late 1903.

Opposite, from top to bottom: beautiful and advanced, the first Mercedes racing car, the 40 PS from 1901; fitted with its 'comfortable body'

Painfully, even for the humble Maybach, he was reduced to writing to Lorenz in June 1904 begging for his job (or even a lesser job) back, and payment of bonuses that he felt had been promised. Lorenz's response was to offer him a role in the inventors' office, alongside his own son, and no bonuses. This must have been devastating for Maybach — and it certainly did not best please Jellinek, still the company's biggest customer. As early as 1903 he wrote to Maybach: 'Your absence from Cannstatt is evident from the low quality of recently released cars. Daimler without Maybach is like Russia without a navy'[8].

Later, in 1907, after Maybach's eventual departure and with car sales now falling, he wrote even more earnestly: 'Daimler Motor Company constructs incorrectly designed vehicles, unloved by the public, but these unloved cars are forced upon that same public; [the company] has a chief designer, an able man in Paul Daimler, but who is unable to finish a design on his own because he lacks what Maybach had in abundance — 1) a sense of form, 2) a feeling for what the buying public wants and, finally — in spite of his promises — he never does what I ask of him.'[9]

But Jellinek's influence too was drawing to a close, and he retired from the automobile business in 1909. His legacy, arguably, was that of bringing the customer into the boardroom. Famously, he wrote to DMG: 'You are mistaken if you believe that the buying public will put up with the whims of your designers. The decision as to what a car should look like lies with the former, not with the latter.'[10] This may have been a little naïve, but the motive was sound. And in subsequent years, periods when the company failed to listen to the customer tended to precede times of commercial hardship. For this plea (which today one would call 'customer-focus') we have to thank Emil Jellinek.

Maybach's career continued, however. He stuck it out in the inventors' office for only a couple of years, using the time primarily to develop marine applications of his earlier designs, but finally succumbed when the politicking reached its peak in 1906. Despite Jellinek's protestations and the offer of an honorary board position he left the company forever in April 1907.

In truth, Maybach had to keep working simply to support his family. He, after all, never shared substantially in the riches that DMG was now generating. His decision to stay on after 1903, despite the humiliations he received, was largely driven by the need to support his wife Bertha, their daughter Emma and his two sons Karl and Adolf. Adolf, in particular, needed constant support since from early adulthood he had been diagnosed as schizophrenic and spent most of his life in psychiatric institutions, finally succumbing not to old age, but to Hitler's euthanasia programme in 1941.

Though an aside to this story of the Mercedes-Benz brand, it's worth remembering

Maybach's later life, because the brand carrying his name enters the story again at the very end of this book. After many years of work before and after the First World War with airships, notably the Zeppelin — and a move in this role to Friedrichshafen — in 1922 Wilhelm and his son Karl once again turned their attention to cars. True, it was Karl rather than his father who led the way now, but even in his late seventies, Wilhelm took an interest and gave his son extensive technical, as well as moral support. Six-cylinder luxury saloons were produced between 1921 and 1926 and in 1929, the year of Wilhelm's death, came the first of the wonderful V12s. The Type 12 was followed in 1930 by the DS7 Zeppelin, and the following year by an 8-litre version: the DS8. These cars, though rare on the roads, set new standards of opulence, luxury and performance that even the Mercedes-Benz of that era struggled to reach. Wilhelm Maybach would have been proud of those cars.

More pertinent, at least from the perspective of the Mercedes brand, is how Lorenz and his fellow

directors managed not only to cope with all the upheaval in the first decade of the 20th century, but also to keep the business viable and on course. Despite the death of the founder, the disaffection and then departure of the principal designer and the murder of the chief executive, the years 1904 to 1906 were a definite high point for the company in sales terms, with between 500 and 1,000 vehicles produced in each year.

The answer lies first and foremost in the cars themselves of course: four models had been launched in the previous three years and the company was reaping the rewards of its great leap forward. The Simplex in particular was leading the way. Despite its name it was, by the standards of the day, quite a complex car technically. As well as effectively putting an end to the era of the 'horseless carriage' (a look that still defined the styling of most cars at the turn of the century) the new Mercedes also set new standards of technical intricacy for the market. Henceforth, technology in all areas would in some senses progress faster even than exterior

GORDON BENNETT COURSE

THE 1903 RACE WAS RUN OVER THE CIRCUIT SHOWN, WITH START AND FINISH AT BALLYSHANNON. THE TWO LOOPS WERE DRIVEN ALTERNATELY FOR SEVEN LAPS, BEGINNING WITH THE SHORTER AND ENDING WITH TWO LAPS OVER THE LONGER, FOR A TOTAL DISTANCE OF 327.5 MILES.

styling. And the Mercedes brand, then as now, would increasingly be associated with the mechanical and electrical complexities that accompanied that progress. For the time being though, Lorenz and his colleagues could at least count on having leading-edge cars to sell.

Nowhere was that better proven than on the racetrack. Partly as a test-bed, partly just out of the spirit of competition, DMG was increasingly involved in motor racing in these opening years of the century. Jellinek's sponsorship and the personal interest of the rich and famous had accelerated that involvement, but it was the public who increasingly

clamoured to see these new metal beasts hurtling around circuits. And the circuits of the day were a far cry from today's slick, regulated Grand Prix venues. Of the tournaments of the time, none was more prestigious (or gruelling) than the Gordon Bennett series. The 1903 race, due to take place in Ireland, was only seven laps long — but each lap was nearly 50 miles in length.

Unbelievably, the Mercedes cars were driven to the circuit from Germany, by way of France, England and Wales — ready to compete the day after their arrival at the circuit. The reason for this dramatic entrance was the fact that DMG's factory

in Cannstatt had burned down just weeks before, consuming the three original cars and necessitating the borrowing of three last-minute replacements from private owners.

To race at all under such circumstances was extraordinary; to win outright, as the Mercedes did, was the ultimate testimony to the powers of the new car. The plaudits followed, the orders came in even faster, and the company rebuilt its factory on the neighbouring site of Untertürkheim, where it is still located today.

For the brand, this too was a key moment. To its already burgeoning associations with wealth and elegance, it now began to add the attractions of excitement and sportiness. All of this set it apart from the field, especially from the Benz brand, which at this time was still struggling to shake off its old-fashioned, slightly frumpy persona.

The Mercedes brand continued to build on these associations over the coming years, and the competitive spirit became increasingly a core value of the brand. As well as confirming its leadership position within the market, racing was also key to the way in which the brand was promoted. As with Benz (but much earlier), Mercedes advertising now eschewed price lists and technical specifications and began promoting the speed and glamour of its cars. The tone was vibrant, the imagery truly liberating.

This page: Mercedes won the prestigious 325-mile Gordon Bennett race in 1903
Opposite: Mercedes advertising in the early 1900s

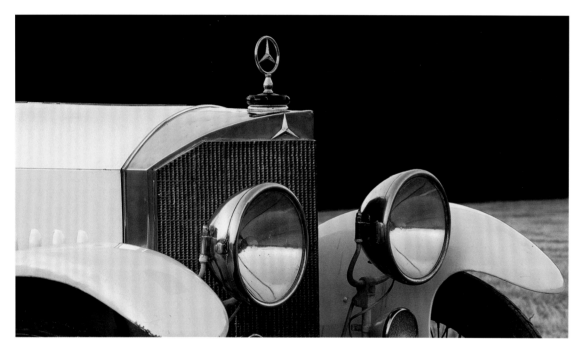

This page: the three-pointed star on the bonnet of the 1922 Sport Phaeton
Opposite: Mercedes raced to victory in the French Grand Prix in 1914

The fact that the company grew, despite the fire and the other problems, from 500 employees in 1902 to nearly 4,000 by 1906 is a tribute to Lorenz and his management team, notwithstanding their brutality towards some of the old guard. Paul Daimler, Gottlieb's son, should take credit too; it was he, after all, who had worked with Maybach on the original 1901 Mercedes. It was Paul too who, as chief engineer, had steered the company's product (now increasingly in commercial vehicles also) in the post-Maybach years.

Though sales dropped back after 1906, partly as a result of the economic situation around the world, they picked up again in 1909 and had reached new and heady heights by 1914. Though still fewer than Benz was producing, DMG's output averaged around 2,000 vehicles per year in each of the four years before the outbreak of war.

Paul Daimler is also the man credited with the inspiration for the now famous Mercedes logo. By 1909 Lorenz had retired, and his replacement Alfred von Kaulla (of Württembergische Bank) had decided that Mercedes (rather than DMG) required a new trademark. Until that time the cars had carried simply the name, originally even with two accents over the second and third 'e's. As various ideas were discussed, Paul produced the famous postcard, the asterisk on which was indeed a star, albeit one of five points.

With hindsight, it may well have been Paul's description of his father's vision of motorisation, and of how this vision extended to land, sea and air that

interested von Kaulla, more than Gottlieb's original scribble. Even then there is a discrepancy: DMG, as we noted, registered both a three- and four-pointed star in 1909, so if the three-pointed version was to be the embodiment of Gottlieb's vision, where had this fourth geographical dimension come from?

The truth of the matter may well be that then as now the whole imagery of stars — reaching for the stars, stars as signs of victory, achievement and fame — was what appealed to the two men. In fact Scott-Moncrieff pointed out that no fewer than 31 other companies were using stars as part of their logo or identity at this time, so the Mercedes design, though classic, was hardly original. Both three- and four-pointed versions (with their distinctive 'relief' designs) were registered on 28 June 1909, bizarrely

just 40 days before Benz & Cie registered the 'laurels' motif for its brand.

The driving force for this logo redesign, at least in von Kaulla's eyes, was in any case probably less to do with a 'visual eulogy' to the founder, as Kimes suggested, than with cementing and protecting the Mercedes brand identity from the competitive incursions of its growing band of imitators.

Imitation of the Mercedes both in technology and design was a growing problem for the company in those pre-war years. Maybach himself, in 1904, had written that the 'competitors now have access to almost all of these achievements',[11] and later the French technical writer Baudry de Saunier wrote in his magazine *Omnia* of how for many companies 'it was the fashion to copy the Mercedes rigidly and

even today many manufacturers find it the best recommendation of their make to refer to its similarities to the Mercedes-type'.[12]

The star, then, was probably born more out of the necessity for legal protection and as a trademark signifier than out of a more ethereal motive. In a sense it doesn't matter — the brand was, by that stage, the sum of all that Mercedes had come to be and stand for over the previous decade; almost any symbol could have been chosen to signify that achievement. In fact, the star used entirely on its own (without a surrounding ring) would only survive another 17 years, after which it was integrated into a new combined logo, that of Mercedes-Benz. And yet, it does seem almost to have created a life of its own. The phrase 'following the star' is still used today (for example

when people move jobs within DaimlerChrysler), and undoubtedly seeing it on the front of a car's bonnet over the years has been a reassuring and inspiring sight to generations of motorists.

A wise choice then, and one that signified Mercedes' leadership of the global car market by 1914. DMG may not have been the biggest seller of cars, but in terms of its performance at the peak of the market, the company and the brand certainly held a commanding position. If, in 1901, Europe had entered the 'era of the Mercedes', then by 1914 the brand really was the leading light on the world stage.

'I don't want the car of today, or the one of tomorrow. I want the car of the day after tomorrow'

So now, finally, we can begin to construct the model of the Mercedes brand as it was in Europe when war broke out in August 1914. First and foremost we have a Mercedes product that had by then combined its outstanding racing and performance credentials with a seemingly unstoppable series of technological advances and increasingly luxurious interiors and designs.

The brand's values, influenced by Maybach and Gottlieb and Paul Daimler, were innovation, a strong competitive spirit and, above all, the ever-present pursuit of quality. To these, via Emil Jellinek in particular, had been added a sense of customer focus that distinguished the Mercedes brand from most others at the time.

On a less positive note, the flip side of these was a sense of inconsistency within the organisation (the years of strife had taken their toll), and the company was still capable of producing some less successful models — the 1908 35 hp Kardan looked particularly awkward for its time. And though by 1914 the cars were still winning races (notably the French Grand Prix of that year) and speeds of over 60 mph were becoming routine, the cars were becoming increasingly complex technically and hence less reliable than the better-selling Benz cars. Gottlieb's arrogance too had found its way through to later generations of owners and managers. His belief in being the best had led to the company increasingly behaving as though it were — with some justification this was true, but then pride often comes before a fall.

The brand's associations for the customer, though, suffered no such setbacks. Mercedes was, for most, the epitome of elegance combined with sportiness. Its special place in the eyes of the public was as much a function of its exuberance of spirit as of its mastery on the racetrack. If it had negatives these were a function of its price and, hence, what would today be called its 'user image'. At a time when, for example, the average DMG worker earned only around 1,500 marks per year and the cheapest Mercedes, the 8/22 hp, cost 6,500 marks, this was an expensive purchase. This meant that ownership was the privilege of the few — exclusivity was very much a trait of the Mercedes brand even in that era.

So, what was the essence of the brand in 1914? Certainly a passion for innovation, for advances in design, for success on the track and in the market-place defined the spirit of the brand. But above all was the sense of leadership. This was a brand that had broken the mould, that had defined the shape of cars as we know them today, that had led the world in terms of technology and design and that, by 1914, was still a leader in its field.

More than ten years earlier, Emil Jellinek had told Maybach: 'I don't want the car of today, or the one of tomorrow. I want the car of the day after tomorrow.'[13] Maybach and his successors had lived up to this demand and had consistently delivered cars that were both ahead of the market and ahead of their time. For Mercedes, leadership was now not only in the heart, but in the blood of the company — and of the brand.

It's important to remind ourselves not only of how different this picture is to that of the Benz brand, but also to recognise that in many respects this difference stemmed from the quite distinct corporate cultures, the internal brands, of the two organisations.

While the progress of Benz & Cie in Mannheim had been steady and to a degree predictable — reacting in product terms only in the later years to Mercedes' triumph on the track — DMG's corporate life

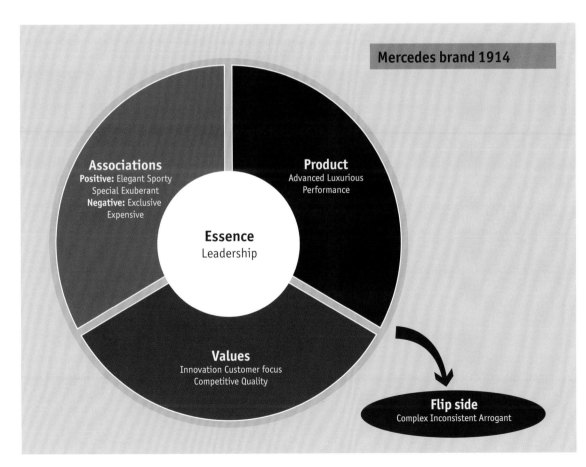

Mercedes brand 1914

Associations
Positive: Elegant Sporty
Special Exuberant
Negative: Exclusive
Expensive

Product
Advanced Luxurious
Performance

Essence
Leadership

Values
Innovation Customer focus
Competitive Quality

Flip side
Complex Inconsistent Arrogant

story had been far more tumultuous. Disputes, management upheavals, even death, fire and ritual humiliation had made life at the company a lot less focused and more chaotic than at Benz.

The consistent strand, returning to my original anecdote in chapter 1, was Schwabian-ness. The company's heartland in Stuttgart, at the centre of that region, had contributed partly through Daimler, but primarily through Maybach, some of the key distinguishing features that one can still discern in the business today.

Attention to detail, frugality, care in construction and an endless focus on quality at every stage — these are the hallmarks of the Schwabian culture. Maybach, and others of his ilk, epitomised these: a God-fearing man, careful to do nothing to excess, with a strong work ethic, he set the pattern for many that followed, not just in Stuttgart but in outposts of the company today throughout the world.

Like Benz, DMG was a beneficent employer — conditions in the newly built factory at Untertürkheim were world-class in their day; the company even had a lemonade factory built to supply the workforce with a non-alcoholic substitute for their usual tipple!

Unlike Benz, though, the internal culture at DMG was even more focused on the detail of its product (the *tüftler* syndrome), even more fascinated with the intricacies of its technological advances. This led to more complex cars, and a more complex culture: Schwabian to its core, but demanding of its employees and, on occasion, seemingly chaotic to the outside observer.

What is interesting though is that it is also a culture that has consistently revered technical skills over managerial abilities. It is commonplace now to celebrate the achievements of Daimler and Maybach as innovators and engineers. Indeed, some rate the latter ahead of the former. (One particularly harsh biographer, Sass, went so far as to say: 'Daimler's only actual invention was the face-cam regulator. Everything else, even those in Daimler's name, came from Maybach.'[14]) But unlike today's world, it is the technicians not the chief executives who are the heroes of history.

Lorenz, in particular, is dealt a harsh verdict as the man who argued with Gottlieb literally into the grave, and then schemed and politicked to oust Maybach. And yet this man (whom Daimler had invited to join the company in 1890) steered the strategy, the finances and the product of the business for nearly 20 years — and ultimately to great commercial success. Arguably, without his managerial hand on the tiller the company would have imploded at some earlier point. Daimler and Maybach may have been full of ideas, but without commercial skills, business strategy and strong management, those ideas would never have seen the light of day. Though much vilified, maybe history should have been kinder to Duttenhofer and particularly to Wilhelm Lorenz.

Opposite: three cars destined for the Gordon Bennett race were destroyed in a fire at DMG's factory in June 1903

CHAPTER SIX

MERCEDES AND BENZ

A MARRIAGE OF CONVENIENCE

The story of Mercedes-Benz is, as noted earlier, the tale of two brands. And the years from the outbreak of war in 1914 to the time of the Wall Street Crash in 1929 mark the period when the two came together to form today's single entity. It is a critical period in the brand's life because the decisions made in the mid-1920s — particularly in respect of how the different parts of the newly merged company would share out production responsibilities — would afterwards fundamentally affect the shape of the company, right up to the present day.

Unlike the cataclysmic effect of saturation bombing in the Second World War, the 'Great War' (as it was inappropriately labelled at the time) had much less serious consequences, industrially at least, for Germany's home territory. Indeed, to support the military effort on land and sea, and increasingly in the air, both Daimler-Motoren-Gesellschaft (DMG) and Benz & Cie actually grew significantly during the years 1914 to 1918.

The Benz plants, switching from producing passenger cars to military and transport vehicles, also began to focus on submarine and aircraft engines. The company's workforce increased from under 8,000 employees to over 12,000.

DMG's transformation was even more spectacular. Its Untertürkheim plant quadrupled its workforce to 16,000 to produce aero-engines, and a new plant, employing a further 5,000 people in nearby Sindelfingen, was built in 1916 to produce the aircraft that would house them. Cars continued to be manufactured, mainly for the military, but in much smaller quantities than before the war.

If Benz and Mercedes had grown to be very different brands by 1914 then the war itself did little to close the gap. Though it meant that both companies focused on similar military priorities, the approach of each remained distinctive. In terms of their cars, the two brands were as different at the time of the Versailles treaty as they had been when hostilities began. But if the war had only interrupted the progress of each brand, it had certainly disrupted the previously expanding German car market as a whole.

As one journalist commentator noted in 1920: 'Compared with Paris, London or Brussels, the first impression received in Berlin is that the use of automobiles has ceased'[1]. Private car registrations were minimal compared to Germany's victorious neighbours: blockades, shortages and rationing of fuel had effectively killed off the domestic market in the war years. And with military needs at an end, DMG (which had invested particularly heavily) had no option but to lay off nearly 10,000 of its so recently swollen workforce. Benz fared better — a pattern we keep on seeing — producing nearly 1,000 cars in 1919, albeit of mainly pre-war designs.

In a further confirmation of how different these two companies and their brands were as they entered the 1920s, while DMG had been working on superchargers to boost the performance of aircraft engines, and now began to transfer that technology to cars, Benz had been concentrating its efforts on the frugal and durable diesel engine. They too were about to take this technology into the arena of passenger cars — to dramatic effect.

It was typical of the brands that Mercedes should come to be associated with the sexy supercharger (or Kompressor as it is called in Germany), while Benz would employ the more robust and reliable technology of diesel. The imaginations of

This page: advertising for Benz and Mercedes during the First World War
Opposite: German stamps showing the extent of hyperinflation in the early 1920s – prices rose from 75 pfennigs to 20 billion marks to send a letter

motoring journalists (probably because of its obvious implications for sporting performance) were clearly caught by the former. The imagination of the motoring public, still desperate for an accessible, economic form of transport, would be caught by the latter.

Both companies, and their respective brands, were far from alone in this shrunken market. For a country 'consuming' less than 20,000 cars a year, there were, in 1920, over 110 manufacturers producing close to 200 models. Adler, Stoewer and, in particular, Opel were the principal competitors — often offering cars at less than half the price of a Benz, one-third the price of a Mercedes.

To put this in context, Langworth calculated that one single factory, using mass production 'would

have sufficed to supply the whole of the German market'.[2] And in Detroit, 3,000 miles away, that was exactly what was happening. Even before the war Ford had been producing 80,000 units a year; now these volumes were even higher. And while the number of cars in Germany at that time was less than 75,000, in France it was 100,000, in Britain a quarter of a million and in the USA a staggering 1.3 million.

Imports too were becoming a fact of life in the German car market, a market that was being squeezed from all directions. Strong brands were what was needed then, as now, to survive, but large-scale production too was becoming a parallel requirement. Big was becoming not just beautiful, but commercially more necessary with each passing year.

Benz and Mercedes, though very different, did at least share a common position at what today would be called the 'luxury' end of the market. So at face value it might have seemed natural for the two to look to each other for partnership; but that was an idea that had already been rejected in 1919. 'Too much pride was at stake on each side,' commented Langworth again.

The squeeze though was about to get worse, but still it would take a third party, Deutsche Bank, to push the two companies towards what, with hindsight, looks very much like a marriage of convenience.

Inflation, as a result of the war alone, had already taken the German mark down from just over four to the dollar in 1914 to 62 to the dollar by 1919.

Initially, that benefited the two brands, at least in terms of export sales if not in the domestic market. Both companies were pleasantly surprised by how old friends of the brands from abroad seemed to have returned. DMG spoke of 'rejoicing' in this, Benz simply of being 'quite astounded' that its cars were again finding favour even with former enemies.

As it would turn out, the foreign currencies thus earned would soon be the only currency of any worth in the companies' coffers. By 1922, and worse still in 1923, inflation had raced to stellar levels: at its height it cost billions of marks to post a letter, and workers were paid half-daily in order to spend their salaries at lunchtime or in the early evening before it became worthless by nightfall. Stories abound of suitcases or even wheelbarrows being used to take home one's pay packet. The effect on the economy was perhaps more catastrophic than the war itself. No wealth held in cash survived; the only things of value were property, possessions and, of course, holdings of stocks and shares, representing as they did percentages of a company's worth, not just cash.

If pride had been the source of DMG's wish to remain autonomous then this hyper-inflation probably destroyed any last vestiges of confidence in the possibility of such 'splendid isolation'.

Although still competitors, Benz and Mercedes did at least offer similar types of cars, at similar prices, to similar customer groups. Now, though, not only were others targeting those same customer groups, but the numbers of such customers were shrinking as personal bankruptcies followed swiftly in the wake of the loss of all savings. For DMG, the situation was exacerbated yet further by the fact that motor racing, by now such a mainstay of the Mercedes brand image, was off limits to the company and the nation.

Racing did begin again after the war, though not until the French Grand Prix of 1921. But then, and for some years to follow, Germany was banned from competing. To Paul Daimler's despair, even the company's most loyal sporting clientele were now at risk too.

'Both Daimler and Benz faced imminent collapse in the early post-war period'

But it was through a third party that the two companies would be brought together — and then only after some pretty heavy arm-twisting and intrigue. The merger was more akin to a shotgun wedding than a romantic union, and holding the shotgun was Deutsche Bank.

The process of bringing the two companies together is fascinating partly for the detail of this classic corporate power struggle, but mostly for what it produced in terms of management structure, production realignment and, most important of all, brand integration.

Essentially, the relationship between both companies and Deutsche Bank can be traced back to much earlier times. It was Deutsche Bank that had acquired Württembergische Vereinsbank, the former employer of DMG Chairman von Kaulla and DMG's bank since 1893. That bank too, through a subsidiary, had also helped set up Benz & Cie and had subsequently handled its affairs. Now Deutsche Bank was to use these long-standing relationships to act as 'matchmaker' for the two organisations. But not without a struggle.

According to Langworth: 'Both Daimler and Benz faced imminent collapse in the early post-war period... Had one or both remained independent, they would certainly have been out of business by 1925'. This is possibly a pessimistic verdict. DMG, it is true, had suffered badly — sales peaked in 1920 at just over 2,000 vehicles and fell below 1,500 in 1922. But the position in 1923 was stable and by 1924 sales were again at 1920 levels. Furthermore the company, more than even in its early years, was diversifying into fields as disparate as bicycles and typewriters. Still, this probably would not have saved it. The truth of the matter was that its all-important car brand was taking a hammering. Hit also by strike action, the company's report and accounts for 1922 are revealing: 'Sales were difficult,' runs the commentary, 'we often encountered a complete stop in orders'. Then more plaintively: 'Our homeland gets poorer and poorer, which results in a narrowing market for our product'.

The situation for Benz was better, if not exactly rosy. Some indeed considered a Benz car a safe place to invest their cash to shield it from the effect of inflation. How typical again that they should choose this 'tried and trusted' brand rather than the more racy (and hence perhaps more risky) Mercedes. Benz & Cie's sales showed a similar pattern to DMG's but (as had been the case in most years throughout their histories) at an absolutely higher level: nearly 3,000 vehicles in 1920 and 1921, only once (in 1923) falling below 2,500. Its company report for 1922 speaks only of 'the constant changes of our economic market having a strong effect on the sales of our product'. Perhaps Benz was also protected by its higher and relatively stable level of commercial vehicle production. This stood at around 1,000 vehicles per year throughout the period — in other words, all the losses were coming from the slump in sales of passenger cars. In fact, by 1923, over 40% of the total volume for Benz was coming from trucks, buses and lorries. Benz, therefore, might just have survived the economic storm that was engulfing the brand's homeland — and it is interesting to speculate as to what kind of brand it would have been today had it gone its own way.

Opposite: Deutsche Bank was instrumental in the Daimler-Benz merger of 1926

As before, Volvo is the one that comes to mind, with its clear market niche, reputation for strength and safety and significant involvement in commercial vehicles. Like Volvo, a solus Benz brand today would probably be a bit dull and worthy, renowned for its sturdiness and longevity, but still with a distinctly committed and loyal user-base.

We shall never know because despite Benz & Cie having, according to Langworth, 'greater commercial drive than Daimler', DMG was inexplicably judged the senior party in the forthcoming joint venture. Emil Stauss (later von Stauss), a board director of Deutsche Bank who had sat on the supervisory board of DMG since 1920, teamed up with Karl Jahr (from the bank's recently acquired subsidiary) who was Deputy Chairman on the supervisory board of Benz & Cie, to fulfil his vision of a new German auto-industry giant, along the lines of the emergent General Motors. Outmanoeuvring other interested parties, the two worked together to put the finishing touches to their plan.

Jahr, with Stauss' backing, presented a proposal for a 'streamlined association of common interest' to the boards of both companies, which was ratified by both on 1 May 1924. Though not yet a full merger, this was in fact the point of no return. Managerially, it threw up some interesting arithmetic. The management board had six Daimler directors, five from Benz; on the supervisory board (a common feature of German companies) the two companies had nine each, including five from within the ambit of Deutsche Bank. Notably, the company's board now included three world-class engineers: Hans Nibel, Friedrich Nallinger and the increasingly ambitious Dr Ferdinand Porsche. The supervisory board included the rehabilitated Karl Benz and the previously much maligned (and now equally elderly) Wilhelm Lorenz.

For the day-to-day running of the joint business, a smaller executive committee was also created, to be headed by a Benz director, Wilhelm Kissel. To Kissel fell the job not just of knocking the new business into shape, but frequently of knocking warring heads together as the politics escalated.

Perhaps, with hindsight, it was a smart appointment. Even though Benz was outperforming DMG commercially and the two companies had virtually identical turnovers, Daimler was the company that seemed, somehow, to come out on top. It feels more balanced for the real executive power to have been placed in the hands of Kissel, the long-time Benz man.

Now the big decisions, the ones that truly shaped the destiny of the single Mercedes-Benz brand, started to be made. Obvious steps were taken first: the sharing and rationalising of sales offices in German cities to avoid duplication, setting up external communications that stressed the shared ambition of the two brands (still at this stage separately identified in their advertisements).

Opposite, from left: even before the merger, DMG and Benz & Cie ran joint advertising featuring both companies' logos; DMG and Benz & Cie advertisement, announcing their association of common interest, 1924

This page: the Benz 16/50, pictured on the
company's final day in 1926
Opposite: the very similar Mercedes 10/40/65
Pullman-Limousine from 1921

Much more significant for the brand in later years were the production decisions now being debated. Initially it was suggested that Benz & Cie's car body operations be closed down completely — with this production being moved to Sindelfingen. Alongside this, it was also proposed that only 2-litre cars would be built at Mannheim, with 4- and 6-litre models coming out of Untertürkheim. In the event, the existing Benz factories continued to build complete cars for some years after the merger, although designs were increasingly coming out of Stuttgart. The aim was complete integration, and this was pretty much achieved within ten years of the merger. Indeed, even by 1930, the company's official history records that 'as a rationalisation measure, car production is concentrated in Untertürkheim, truck manufacture in Gaggenau and body construction in Sindelfingen'. Poor old Mannheim doesn't even get a mention in that year. While the economics of all of this probably made sense, the cultural impact would have been harder to calculate. The legacy of those decisions, particularly in respect of the internal brand within DaimlerChrysler's various plants, is still felt within the company today.

It was to take two more years for the full merger to be consummated (in June 1926), but for all intents and purposes by then the marriage of convenience was a done deal.

Economic factors again explain why the association of common interests had to be firmed up so quickly. With the halving of tax levels on luxury cars in 1925, foreign competitors started making massive inroads into this end of the market. American imports were undercutting prices even on the smaller Benz models and certainly up the ranges of both brands. Supercharging may have injected yet

more performance into Mercedes, but it didn't stop rivals exploiting the lack of economies of scale in DMG's plants.

Even when both brands cut prices drastically, demand failed to recover fully and Benz laid off a further 1,000 employees at Mannheim while DMG laid off 1,500 in Stuttgart. By now, the merger was a necessity — and nowhere more so than in the product line-up. If prices couldn't be kept low through mass production, then at least savings might be made by eliminating duplication in the two model ranges.

The core Benz model was the four-cylinder 10/30 hp, which with the six-cylinder 16/50 hp was the mainstay of its range, together with the less successful 11/40. The closest Mercedes was the supercharged 6/25/40, but more significant in sales terms were the Porsche-designed and much bigger 100 hp Type 400 and the 140 hp Type 630.

The overlap between these two model line-ups was not huge, although there were still some remarkably similar-looking cars. Savings, if they were to arise, would have to come from future shared product developments as well as cutting the current

ranges — but those developments were still some way off. It was an early decision by both companies that they should not only withdraw slow-selling models (especially where there was any duplication), but also develop wholly new ones to take their place. Though it was the Benz models that tended to be dropped, the new cars (already under development in 1925) more closely resembled former Benz designs than 'typical' Mercedes. Notably, all had flat-faced radiators (clearly reminiscent of earlier Benz models such as the 16/50) rather than the angled radiator front more often associated with Mercedes.

Mercedes could lend Benz outstanding performance credentials. Benz could underpin Mercedes with its rugged build and reliability

With all of these changes in contemplation — and the political somersaults going on internally — what was it then that made this marriage work?

The short answer of course is necessity, but that doesn't explain why these two companies (rather than another pairing) should have got together. True, there was the Deutsche Bank link — it met all the substantial borrowing needs of both operations, and viewed it as the bank's duty to 'risk losses in order to ensure the survival of a company of vital importance to the national economy'. (This incidentally is a viewpoint confirmed by my interview with Hilmar Kopper, former CEO of Deutsche Bank, who like his predecessors sits on the board of Daimler-Chrysler.) More fundamentally there was something deep in the values of both companies that could, whatever else might divide them, unite the two in mutual respect for each other. And that something was quality — the continued, consistent, deeply held belief within both organisations that the pursuit

of excellence, particularly in respect of product, was a worthy goal. The expressions of that excellence, the definitions of quality if you like, may have been different, but the ambitions were very similar.

If little else united the two brands as they moved inexorably closer, quality at least was common ground. It generated respect, but also understanding, a unity of purpose — and even the beginnings of a common language. Think back to the models of the Benz and Mercedes brand and it is clear that, in respect of values, quality is the one word that unites the two.

Each had talked for a generation about being 'the best of the good' (Benz) or about aiming for 'the best or nothing' (Daimler). Now was the chance to put that shared language and belief into practice. Now was the moment to recognise that these were not just two brands that would happen to co-operate, but rather, that they were two truly *complementary* brands.

Who knows whether at the time the key people saw this opportunity? There seem to be no quotes that hint at this potential being consciously recognised. And yet now it seems so obvious: Mercedes could lend to Benz some of its outstanding performance credentials, Benz could underpin these for Mercedes with its reputation for rugged build and reliability. Mercedes could bring some glamour to Benz's staid image, Benz could bring consistency to the more 'flighty' Mercedes brand. Mercedes could sharpen up Benz's product through its heritage of innovation, Benz could deliver the virtues of durability and simplicity to underpin it. In design terms, the elegance of the Mercedes look could sit happily with the sturdiness of the Benz frame. And so the list and the logic go on — with quality underpinning each and every complementarity between the two brands. Other writers have spoken about the shared engineering skills of the two companies. To me the shared ethos of quality is far more important. This was what provided

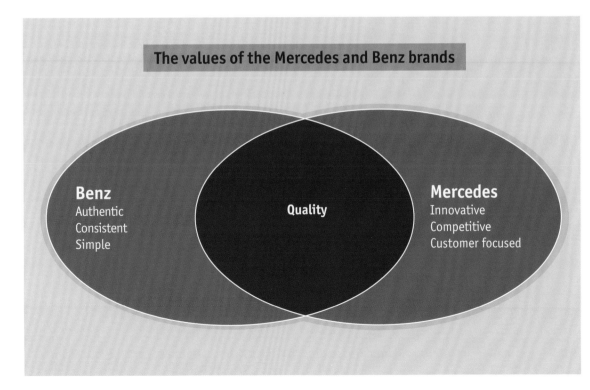

The values of the Mercedes and Benz brands

Benz
Authentic
Consistent
Simple

Quality

Mercedes
Innovative
Competitive
Customer focused

the foundations of the Mercedes-Benz brand that was to emerge.

Today, some might call this kind of amalgamation 'synergistic'; I prefer the word 'symbiotic'. The truth is that two plus two did not equal five for the new Daimler-Benz company — the ambition in the short term, if anything, was for two plus two to equal three (in terms of product range, production costs, workforce and sales network at least).

The real achievement was symbiosis: a mutually beneficial relationship where each partner thrived off the other, and the two grew stronger together. Of course, in this case, the two eventually became one — but that was not achieved overnight. Particularly in the difficult years that still lay ahead, this sense of being in it together was a key factor in the brand's survival as a single entity. Arguably, in sum, it was Benz's 'groundedness' that gave *Mercedes*-Benz permission to fly and Mercedes' exuberance that lifted Mercedes-*Benz* to spirited new heights.

"ÜBERALL MERCEDES-BENZ"

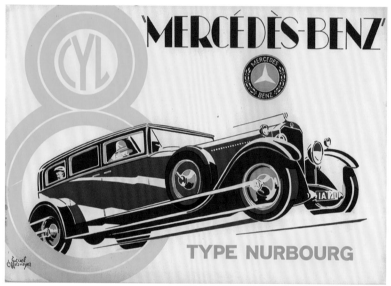

'MERCÉDÈS-BENZ'

TYPE NURBOURG

MERCEDES-BENZ
TYPE STUTTGART 260

Wilhelm Kissel takes much credit for making the merger happen, and holding the disparate corporate structures together

The full merger, when it came in 1926, was not a simple achievement. The shareholding machinations are bewildering. But Wilhelm Kissel takes much credit for making the merger happen, and holding the disparate corporate structures together in its aftermath. It seems to have been quickly agreed that his office (though he hailed from Benz) would be in Stuttgart, Daimler's heartland for 40 years. (This would be symbolic in terms of where the future power base would lie geographically.)

According to Dr Harry Niemann, Kissel's arrival at Untertürkheim was far from celebratory. He was picked up from Stuttgart station by one of the smaller cars available in the company pool, and directed, without ceremony, to a modest office in the factory complex; so modest, in fact, that there was only room for a desk, a chair and a single filing cabinet. Perhaps it was to make a point about his deeply felt Benz values of durability and simplicity that he chose to remain in that office for the next 16 years.

The Stuttgart culture didn't exactly welcome Friedrich Nallinger's son, Fritz, with open arms either. Given Dr Porsche's overbearing presence there and his deep suspicion of all ideas emanating from Mannheim, this would not be an easy relationship. Yet out of this pairing quickly emerged those new designs that the two companies, now one, had so eagerly anticipated to allow them to thin out their combined product range.

Initially introduced at the Berlin Motor Show in October 1926 as the 8/38 and the 12/55, these models were later re-christened 'Stuttgart' and 'Mannheim' respectively and became the mainstay of the new company's range for many years. Both originally had six-cylinder engines — 2.0 litres in the 8/38, 3.1 litres in the 12/55 — though these were enlarged in 1928 at the time of the renaming.

Clearly named after their factories of origin, the Stuttgart in particular sold well: 13,000 units, many of which were put into service as taxis in the

late 1920s. The larger Mannheim evolved from a two-seater cabriolet into a bigger four-seater saloon, very much in the style of the models coming out of Detroit at the time.

The Nürburg, an even larger saloon, with an in-line, eight-cylinder engine was launched in Paris at the end of 1928. Sometimes described as the last of the classic models, it was certainly a lot less exciting than some of the new sports models coming from the former Mercedes stable at about the same time. Noteworthy among these was the 6.3-litre K model (K standing for *Kurz*, or short wheelbase) and the six-cylinder supercharged S (Sport) model.

Opposite: the Mannheim, Nürburg and Stuttgart, the first cars produced by Daimler-Benz AG

Despite all the economic and corporate upheavals of these years, DMG (and to a much lesser extent Benz) still managed to retain its interest and involvement in motor racing. And even though Germany was banned from competing in Grand Prix after the First World War, Paul Daimler's appetite for competition was, if anything, increased by the recently available supercharger technology. He and his fellow directors were very aware of the damage that could occur to the Mercedes brand if it was out of motor sport entirely for a protracted period.

The first opportunity to compete in any kind of tournament came in 1922 with the gruelling Targa Floria event. As at the Gordon Bennett nearly 20 years earlier, the Mercedes cars performed spectacularly well. Encouraged by the performance of superchargers in this race, the technology was increasingly embraced in the road cars. Superchargers were also hooked up to a 2-litre, eight-cylinder engine, to develop 170 hp in a race car designed to take Mercedes back into Grand Prix when the ban was lifted in 1924. In that year success eluded the company, but in 1926, as if to coincide with and announce the merger on home soil, Caracciola drove the car to victory in the German Grand Prix in Berlin.

In 1927, the newly combined Mercedes-Benz brand competed in no less than 90 motor-sport events, using the new K and S models. Derivatives of these, notably the SS, SSK and SSKL models, continued to carry the flag (and often the winner's trophy) for the new brand until the end of the decade and beyond. Mercedes' competitive streak and the performance credentials of its cars were clearly two features of the brand that would survive the merger, come what may.

What, though, did the customer make of all of these mixed messages? Success on the racetrack, near-failure commercially, ever more intense market competition, wildly fluctuating prices — and ultimately two brands, seen as quite different, fused together into one. Deutsche Bank may have seen the two as of vital importance to the national economy, but to the potential customer the choice of car brands, even German

1316:0

Opposite, from left: Mercedes-Benz Type SS, 1928-33; the Mercedes-Benz Type SSK, 1928-30 This page: the Type S sports car from 1927, with supercharger engine

brands, went way beyond Benz and Mercedes. From 110 or more in 1920 there were still no less than 86 in 1926, plus an enormous array of imported marques.[3]

True, Mercedes had a special (not to say, exclusive) place at the top of the market that probably made it prominent beyond its actual volumes. And Benz was still the authentic, the original — no one could take that claim away. But for the customer there was still lots of choice — and certainly most were cheaper than either of these two.

Perhaps for both brands, for different reasons and for different people, it was brand loyalty that carried them through this difficult period. Quality was probably at the root of this too, but for whatever

reason the two both seemed to enjoy high levels of heartfelt support from their respective owners.

Looking through customer letters from that period held in the company's archive, one is struck not only by the stories told but by the degree of emotion expressed towards both brands. Owners speak of 'never having experienced such pleasure', being 'lucky to own one', being 'pleased to be back with our old company' after having sampled a competitor's make. Of course, as would be expected, there are the identifiably different brand virtues: the Mercedes owner who praised the 'speed when wanted, power at all times and marvellous riding qualities'; the Benz owner who talks of his personal experience

'providing convincing evidence that the strength and durability of a Benz are unequalled by any other make'.

But over and above all of these, one senses a genuine warmth towards each, a desire to see both succeed and almost certainly a preparedness to give each separately — or the two together — the benefit of the doubt.

Though the brands' positive and negative associations — except for quality — were markedly different, consumers seem to have been supportive of the merger, and quick to accept the reality of the new combination.

In the course of my research, I was fortunate to be able to interview Fritz B Busch, the renowned

This page: 1926 advertisement from the newly merged
Daimler-Benz AG

German motoring journalist, now retired and running his own small motor museum in the south of the country. At the age of 81, he was one of the few people who, though as a child, could remember the 'new' Mercedes-Benz brand first hand. 'Benz was the weaker marque,' he told me, 'even though Karl Benz had been the inventor of the car. The Benz brand had lost its way, but Mercedes was still pre-eminent.' In his view, people were quickly able to assimilate the two brands becoming one, at least in part because they could see the contribution that each could make to the other. Mercedes' strengths were perhaps more visible and exciting, but as we now know the contributions could potentially travel in both directions. The result, according to Busch, was a united Mercedes-Benz brand that emerged 'at the top of the pile', a good metaphor for the crowded car market of the time.

When you sat in the new Mercedes-Benz, according to Busch, 'steigen die Glückshormone' — it set the happy hormones racing! Advertising from the time actively promoted this sense of joy and achievement. But before that, the two brands had separately used paid-for communications in quite different ways. Benz, having initially returned to its 'Mein

Benz' theme after the First World War, seemed thereafter to revert to more mundane subjects, often featuring commercial vehicles or references to its factories. Mercedes, by contrast, continued in its pre-war vein of romance, glamour and speed. And these virtues seem to be the ones that won out for the Mercedes-Benz brand after the merger.

During the period of association, advertisements were clearly preparing the ground for a closer union in featuring both logos, even both companies' addresses. But when the two finally did become one, the new joint advertising reached new heights of exuberance, even triumphalism.

These executions must have seemed in sharp contrast to the austerity of mid-1920s Germany — but through films like Cabaret we've been made aware that there was also a decadent, romantic, colourful side to German life in that decade. And for those who could afford one, ownership made a bright, vibrant, powerful statement in this otherwise grey world. The advertisements reflect this — in the main they are beautiful pieces of art even by today's standards — and they also literally raised the 'star' to new heights, as a symbol of achievement and success.

1909

1909

1916

1926

1933

But the star had changed too. With hindsight it all looks too easy — almost as though the two brands were made for each other — at least in logo terms. First, there is the Mercedes logo, which after a number of evolutions has the word 'Mercedes' sitting beneath the three-pointed star in a circle but, rather gratuitously, with four other smaller stars dotted around the upper edges of the circle, looking a bit lost. Then there is the Benz logo, with its four quite harsh-looking letters sitting at the centre of a ring of laurels that either soften the effect of the name or conflict with it, depending on one's view.

Simply, elegantly (but no one knows by whom) the two are comfortably brought together:

the outer circle embracing the laurels, the inner core highlighting the star, the words 'Mercedes' at the top and 'Benz' at the bottom completing the symmetry of the new design. On this badge the two names carry no hyphen. In the written name of the brand after 1926 they did: Mercedes-Benz, a symbolic 'linkage' between the two former competitors. This final design was registered on 21 August 1926, and still features in blue and silver flat on the bonnets of the majority of the company's models. Significantly though, within just seven years the star alone within a ring was also registered for use by the new company, now called Daimler-Benz. This 'solus' star had been used as an upright badge on the radi-

ator cap of Mercedes cars since 1921, and its use in this way seemed to continue after the merger — presumably sanctioned by the new management. From 1933, however, it was employed as a flat badge on the rear of passenger cars, on race cars and on the company's print materials. Symbolically again, therefore, one is left with the feeling that it was the Daimler/Mercedes half of the partnership that came to the fore in the crucial post-merger years.

Of those years, 1929 was without doubt the most significant. In that year Karl Benz died, as did Wilhelm Maybach and indeed Mercedes Jellinek, the lady who in childhood had given her name to this now-singular brand. It really did seem that an old

For now, Daimler-Benz could celebrate. The marriage seemed to be working

era was ending. The new company certainly felt a sense of history — it built a museum to house its now much larger collection of classic vehicles... in Stuttgart, of course.

In 1929, the economic forecast looked bleak too: recession, and with it new levels of unemployment, were on the horizon. Following closely behind, another storm cloud, much bigger and darker, was also looming. Adolf Hitler, gathering the support of the disaffected from all around, would briefly become something of a saviour for the German car industry, but thereafter would plunge it into a gloom that would be beyond anyone's imagination.

For now, Daimler-Benz could celebrate. The marriage seemed to be working. For the Mercedes-Benz brand, the early signs were good too: passenger car sales leapt from around 2,000 in 1926 to almost 8,000 in 1927, partly as a result of the new cheaper and more economical models. Both 1928 and 1929 brought similar volumes, and commercial vehicles too more than doubled in sales in these three years.

By 1929 the company had many reasons to be cheerful: management integration had been achieved with minimal fall-out (only Dr Porsche had been a significant casualty of the post-merger years), the company's scattered plants now had a semblance of logic to what they produced and where, and the public had assimilated the new union and bought into its new brand.

Though still highly priced (in 1928 the cheapest Mercedes-Benz was 7,600 marks while the most expensive Ford was only 4,800 marks), the cars were selling well. Public and press reaction to new models continued to be adulatory, although if anything the cars were getting bigger at a time when practicality was still the buying public's principal concern. Still, with Kissel at the helm, the company's fortunes looked to be set fair for the immediate future at least.

Then, on 24 October 1929, the Wall Street Stock Market crashed. Shockwaves travelled around the world, particularly to the still-fragile economies of Europe. For the new-born Mercedes-Benz brand, things were about to get a lot tougher again.

The last three chapters have covered a fundamentally important period of the Mercedes-Benz brand's life. The 50-odd years from Benz, Daimler and Maybach's early work to the eve of the Great Depression help us understand not just the origins of the brand, but also the way in which its character was shaped. It is the story of two brands that became one, but vestiges of each were very apparent in 1929 and many still are today. We've examined the detail of each — its product, values, associations and essence — and the differences and similarities between the two.

We've seen how they came together — neatly in terms of the brand logo, much less neatly in almost every other respect. Nevertheless, what becomes increasingly important is the complementarity or symbiosis between the two brands which made their union so productive.

This duality, akin to the more recent theory of 'left brain' and 'right brain', was above all what equipped the brand to survive and even prosper over the coming years. Though probably more unconscious than deliberate, the fine-tuning of the brand's response to the difficulties it subsequently faced will remind us time and again of the twin roots of the brand's character.

The next 40 years of the brand's life, from 1930 to 1970, were less character-forming than character-strengthening. This period placed obstacles in the path of the company and the brand that few would have survived — and indeed many other brands did not. The company had to plumb new depths of resourcefulness. The brand had to count on new reserves of loyalty and resilience. The company had, on occasion, to deploy strategies of which, with hindsight, it was less than proud.

The Wall Street Crash of October 1929 had more impact on Germany than on most other European countries because the German economic recovery since the period of hyper-inflation was built largely on American loans. As the US banks called in these loans, businesses once again began to collapse and unemployment rocketed. From a manageable 1.5 million unemployed in 1928, Germany's jobless reached a massive 6 million, 40% of the entire workforce, by 1932. Homelessness followed for many, and the already creaking Weimar government, desperate to avoid another period of inflation, fuelled the popular anguish yet further by raising taxes, cutting public-sector wages and reducing unemployment benefits. This was a heady and provocative mix of policies that drove even more of the disaffected into the arms of the extreme left and right.

The effect on the car market was predictable. Though still way behind other countries in terms of per capita ownership (one in a hundred Germans owned a car at this time compared with one in five Americans), the market had just about clawed its way back from the all-time low in the early 1920s. Now, from 156,000 cars sold in 1929, sales again plummeted to less than a third of this figure in 1932. For the new company Daimler-Benz, and its new brand Mercedes-Benz, the effect was almost as severe — total sales down from nearly 15,000 to under 10,000 over the same period. Relative to its competitors though, this performance was at least better than average.

Hitler saw motor racing as a crucial mechanism for rebuilding pride at home and status abroad

Still slightly schizophrenic after its recent merger, the company responded in product terms in two very different ways. At the very top end of the market, probably the bit least affected by the Depression, 1930 saw the launch of the 770 Grosser Mercedes — a gigantic car, as its name implied, with a 7.6-litre, eight-cylinder, supercharged engine. Planned during the 1920s, this car looked hopelessly out of touch with the times on the day of its launch. Its appeal was limited to those still rich enough to 'always view a maximum achievement as just sufficient for their needs' (according to the sales brochure). Just 117 were sold.

Much more significant, and very much in tune with the times, was the following year's launch of the 170 — the car whose double life-saving role was described briefly in chapter 2. At 4,400 marks it was accessible like no Mercedes or Benz before. Yet it was technically advanced and typically durable. While it couldn't match the opulence or beauty of the 770, it was still a luxury car by the standards of the day. More importantly, it sold like hot cakes — over 80,000 cars in all variants up to 1939.

It is inconceivable why this car, which sold as many as all others before it put together, doesn't attract more fame in the history of the company. It wasn't beautiful, sexy or fast, but certainly it was important.

The turmoil in the German economy finally exploded into the political arena in 1933 when Adolf Hitler became Chancellor. The era of National Socialism, with its promise of a 1,000-year timespan, had begun. The new certainty, pride and, with it, economic success, transformed the fortunes of the car industry once again.

Hitler had always been interested in cars, although he was not a driver himself. Having read Henry Ford's biography much earlier, he saw cars as liberating and potentially unifying in terms of their classlessness, but only if they could become genuinely popular. At the 1934 Berlin Motor Show he reportedly said: 'It is with bitter feelings that we see millions of honest and hardworking men, whose opportunities in life are already limited, cut off from the use of a vehicle which would be a source of yet unknown happiness to them'.

He wasted no time in making his intentions to pursue such a vision clear. The building of *Autobahns* (though virtually empty of cars at first) was a key way of getting people back to work. Tax breaks for the industry, and lower taxes on cars themselves were announced in April 1933. Motor-racing programmes were to receive special subsidies since Hitler saw these as a crucial mechanism for rebuilding pride at home and status abroad. Daimler-Benz was to receive nearly half a million marks a year, plus bonuses for podium finishes.

Ferdinand Porsche, himself a party member, but by now working at Auto Union, quickly approached the Führer and requested similar support for that company. Hitler, keen on such competition, agreed and the funding was split between the two companies. (In reality, the subsidy only represented about 10% of the annual cost of racing.)

All of this benefited the German car industry considerably. Around 70,000 new jobs were created in the industry. Employment at Daimler-Benz rose to over 14,000 again — and production capacity was full.

Opposite: Mercedes-Benz winning the 1935 Monaco Grand Prix

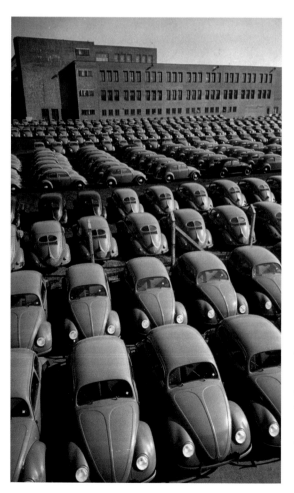

Exports too were growing, though more because of the new government's need for foreign earnings than because of their innate profitability. In every respect though the brand was on the way back. Largely through the 170, sales just kept on growing: over 20,000 in 1935, and over 40,000 in 1937. Success for the brand made it the car of choice for the new elite in both the commercial and the political world. Hitler, in particular, was seldom seen in any other marque — an enduring image: for better at the time, for worse later.

But political involvement with the company didn't stop with selecting its brand as the principal vehicle for both government and, increasingly, the military. Kissel, still at the helm of Daimler-Benz AG, had joined the party in 1933, partly to shield the company from government intrusion. The company spoke in its 1936 annual report of its 'profound gratitude towards our Führer' for its new-found success. More significant than both was the appointment of Jakob Werlin, a personal friend and adviser to Hitler, to the board in 1933.

This appointment, at the Nazi government's instigation, was a clear attempt to stay close to the heart of the business and was followed, in 1936, by a detailed examination of the company's books,

leading to allegations of mismanagement. With the odds very much stacked against him, Wilhelm Haspel (himself a recent appointee) wrote a 176-page rebuttal and, remarkably, Berlin backed off. Haspel's reward was to be appointed to the board and later to become general director, despite having a Jewish wife. The two were effectively protected by Werlin, such was the importance of a successful Daimler-Benz. Government interference was also seen in the commercial vehicles side of the business — the *Reichsverkehrsministerium* (the Reich Transport Ministry) was being quite prescriptive about sizes of trucks, and specifications for off-road and tracked vehicles — for obvious reasons.

For the time being, the brand rode out these obstacles and continued its upward progress. Model after model was launched — to feed a seemingly endless customer appetite. The breadth of the range was by now enormous, stretching from the 170V (still the biggest seller), through the 230 and 260 models, up to the opulent and powerful 500 and 540K.

The most significant new models though were the 260D, the world's first diesel production car (building on Benz's focus on this area a decade earlier), and the 130. Designed from scratch as a new, economical car for the mass market, the 130 is

remarkable in more ways than one. The DaimlerChrysler website simply says that the technically innovative rear-engined design 'did not catch on at Daimler-Benz'. Yet the truth of the matter, as early prototypes for the 130 show, was that this car was very much the design forerunner of what was to become the 'Volkswagen', the people's car.

Though never a great sales success for Daimler-Benz, the 130 (the smallest Mercedes-Benz ever) nonetheless planted the idea and defined the shape of the now-more-famous VW that was to follow. Claim to that concept has traditionally been given to Ferdinand Porsche. But in fact a protracted libel battle between 1952 and 1955 established its true ownership: that of Béla Barényi, of whom much more later.

Ironically, Daimler-Benz was also charged with building 30 prototypes of the VW that Porsche (and Hitler) were responsible for in 1937. Look no further than the 170H, a derivative of the 130, to see how the VW so closely resembled earlier Mercedes-Benz models.

Opposite: the Volkswagen factory in Brunswick, Germany
This page: the 1936 Mercedes-Benz 170H convertible

This page: a 1939 advertisement celebrating 'Three new international records for Mercedes-Benz with the DB 600 aircraft engine'

Motor racing too, as Hitler had intended, was playing its dual role: valuable publicity for the brand, and internationally a showpiece for the Nazi government. Though retouched or cropped out of most of today's photographic references from that era, the swastika featured prominently on the company's race cars. The 'Silver Arrows' may have had their white paint stripped bare to cut weight (thus earning Daimler-Benz its famous team name), but the infamous Nazi symbol was still emblazoned on the side of the cars.

Seven out of the 13 Grand Prix in 1937 were won by Mercedes-Benz. In the German Grand Prix of that year, the team took first and second place. At Monaco, they scored a hat trick and, remarkably, at the Swiss Grand Prix, Mercedes-Benz secured first, second, third and fourth places. Just ten years after its fitful merger, the company was now truly a star performer. But such details were soon to become utterly irrelevant.

The story of Mercedes-Benz in the war years of 1939–45 is something of a dark chapter in the company's history. Although more the story of Daimler-Benz AG than of the brand, it's important to recognise that the company (like so many others in that period)

did employ significant numbers of forced labourers. Daimler-Benz subsequently commissioned independent researchers to conduct a comprehensive inquiry into what happened during the time of the National Socialist regime, and the results have been published.[1] Daimler-Benz and, later, DaimlerChrysler have also consistently expressed regret for the suffering inflicted upon those who worked as forced labourers during this period in plants belonging to the company.[2]

From the outset of the war, in September 1939, sales of private cars were forbidden and all of Germany's car manufacturers switched to military production. For Daimler-Benz this, of course, included trucks, pick-ups and staff cars. But it also increasingly included aircraft and aircraft engine production. It was this in particular that attracted the attention of British and American bombers, and from 1943 onwards Daimler-Benz various plants were targeted repeatedly.

Even at the beginning of the war, the situation inside the company was difficult. Werlin, sidestepping Kissel, conspired to have Daimler-Benz produce trucks for arch-rival Opel in its Stuttgart factories. Kissel, already exhausted from nearly 20 years of running the business, died of a heart attack in 1942 at the

The story of Mercedes-Benz in the war years of 1939-45 is something of a dark chapter in the company's history

age of 56. Haspel, his Jewish wife still protected by Werlin, took his place as CEO. Others were less fortunate. Four Jewish members of the Daimler-Benz supervisory board (most from Deutsche Bank) had been ousted in the mid-1930s. Otto Hopper, on the main board, was forced out — his wife too being Jewish. And in 1943 Herman Köhler, another Deutsche Bank appointee, was executed for 'making remarks critical of the regime' after being overheard by fellow passengers on a train from Munich to Stuttgart.

This was the year of Stalingrad — and from that moment the tide turned and the heat on the company intensified. Bombs fell on Mannheim for the first time in April 1943. No less than 38,000 bombs rained down on Gaggenau. Sindelfingen and Untertürkheim would become targets in their turn.

Importantly for this story, it is clear that Haspel and his colleagues could by now see the inevitability of the outcome — and began to prepare for it. Though the company reports from post-war years talk of it having 'effectively ceased to exist' by 1945, in production terms this was far from the truth. The company, daringly, chose to ignore Berlin's scorched earth policy in the face of the Allied advance. By now the company's major assets, its machine tools and manufacturing equipment, were buried. It had been a necessary precaution to move these engineering facilities into deep underground factories to protect them from the nightly bombings. It would prove prudent (or perhaps just lucky) that among this equipment were also the dies and tools for the pre-war 170.

My father was himself among those who inspected the Daimler-Benz underground factories after the war, as part of his work with the UK's Ministry of Aircraft Production in 1945. His diary from that time notes: 'Intact. In an old mine in a hillside overlooking the River Neckar. A large and formerly very active Daimler-Benz engine factory. Normal complement was 5,000 persons and there are said to be 2,000 machine tools here'. He describes no less than 16 alleys and 14 traverses within the complex and notes that: 'the tools are mostly in good condition and are greased... a considerable number of good standard machines, particularly some fine radial drills'.

In fact, Neil Gregor estimates that only around 15% of Daimler-Benz machine tools were destroyed by the bombing, and concludes that therefore 'the essential substance of the company remained intact in 1945'.[3]

Above ground, the devastation was tremendous — over 70% of both the Stuttgart factories were destroyed, though less than 20% of the Mannheim plant.[4] Below ground it was a different matter, and

Opposite: the bombed Mercedes-Benz factory at Untertürkheim, 1944
This page: the 170 went back into production in 1946, and was central to the company's post-war recovery

in the vaults of the company's Stuttgart banks sat 250 million Reichsmarks to fund the rebuilding.

Alongside these, Gregor also attributes the company's ability to survive to the fact that it had made a 'clear strategic shift' in 1944 to commercial vehicle production (anticipating the post-war need) and was blessed with machinery (for example, for aircraft engine manufacture) that could easily convert back to peacetime uses. But what of the management and the workforce to put all this fortuitous resource to use after the war ended in May 1945?

Haspel was still in place, and set to with the rebuilding — only to be removed by the Americans in October 1945 for 'de-Nazification'. Fittingly, he was replaced by Otto Hopper until his return in 1948. Even Werlin got a job: running a dealership in Bavaria until 1948. More extraordinary though — and here again we see the power of the internal brand — was the fact that, within a fortnight of VE Day, over 1,200 former employees had voluntarily

returned to the plant to begin the clean-up operation. Twice this number had died in the war and a further 800 were missing.

By the spring of 1946, after nine months of reconstruction, supported in part by contracts to repair American vehicles, the company once again began making the 170V, its best-selling pre-war model. Officially retailing at 6,200 marks, these cars were selling on the black market for over 100,000 marks because of limited supply. The UK's *Autocar* magazine in 1947 commented: 'Some 200 apprentices are being coached in the finesse of the trade by former racing mechanics'. They had 'the grey look of under-nourishment on their faces [and were] dressed in clothes held together by patches. Their attitude, however, still breathes precision, speed and pride in their work.'

By 1949 the company had launched the 170S and D — both effectively pre-war designs — and had been given permission again to build diesel engines.

Export orders came first from Sweden (which had been neutral), then from Argentina. In other countries though, the image of Hitler was still so closely associated with the brand that in the eyes of many, according to Dennis Adler, 'Mercedes-Benz still bore the stain of the Third Reich'.[5]

But if exports to former enemies would have to wait, sales in the home country came flooding back. It is almost unbelievable now to realise that by 1950 Daimler-Benz was producing nearly 34,000 cars, its highest ever annual output — 80% of which were for the domestic market.

The reasons for this remarkable recovery are worth exploring. Some were pure luck, like the location of all plants (except Gaggenau) within the American sector of occupied Germany. Some were endemic: yet again the Schwabian work ethic shone through and the ownership of the company (still largely in private hands) was supportive of long-term reconstruction and growth.

Others though were due to company actions: the decisions made before the war's end, and the pursuit, once more, of export markets, for example. Probably more significant was the bond of loyalty that was created between the company and its work-force in those years. From the company's reports for the post-war period we get a strong sense of the kind of contract that was emerging.

The company placed simple food supply at the top of its agenda, noting that 'we sacrificed a good deal to follow this promise through'. The workforce reciprocated with what the annual report describes as 'endeavour, performance and loyalty'. Thus are strong brands built: by belief from within and a powerful internal culture.

Externally the brand was rebuilding its former loyalties too. The sporting image survived, of course, but more important was the continued commitment to, and perception of, quality. Even in these difficult times, Germans could still be proud of the brand as a symbol of national renewal and regeneration. The 'economic miracle' would follow, but by the 1950s, Mercedes-Benz was something of a beacon of hope for the nation. But if customers were flocking back, it was also for more mundane reasons — and often they were new sorts of customers too. Fritz B Busch remembers how, at first, it was the successful company directors and business owners who bought back into the brand, just as they had before the war. But 'then came the wholesalers, the tradesmen, often people living off the black market — and after that the butchers and shopkeepers... they even used the cars to pull trailers!' This new democracy was short-lived and by the early 1950s, with prices rising again, the traditional clientele was once more in the ascendancy. As if to give the brand a seal of approval, Mercedes-Benz (in preference to BMW) became the chosen car of the first Chancellor of the new German Federal Republic, Konrad Adenauer.

Amusingly, it seems that this choice was only made after Adenauer had viewed both cars and, on looks alone, had taken a fancy to the BMW. However, on climbing into its rear seat, the low roofline knocked his hat off — so he plumped for the taller and more stately Mercedes-Benz.

Opposite: Konrad Adenauer (right), first Chancellor of the German Federal Republic, selected a Mercedes-Benz 300D as his official car. He is pictured here with President Dwight D Eisenhower in 1959

Opposite: the rich and the famous were quickly reassociated with Mercedes-Benz after the war. Clockwise from top: Zsa Zsa Gabor, Yul Brynner and Bing Crosby
This page: Karl Kling and Hans Klenk repairing the windscreen of their 300SL after a vulture crashed into it during the Carrera Panamericana race, 1952. They went on to win the race

How extraordinary. Against the odds again, the car so closely identified as one of Hitler's trappings of power less than ten years before was now the apparently acceptable choice for the leader of the new Germany.

The earlier Benz values were clearly to the fore in this period: durability and economy of build, simplicity and consistency of running were all-important, underpinned by the sense of authenticity of origin. Again this was instinctive rather than orchestrated. Just as the workforce needed their more basic needs to be satisfied first, so too did the brand have to fulfil, first and foremost, the functional requirements of its buyers. Benz's essence of 'fitness for purpose' was exactly right for the times.

It is also clear that as the workforce rediscovered their earlier pride in the product and the company's renewed commercial success, their needs too changed. The German expression '*wir sind wieder wer*', meaning 'we are someone again', characterised this period — employees could once again raise their eyes to higher-order goals. So too with the public and the cars. As the austerity of the early 1950s began to diminish, the Mercedes side of the brand again started to shine through.

In 1951, the company launched the 220 and 300 models, both wholly new cars, the first luxury models since the war. It was the 300 that Adenauer had selected, but he wasn't alone. This was after all, as Adler describes, 'a car so beautiful that it eclipsed the Nazi stigma that had clung to the earlier models'.

No wonder that it became the choice too of glamorous stars of the day like Clark Gable, Yul Brynner, Bing Crosby and Gary Cooper, not to mention countless heads of state and embassies around the world. Mercedes' image of romance and power was coming back.

It would be easy to assume that the 300SL, the famous 'Gullwing' sports car, was the product of this resurgence of 'Mercedesness'. The car certainly was stunning, especially coming so soon (1954) after the post-war gloom. But in fact its genesis was the 300SL racer of 1952, a car very much built in the Benz tradition of 'function before form'. It happened to look pleasing aesthetically, but was, according to Kimes, 'cobbled together' from the parts bin of other cars, under the watchful eye of Fritz Nallinger — now at Daimler-Benz for over 25 years. The distinctive door design was a function of the space-frame chassis which meant the doors had to be hinged on the roof.

This was a car that, in the true Benz tradition, was built to do a job. The fact that it looked sensational was simply a bonus. For Mercedes-Benz the brand, though, the SL did a fantastic job. Fritz B Busch described the moment when he took delivery of a production version in 1954: 'I remember to this day how I felt when it arrived. I was 30 years old at the time and had something of a head for cars. But this one embedded itself deep in my heart'.

Head and heart, Benz and Mercedes, the perfect duo to appeal to both the rational and the emotional. Right brain and left brain. This is the

Mercedes-Benz brand at its best: balanced, complementary, symbiotic. When either side becomes too dominant, and the other is weakened, the brand suffers. When the two are in harmony, the brand is unbeatable.

On the racetrack too the brand seemed unbeatable. Excluded now for 12 years, the 300SL picked up trophies around the world, most notably at Le Mans, in 1952. The company then switched its attention to Formula One (as it was now called). A completely new car was built — still employing the space-frame construction for the 1954 season and, magically, Fangio took the world championship for Mercedes-Benz. The list of victories continued through 1954, but in 1955, after a horrific accident at Le Mans in which its car killed 80 spectators, Daimler-Benz announced its withdrawal from competition.

In truth, the decision to withdraw from Formula One had nothing to do with the team's involvement in the Le Mans tragedy. Indeed, the decision had been made by the board much earlier and related to the company's desire to focus its

efforts on series production. However, the timing of the announcement was unfortunate.

None of this, however, diminished the popularity of Mercedes-Benz in Germany or around the world. By the end of the 1950s, annual passenger car volumes had passed the 100,000 mark, of which more than 50% were being exported. What would change though was the focus on safety, perhaps as a result of the events at Le Mans. Ahead of any other manufacturer in the world, Mercedes-Benz undertook research that led to safety becoming an integral part of the development of new cars. And safety would start to add, for the brand, a wholly new dimension to its product credentials.

Pioneered by Béla Barényi, the owner of the original Volkswagen concept, the engineering teams at Daimler-Benz began to explore new ways to protect both passengers and pedestrians. From early observations of the dangerously pointed design of Ford steering wheels, Barényi and his team began to develop passive safety concepts that would change the shape of cars to come, and set new standards for the industry worldwide.

In quick succession came side impact protection, crumple zones, the concept of a passenger cell, energy absorbing interiors, deformable switchgear and handles — all the features we take so much for granted in the cars we buy today. But in 1959 (the year that also saw the world's first crash testing in Sindelfingen), only one car embraced all of these features: the Mercedes-Benz 220, launched in that year. It was the first car in the world to truly redefine safety — and confirm Mercedes-Benz's leadership in this area — but it wasn't to everyone's taste.

Although the 220 was a technological leader, it was a design follower. The 1950s had been the heyday of the American car, and as the decade wore on American cars were getting not only bigger but also more extravagant in their design. Above all 'fins', notably tailfins, were the defining characteristic of the New World's new cars. This fashion though seemed to have stuck, and was now beginning to influence strongly the shape of European cars. Subsidiaries of the US manufacturers were the first to emulate it — now Mercedes-Benz followed suit. To the horror of the traditionalists, the 220 had fins; discreet fins,

Opposite, from left to right: Mercedes-Benz 300SL coupé, 1954–59; launch of the 'Pagoda roof' 230SL at the Frankfurt motor show, 1963; Mercedes-Benz 220SB with infamous 'tailfins', 1959
This page: section drawing of Béla Barényi's safety cell (patent granted in 1952)

but fins nonetheless. Famously, the distinguished German architect, Professor Egon Eiermann, reputedly said at the car's launch party: 'This car is a whore — this is all stolen from American cars'.

Purists may have shrunk from the 220; the public didn't. If anything, this gave the brand a little more modernity, a little more glamour. Sales boomed and a few years later the even more American-looking Opel Kapitän would pose a serious competitive threat. For now though, things were looking good, and at the dawn of the 'swinging sixties', the contrast with where the brand had been ten years earlier could not have been more acute.

If the 1950s had been the decade of renewal, then the 1960s — for the country, the company and the brand — was the decade of pure achievement, perhaps to the surprise of some observers. After all, the first three years alone had seen the Berlin Wall erected, the Cuban missile crisis and the assassination of John F Kennedy. The world suddenly felt a more dangerous place. Yet in those same years, Mercedes-Benz launched no less than six new models: the elegant 220SEb convertible, the

luxurious 300SE, the smaller 190C and DC, the famous 'pagoda-roof' 230SL and, finally, three months before Kennedy's death, the fabulous 600. What an array of models: sleek cabriolets, sexy roadsters, luxury saloons, practical family cars and then the ultimate limousine.

Again though, the balance of Benzness and Mercedesness seemed to be retained across these models — so the success continued. The pagoda roof looked good, but its concave shape was designed (by Barényi) to provide structural strength in the event of a roll-over accident.

The more traditional saloons came with advanced features like power steering, air suspension and four-speed automatic transmission. Benz-like build qualities were still marching hand in hand with Mercedes' tradition of innovation. Even the finned designs, now extended to include smaller models like the 190C, kept the look fresh and contemporary.

The 600 took the brand to new heights of opulence, especially in the six-door 'Pullman' version. In production for 17 years, it became the car of royalty, show business and political leaders the world

over. From King Hussein to the Shah of Iran, from Queen Elizabeth II to John Lennon, from Prince Rainier to the Pope, this was Mercedes exclusivity at its peak.

Small wonder then that Graham Robson, in his book *Magnificent Mercedes, The Complete History of the Marque*, reported that 'the suspicion that they might be able to build the world's finest cars had been lurking around the corridors of Daimler-Benz top management for some years but it was not until the 1960s, when the vast prestigious 600 limousine had been launched, that the firm knew it could build the best'.

Commenting recently on the whole period from the SL in 1952 to the 600 11 years later, Volker Steinmaier confirms this view, but with an interesting aside about the two subcultures: 'What counted was the dream of a better future and the feeling of everyone at Daimler, as the company was commonly referred to in Stuttgart — or at Benz as it was referred to in Mannheim — that they were involved in producing something very special. This is a feeling which is still widespread in large parts of the giant concern to this day.'[6]

This revealing use of different brand languages is still widespread today — but more of that phenomenon later. The company did indeed take giant steps forward in this decade. Barényi's work delivered yet more firsts, especially now in terms of active safety. The brand's reputation in this area was developing apace. And though Mercedes-Benz was still absent from Grand Prix, the cars regularly performed in rallies and marathons, as they had done since the early 1900s.

Sales continued to climb: from 100,000 passenger cars per annum in 1960, to nearly 300,000 in 1970. The brand really did seem unstoppable. More and more sales were going abroad; to other European countries and to the USA, which was now a key market.

Diesel was becoming ubiquitous, and the brand built on its early leads in this area. The diesel Mercedes-Benz was a German taxi-driver's dream: with an engine that turned over at 3,800 rpm

compared to the average petrol engine's 4,800 rpm, the cars simply lasted longer. Taxis covering over a million kilometres were not unheard of. And with petrol then costing 45pf per litre, compared to diesel's 15pf, no wonder the latter engines were becoming so popular in the domestic market. Then, as now, Mercedes-Benz dominated this lucrative sector.

But the brand didn't have everything its own way. The Opel Kapitän, mentioned earlier, for a time posed a serious threat to the company. Its 2.5-litre, six-cylinder engine outperformed the equivalent (but more costly) 220.

The Opel even began to create something of a style statement through its American-influenced design. Fritz B Busch talked about Mercedes-Benz 'curious reluctance' to respond in the most obvious way: increased engine capacity. Instead, says Busch, 'Mercedes-Benz tried to reply with innovation and clever ideas rather than capacity. The engineers played at trying to create crazy new things for the

car.' Here's the first hint of how the company would increasingly behave over the coming 20 years: more and more engineering inventions, rather than perhaps more obvious, customer-orientated steps forward. The Opel threat finally went away — by the end of the decade its styling looked increasingly redundant — but this is a telling episode.

Mercedes too had begun to abandon fins, firstly with the new S and SE models in 1965, then with the mid-size 200 series launched in 1968. But 1968 was the year when the ground subtly started to shift beneath the company's feet. Not because its cars changed, but perhaps because they didn't. Not fundamentally at least. What was beginning to change was the world around the brand: politically, socially and culturally.

This page: Opel Kapitän, 1960
Opposite: Queen Elizabeth II of England in a
Mercedes-Benz 600 on her visit to Stuttgart, 1965

The emerging exciting world of 'sex and drugs and rock 'n' roll' was not a world that Mercedes-Benz felt comfortable with

In 1968, the Vietnam War was at its height — as were the worldwide protests against it. Lyndon Johnson's policy of saturation bombing of Hanoi sparked student riots at Kent State University in California in May 1970 that left four dead. It also prompted 'Red Danny' Cohn-Bendit's protests in Paris that ultimately grew into full-scale riots in that city. And in Germany too, people and not just students took to the streets to oppose America's 'new world order'. From this emanated Baader-Meinhof, who for a time at least had a kind of chic appeal to the ever-more outspoken left among Germany's youth.

Culturally too, things were shifting: Timothy Leary's advocacy of 'turn on, tune in, drop out' was creating waves, just as was Andy Warhol in art, and the Beatles' *Sergeant Pepper* in music. When Scott McKenzie, in his anthem to the 'Summer of Love' sang: 'There's a whole generation, with a new explanation', he received a sympathetic ear from young Germans in particular. The emerging exciting world of 'sex and drugs and rock 'n' roll' was not a world that Mercedes-Benz felt comfortable with, or even understood.

Nor did vast swathes of middle-class, middle-aged Germans: the 'economic miracle' for which they'd worked so hard was now really beginning to deliver the goods. Incomes were rising rapidly and with them

the phenomenon that Thorstein Veblen, the American economist and social philosopher, had identified over 60 years earlier: conspicuous consumption.

Few things are more conspicuous than cars — and Mercedes-Benz, for the first time, looked prominently out of step with the new social values that were emerging, at least for the young. In their eyes, the brand looked aloof: its traditional, responsible image in stark contrast with the vibrant, and sometimes angry, mood of the times. Life, even in hard-working Germany, was becoming lighter, looser, more relaxed. Mercedes-Benz as a brand felt tighter, more upright — designs that had seemed classic now looked formal.

It would be some years before this new generation of Germans would be family car buyers themselves, but the whispers of a lingering disenchantment with the brand had started — and Mercedes-Benz wasn't listening. Ask any 50-something German today (and this is a key age group for the brand), and they'll likely as not describe themselves as a '68-er', one of the generation that witnessed or even took part in the profound social change that began in Germany in that year.

Even while researching this book in 2003 and 2004, I came across stories of people, perhaps meeting again after many years, who apologised for

arriving at the reunion in a Mercedes-Benz. As if to say, 'given our history, I bet you never expected to see me driving one of these!'

The effects of this new attitude wouldn't be felt until the 1980s — but when they arrived they put yet more pressure on what was by then something of a beleaguered brand. The 1950s and 1960s had been golden years for the brand. But they had been earned on the back of extraordinary struggles in the 20 years before that. The shape of the world's car industry had changed fundamentally since 1930 — most notably in the concentration of market power in the hands of a much smaller number of companies. That Mercedes-Benz should have survived and ultimately prospered in these 40 years was a tribute to its management, its workforce, its product and, I would argue, its brand. Clouds might be on the horizon, but the story so far was, in total, an impressive one: success, indeed, against the odds.

Opposite: German student protest against the Vietnam War, 1968

CHAPTER EIGHT

INTO THE CRISIS

240 TD
300 TD
230 T
250 T
280 TE

BB·NT 250

From 1970 onwards, the story of the Mercedes-Benz brand relies less on the interpretation of history through what has been written, more on living memory and the spoken word. From this point on, the impressions, thinking and judgements are drawn as much from the 40-plus interviews conducted within and outside the company as from company histories. Every interview was recorded and together they provide an immensely rich impression of these more recent years. Above all, the picture they paint is of a brand that underwent enormous upheavals, and is still in many ways a brand in transition.

Looking at the sales curve for the 1970s doesn't suggest that much is amiss. Annual passenger car volumes seem to climb relentlessly upwards, breaking through the 300,000 car barrier in 1971, passing 400,000 before the end of the decade.

New models continue to appear: the 350SL in 1971, the 280 S-Class in 1972, the 200 series mid-size saloons in 1976 — with a new S-Class (the 500SE) arriving in 1979. Success on the track was consistent too: more wins in the 1970s came in long-distance rally racing, but still not yet — not for another 20 years — in Formula One. Innovations, though by now primarily in the area of safety, were still coming through, albeit at a slower pace than in the 1950s and 1960s.

But look more closely and the picture is less rosy. The new saloons, still largely of a 'three-box' design, are starting to look a little ordinary by the standards of the competition at that time. Each is slightly too reminiscent of earlier models and each is starting to look more similar to other models within the same range.

The utterly confusing model-numbering system employed at the time probably served only to heighten this latter problem. With nine versions of the S-Class described as S, SD, SE and SEL, and no less than 22 versions of the 200 series (called variously E, D, C, CE, T, TE and TD), it was quite possible to see, for example, a 280CE parked next to a 280SE. Yet while the former is a 2.8-litre 200 series, the latter is a similarly engined S-Class. To most ordinary people these designations would suggest perhaps only a difference of trim level, not a wholly different model. Consumers must have been baffled, and left unclear both about the hierarchy of models and about which models replaced which others.

To confuse things further, within the company and among its dealerships, a whole separate numbering system is employed (the 200 series, for example, was referred to as the W123), thus creating a kind of 'secret language' within the company and for its dealers that is almost impenetrable to anyone from outside. More significantly, it betrays a focus on engineering specifications that is anything but customer-friendly. (With today's trebly large model line-up, this is still an issue that the company should probably address.)

New Mercedes-Benz cars in the 1970s were looking less new than they had previously. The designs, still 'classic' to some, were 'traditional' to most, 'conventional' to the brand's critics. And it was among the young that those critics were now most likely to be found. After all, Mercedes-Benz was, for those coming out of universities particularly, the brand of their fathers. (Seldom of their mothers, since then, as now, the cars were predominantly bought by men.)

The 1970s, prompted by the events of 1968, was even more a decade in which parental values were questioned or rejected. This new generation not only had new explanations of their own, but sought new explanations from their parents. By the 1980s they would be the market — but Mercedes-Benz wouldn't necessarily be their brand of choice.

The first shock to the system came with the fuel crisis of 1973, prompted by the Arab–Israeli war. Petrol shortages occurred throughout the world; in the US a blanket 55 mph speed limit was imposed

and, almost overnight, the market for large, high-performance (and hence thirsty) cars started to look decidedly less optimistic. US consumers, followed by those in Europe, began to look for more economical alternatives. In California, by now a world leader in consumption trends, even the Honda Civic, with its outstanding fuel economy, became chic.

Though apparently unaffected in sales terms, the effect on the Mercedes-Benz brand was more subtle. New concerns about economy swiftly led, in Germany especially, to new concerns about ecology. For the first time people began to question the values of expensive 'gas guzzlers'. The political response to the fuel crisis — to lessen the dependency on oil by developing the nuclear industry — didn't go down well either. Again led by the young, sporting the badge '*Atomkraft? Nein danke*' (Nuclear power? No thanks) became quite a fashion. True, they tended to adorn the rear windows of 2CVs and second-hand VWs, but the statement (and the sentiment) was very public.

For the management of Daimler-Benz, this too was unfamiliar territory. While order books were still full, and customers routinely had to wait for two years or more to pick up the car they'd ordered, there seemed no need for a panicky response. But even then, while changing values could perhaps be ignored, changing needs in the car market probably couldn't.

Joachim Zahn, Chairman since 1965, came under pressure from the sales department headed by Heinz C Hoppe, and in late 1975 decided to begin the development of a new, small Mercedes-Benz saloon. But it took a full seven years for that car to materialise as the 190 — and by then the world was again a different place.

Perhaps the lack of urgency reflected, still, some feeling of complacency at these higher levels of the company. The focus was still primarily inward, on production and engineering, not outward, towards customers... or competitors.

This page: 'Nuclear power? No thanks'

Almost overnight, the market for large, high-performance (and hence thirsty) cars started to look decidedly less optimistic

The competition, by contrast with Mercedes-Benz, was far from static. The 1970s saw not only the rapid growth of BMW (still Stuttgart's most heartfelt rival) but also the renaissance of Audi. On the rally circuit, and then on the road, the Audi Quattro set new standards of grip and performance. Jaguar too was 'coming back from the dead' and even staid marques like Saab and Volvo were making inroads into Mercedes-Benz heartland. The Saab Turbo stole a march on Mercedes-Benz now largely discarded super-charger technology. And it was Volvo rather than Mercedes-Benz that was developing, in both Europe and the USA, the stronger reputation for safety.

Finally, from further away were coming serious contenders for consideration, at least for the mass market, in the shape of Toyota, Honda and Nissan. It would be another 15 years before Toyota's luxury brand Lexus would seriously challenge Mercedes-Benz in the quality stakes — but again the die was being cast in this decade.

Thinking back to some of the key criteria for successful brands discussed in chapter 1 perhaps helps to explain how and why Mercedes-Benz began to lose its way in the 1970s. Those criteria were *clarity*: having a well-defined vision and set of values for the brand; *consistency*: of both literal product delivery but more importantly of what you are as a brand; and *leadership*: the ability to reinvent and exceed customer expectations. How well did the Mercedes-Benz brand in the 1970s score against each of these?

Of clarity, there is no doubt. The brand had stuck to its core value and competency of quality engineering pretty rigidly. 'The best or nothing' was still a strong internal mantra — the company itself was one that many a young engineer would dream of working for. But in a sense it was this very rigidity that was beginning to become a problem. Like Benz at the beginning of the century, the company was sticking doggedly to tried and tested designs and resisting external pressure to change. The brand therefore retained its clarity, but looking within rather than to its customers. The parallels with Benz & Cie, both internally and externally, are tantalising — and within the next few years, just as with that company, Daimler-Benz would need to redefine its internal culture.

For consistency too, the company would have got full marks. Delivery in terms of product was still

to an exemplary standard, even if actual delivery times were irritatingly long. Consistency in terms of what the brand stood for was pretty robust too. But it was probably that failure to change, rather than the wrong kind of change, that sowed the seeds of the brand's later problems in the 1980s.

It was in the area of leadership, though, where we can clearly see, even in the 1970s, the problems for the future starting to stack up. If leadership for brands is about 'exceeding expectations' then in this decade at least, Mercedes-Benz failed the test. No longer was it a design leader — design at this point was still largely in the hands of engineers. The cars looked tired, and in some ways over-engineered, and consequently heavy in their styling. Neither was it a performance leader: BMW, Audi,

Saab, Jaguar (and in the USA a multitude of others) were all challenging for that crown.

And nor was it a leaders in terms of brand 'attitude' (what would be called a 'thought leaders' today). If anything, the brand had set its face against the changing social attitudes of the day. Doggedly, as with its designs, the company dismissed the trendiness of new ideas, new social mores. It can't be an accident that then, as before, this was a business run at the most senior levels by respectable, besuited men in their fifties who had little personal contact with the new lives that were now being lived beyond their elegant but insulated offices.

What we can see here is that the Benz side of the brand is alive and well — flourishing in the engineering division of the company — and apparently

oblivious to the changing world outside. By contrast, the Mercedes side — the elegant, sporty and innovative aspects of the company — look to be in full retreat. Mercedesness had receded, perhaps, precisely because the brand had been so successful. Just as with IBM, maybe the incentive to improve had gone away a little. Or maybe it was just simple laziness. Either way, as the saying goes, if you always do what you've always done, you always get what you've always got. For now, that seemed just fine by the Benz men.

Opposite and this page, from left to right: Audi Quattro launched 1980; Saab '99' Turbo launched 1978; Jaguar XJ6 launched 1968; Volvo 240 launched 1974

Leadership, in all these senses then, was the principal problem for the brand as the 1970s drew to a close — a weakness that would be increasingly disabling and then one that would be matched by a loss of consistency and finally by a crisis of clarity too. It is clear, with hindsight, that lack of customer focus, lack of even simply listening to customers was a significant issue. Marketing as a discipline within the business hardly existed, its status other than as a provider of research statistics hardly recognised. Hans-Georg Brehm, Head of Strategy for the brand until 2004, remembers that '25 years ago marketing people got kicked out of meetings if they talked about "positioning"'.

Such was the apparent confidence of the engineers, bordering on arrogance, that, according to Dr Dieter Zetsche, now President and CEO of the Chrysler Group, their attitude was that 'marketing is only for when you have a flop and need to re-wrap the product. We don't need that'. To get an outsider's view, the interview with Dr Wolfgang Reitzle (former Head of R & D and then also Marketing and Sales Director for BMW) was very valuable. His perspective on the brand in the 1970s is both insightful and disturbing: 'When you saw Mercedes-Benz people at motor shows they wore dark-blue suits — proud and

elegant, like the cars. They thought they had a brand that was indestructible, bullet-proof.' This, after all, was a company that seemed to have the Midas touch — that could sell cars to the Pope and to pimps, to communists and capitalists, from Nobel Prize winners to farmers.

No wonder these men felt on top of the world, no wonder they had little time for marketing, and few jobs to offer in this area. When Dr Joachim Schmidt, until recently Head of Marketing and Sales at Mercedes-Benz, applied to join the company in 1979 from Procter & Gamble, his interviewer told him that: 'We don't really do marketing here. We do research but no one listens. Why don't you try for a job in engineering?' Schmidt, as we shall see, was undeterred — and went on to become one of the architects of the new Mercedes-Benz brand in the 1990s.

But Schmidt's report of the interview is revealing — it is almost as though the company, particularly the engineering side of the company, thought it knew best, even *knew* it knew best. Brand wasn't part of the language — as Professor Hubbert pointed out, in those days 'the brand was the company and the company was the brand'. This almost biblical certainty about the fusion of the two, perhaps more than anything else, explains

how the company got into such difficulties in the decade that was to follow.

Perhaps it was also symbolically significant that the new decade began with a change of management that was to be the first of many such changes over the coming years. On 31 December 1979, Professor Joachim Zahn retired as Chairman of the board of management, having steered the company through some of its most successful years since 1965. On 1 January 1980, the chairmanship passed to Dr Gerhard Prinz, the man most closely associated with the yet to be launched small car, the 190. But while Zahn had been the only chairman in 14 years, over the next 14 years the company would, for a variety of reasons, have no less than seven men in that role. The 'consistency' identified earlier as so crucial to successful brands was about to be well and truly broken, at least managerially.

The world outside was changing rapidly too: the now not so young '68-ers' were swapping their *Atomkraft? Nein danke* stickers for a new badge: *Baby an bord*. 'Baby on board' signalled not only a change in that generation's life stage, but also perhaps a change in priorities: economy, responsibility, safety — all of these were becoming as important as prestige and performance.

Thus we have the makings of a decade of difficulties for the brand: a company still focusing inwards, a market outside changing ever more rapidly — and a new audience that Mercedes-Benz as a brand would have to appeal to if it were to survive. Horx and Wippermann in their book *Markenkult-Kultmarken* paint a vivid picture of the out-of-touchness of the Mercedes-Benz brand at the beginning of the 1980s, and contrast it to BMW's position: 'Mercedes was not "status" anymore, it was "status quo"... you needed patience [to buy one]. This after all was not a product but a hand-crafted holy artefact of the upper strata. Mercedes told of the power of inviolable values...

BMW told of influence, of motion, of dynamics'[1]. Mercedes-Benz, Horx and Wippermann observed, 'had remained in the age of steel and mechanics [and] took no interest in design'; BMW by contrast 'banked on technology' and 'bet entirely on design'. Mercedes-Benz drivers increasingly were 'proprietors', 'people who buy themselves a Mercedes when they reach the top'. BMW drivers were 'achievers': 'flexible, dynamic people — the high performers', those yet to reach the top: in other words trend-setters, to Mercedes-Benz trend-followers.

But are these harsh judgements? How much trouble was Daimler-Benz really in at the start of this

new decade? True, sales had briefly dipped in 1978 but, taken in the round, progress here was pretty unrelenting. In 1980 annual volumes of passenger cars were approaching the half-million mark, soon to reach that figure and peak at 600,000 in 1986. New models were still coming through strongly: the 1979 S-Class was selling well and had been followed by the SEL coupés in 1981. Interestingly, for the first time, these cars included air bags and seat-belt pre-tensioners, passive safety features developed by Béla Barényi, as well as improved fuel consumption and pollution-reduction features. These perhaps were a reaction to the demands of the 'baby on board' generation.

It was not until 1982 that the company unveiled its first significant response to changing customer needs: the long-awaited 190 series. And it was significant, as the company's website acknowledges: 'For the first time since post-war production resumed, a compact class vehicle [that] adds to the sales range a third series beside the mid-range and S-Class'. Traditionalists may have bemoaned this 'Baby Benz' as 'not a true Mercedes', but the public reaction was more positive. Here at last was a car within reach of a new demographic group, in Germany and in the company's European export markets. The car may have looked a bit boxy, but at least the price was right.

But it was not enough. The 190's design, especially by contrast with its contemporary, the new BMW 3 series, still looked formal, even frumpy. The car sold well, but did little to address the by now quite deeply held perceptions of the brand. In 1983, the man responsible for this car, Gerhard Prinz, died and the chairmanship passed to Professor Werner Breitschwedt. A year later, as if to compensate for the bravery of the 190, the company started producing its first estate cars, the T-models, that would so epitomise the solidity of Mercedes-Benz design in this era.

In motor racing too, the star was shining less brightly. The 1960s and 1970s had been dominated by private teams with only the occasional official 'works' involvement. But in 1980, citing 'capacity reasons', the board decided to withdraw from rallying too. Excitement, it seems, was not a priority for the brand in these years. Perhaps some of Horx and Wippermann's claims are justified.

Opposite: the new and compact 190, launched in 1982
This page: the BMW 3 series, 1982

From the perspective of a chronicler of the brand, there is a pattern continuing to develop here. Boxy traditional designs, respect for 'steel and mechanics', the ascendancy of engineering over marketing and aesthetics, the unwillingness to listen, let alone respond, to changing customer needs — all of these are reminiscent of the Benz brand of years before. Riding high in 1900, Benz & Cie too stuck doggedly to its outdated designs and proven engineering. Karl Benz's belief in 'the best of the good' had set the business, and the brand, on a course that took it away from the heart of the market — appealing to the functional, rational side of people's nature, but leaving the emotions unmoved. In the early 1980s history was repeating itself. The company's headquarters and principal car-production facilities might have been long-established in Stuttgart, but it was the values of Mannheim that seemed to predominate in these years. Confidence had subtly shifted to arrogance — it was almost as though the company didn't want to change. And the new Chairman, Professor Werner Breitschwerdt, was certainly not the man to turn the tables on the traditionalists.

At the time of his appointment, Breitschwerdt had been with the company 30 years, since 1953. He was first and foremost an engineer — more than proud of the engineering tradition and of engineering's dominance within both the culture and the board of the company. And he had a strong sense of history. When interviewed for this book, he still spoke proudly of 'my company always putting function before form'. Citing the offset pedals in a Ferrari, he claimed that such an arrangement (though essential to the beauty of that marque) would be 'unacceptable' for Mercedes-Benz. '1926', he said, 'is not such a long time ago. We've always worked to make the best cars, the most excellent workmanship, not to the brand.'

This latter statement is perhaps less extraordinary when one realises that to Breitschwerdt the brand was first and foremost the logo — not the holistic concept that we would define it as today. Nonetheless, the sentiment is important and when I interviewed him, Breitschwerdt underlined the point when he talked about what had made him most proud over the years. 'That we made the best engineered cars in the world,' came the reply, 'and that still today four out of the six main board directors are engineers. For that, I'm so happy.'

Events in the mid-1980s began to move rapidly. The brand had lost a lot of its leadership credentials in the previous decade; with the possible exception of the 190, it was no longer 'exceeding expectations'. Now though, the pressures began to build in the other two areas: consistency first, then clarity.

Management inconsistency has already been touched upon. Even though the job description varied from person to person, the title of Chairman had passed from Zahn to Prinz, and then to Breitschwerdt in 1983. Reuter would succeed in 1987, Niefer in 1989 and Werner in 1993. Only with Jürgen Schrempp in 1995 would stability be regained — but these next ten years would be absolutely crucial, and the revolving door in the chairman's office didn't help.

But it was inconsistency of a different kind — that of its cars — that would most vex the company's management.

Opposite and this page, from left to right: successive Chairmen of Daimler-Benz AG. Dr Joachim Zahn (1965-79), Dr Gerhard Prinz (1980-83), Professor Werner Breitschwerdt (1983-87), Edzard Reuter (1987-89), Werner Niefer (1989-93), Helmut Werner (1993-95)

Bonanza was the title of a popular US television series that followed the exploits of a Wild West family. It was not so much 'blood and guts', as good family fun. Perhaps therefore it was at least a little bit tongue-in-cheek when 'the Bonanza effect' became the label applied to the behaviour of Mercedes-Benz latest model, the new 200 series (W124), forerunner of the E-Class, launched in 1985.

It was the German taxi-drivers who gave the car this label, but it was a problem that afflicted all the diesels with manual gearboxes coming out of the Sindelfingen factory. The problem was one of balance within the drivetrain, but the way it manifested itself was that, at low torque, the car could jerk forward and then, suddenly, back off — rather like the bucking horse that featured in the TV programme. This embarrassing characteristic struck right at the heart of one of the brand's core values, one that was paramount for both Mercedes and Benz — quality.

Taxis, as we've seen, are highly visible in Germany — and this erratic behaviour equally so. It called into question the very 'fitness for purpose' that Benz in particular had built its reputation on.

Basic-looking the cars might have been, but they were well engineered and durable. Consistency in these respects was fundamental to the brand's appeal by this time — especially to taxi-drivers routinely covering over 60,000 miles a year. Suddenly that consistency was broken — here was a product that just didn't work very well.

Interviews with drivers told how the situation got worse rather than better in the two years after the car's launch. Individual drivers hung bags of lemons from the star or picketed showrooms. There was even a protest drive and occupation of a service

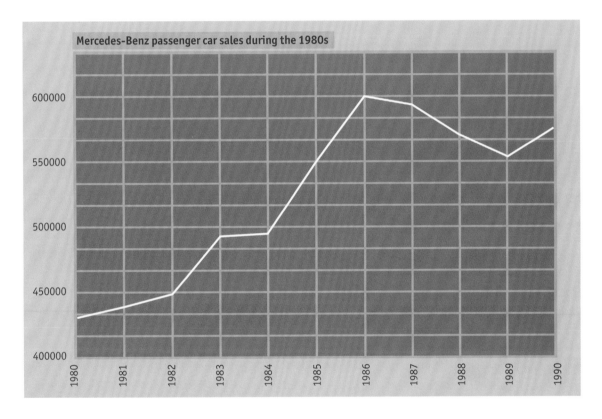

Mercedes-Benz passenger car sales during the 1980s

centre in Cologne. By that stage though, the complaints were as much about the company's failure to respond as about the original problem. And although the drivetrain issue was resolved by early 1987, the effects were potentially longer-lasting. As one driver interviewed said: 'A hundred people a day ask me how I like my car. We are Mercedes-Benz best advertising'. But in the mid-1980s they were the worst.

Inconsistency of product and, though less visible, inconsistency of management both conspired to put a serious dent in the previously untarnished image of the brand. But this time the effect started

to be felt in sales terms too. An interview with Manfred Merkel, the former Chairman of Mercedes-Benz oldest dealership, confirmed that they 'had a hard time with the W124 and the Bonanza effect — when this happened, for us the world collapsed a little bit. That such massive complaints about one of our cars were possible... this was unbelievable.'

The complaints in these years highlighted a new uncertainty: uncertainty about quality — not just for the 200 series, but for the brand as a whole — and it was inevitable that sales should start to falter. Although also impacted by the changing market situ-

ation in the USA, the relentless upward sweep of the sales graph here hesitates in 1986, plateaus in 1987, then starts to drop in 1988 and 1989.

The new 200 series had not been a flop, so the engineers didn't yet feel the need (as Dr Zetsche had pointed out) to bring in the marketers. But the brand's reputation for consistently bullet-proof engineering had been damaged. The Bonanza gunshot had at least wounded its target.

Opposite: the 200 series, prone to 'the Bonanza effect'

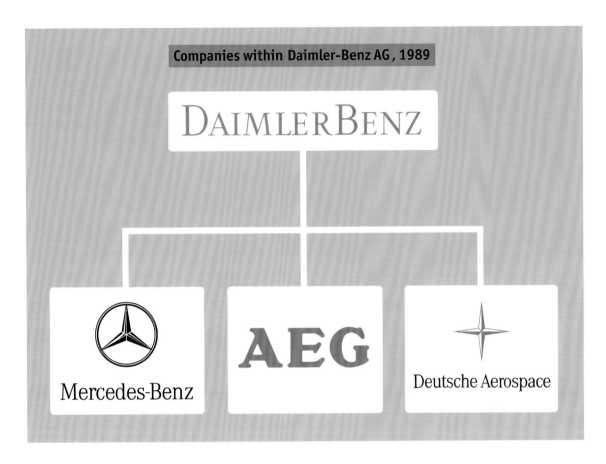

Companies within Daimler-Benz AG, 1989

DAIMLERBENZ

Mercedes-Benz

AEG

Deutsche Aerospace

Now, though, the company would start to come under attack on a third front — clarity. Clarity here is about having a single-minded vision for the brand and, although there were doubts about how customer-focused this vision was, at least the company had been single-minded in its business focus on the luxury end of the world car market, certainly until 1985.

In that year, Daimler-Benz bought up a majority of shares in Dornier (the German aircraft company) and MTU (the country's top aero-engine maker), followed by AEG (the electrical goods manu-facturer) in 1986. This new direction for the busi-nesses was to culminate in 1989 in the creation of Deutsche Aerospace AG (DASA) and AEG as two sepa-rate divisions of the company. Alongside them would sit Mercedes-Benz AG, all three now under the new holding company: Daimler-Benz AG. The 'integrated-technology concern', as it was called, was born.

The key point here is that from having a 'single-minded business focus' on cars, by the end of the 1980s the company had three focuses and a portfolio of brands of which Mercedes-Benz was but one.

How did this situation, and with it the loss of corporate clarity, arise? Was it just an instinctive Mercedes-like reaction to the ever-narrower focus of the engineers on Benz-like cars? Gottlieb Daimler had had a much broader vision of engines and trans-portation — maybe aerospace in the 1980s was the equivalent of lorries, boats and trams in the 1880s. Even AEG, it could be argued, allowed the company to reduce its dependency on the auto business.

Some argue, as does David Lewis, the business historian, that the architect of this major strategic shift, Edzard Reuter (the Finance Director and a candidate for the chairman's job before Breitschwerdt won that post), was driven by his socialist principles towards a dream of diversification. Others are less charitable.

Privately, I've been assured that this so-called strategy was actually the result of a power struggle in the boardroom of Daimler-Benz. Reuter, it seems, was not the only director unhappy with Breitschwerdt's

The brand had lost its leadership, was becoming inconsistent in its quality and was being hampered by the lack of clarity from the top

appointment. Werner Niefer too coveted the chairman's role and apparently the two men sought to topple the incumbent. The acquisition of Dornier, driven by Reuter, was the first step in creating a conglomerate that would go well beyond Breitschwerdt's vision for the company.

The event that brought things to a head was the calamitous 1986 centennial celebration that went out live on German television. After a succession of technical hitches, embarrassing presentations and clumsy hand-overs between compères, the German Bundespresident (Richard von Weizsäcker) sitting next to Breitschwerdt, is said to have told the latter that if things didn't improve within the next 20 minutes he would leave the event. Eventually the transmission was ended by the broadcasters themselves. Such humiliation was unbearable for many at Mercedes-Benz, most of all Niefer who then, I was told, with his finance director set about buying AEG to add yet another burden to Breitschwerdt's shoulders. The pressure told, and Breitschwerdt asked to

be released prematurely from his position as chairman the following year. Not surprisingly his successor was Reuter — but only until Reuter himself took over the holding company in 1989, allowing Niefer to become Chairman of the newly founded Mercedes-Benz AG.

How neat and symmetrical these management changes all look with hindsight — lending considerable weight to the veracity of the earlier story. Also tending to confirm this extraordinary tale is the fact that almost immediately these new businesses started losing money. According to Lewis: 'DASA's profitability depended on Government contracts and, with the end of the Cold War, these began to dry up. Daimler was a colossus on paper, but the car operations that Reuter disdained were the only island of profitability in a sea of red'[2]. (It would be the newly appointed Jürgen Schrempp who would be charged with clearing up this mess, and who would also be the man to replace Reuter in 1995.)

The sheer cost of this diversification strategy alone would have been damaging enough. The greater

damage, though, was just how much it distracted all concerned from the core business of car making. At the very moment when attention should have focused on the worsening market situation, top management lost sight of this goal — and the clarity that had characterised its boardroom for so long was lost for nearly a decade.

As part of the research for this book, I had the opportunity to interview David E Davis, the eminent American auto journalist and a fan of Mercedes-Benz for the last 45 years. His view of the events unfolding in Stuttgart, even from across the Atlantic, is revealing. 'Mercedes-Benz', says Davis, 'built wonderful cars from the 1960s to the 1980s... but they had it all their own way. Suddenly there was uncertainty about what business they were in. Reuter and the others were impatient with all of the historic crap that Breitschwerdt talked about; they wanted to do all the other things, like Dornier and the rest.'

In the car market things were about to get a lot worse for Mercedes-Benz. The brand had lost its leadership, was becoming inconsistent in its quality and was being hampered by the lack of clarity from the top. What *was* the brand now in the late 1980s? Its management was certainly unclear and customers were unsettled.

'Until 1986,' claims Dr Wolfgang Reitzle, formerly Head of R & D at BMW, 'people just believed that what Mercedes-Benz did was right.' From that moment on (perhaps because of the centennial event) Reitzle suggests that 'people were less certain. The look of the cars, the experience of neighbours, what was being written in the press, all of these meant that Mercedes-Benz owners, for the first time, had to defend themselves' in their brand choice.

The only people who did seem to have a clear answer were the engineers, still the pre-eminent force within the company. Even with sales now falling, they were fully in control and planning their next big venture, the new S-Class — due in 1989. Talking to senior managers and directors today about this period, one gets a sense of almost Nero-like disdain among the engineers of the day for the fires that seemed to be burning all around. They, it seemed, had fully taken over what others saw increasingly as an asylum. And unlike the new electronic technologies that BMW was pursuing, the 'steel and mechanics' of traditional Benz-like engineering was still their focus.

Dr Hans Joachim Schöpf, until 2004 Head of Research and Development, described the climate thus: 'Attention to detail, this *tüftler* quality of our engineers, had become a disadvantage. If engineers go too deep or work at something too long it becomes a problem. In the mid-1980s we were producing parts that went beyond what customers wanted or needed — producing, for example, transmissions that were 40% more expensive than other manufacturers', receiving customer complaints that were not being fed back to the production people, and delivering significantly lower added value in our cars than were our competitors.'

It is not a pretty picture, but unfortunately it is one with which almost all the interviewees concurred.

Dr Dieter Zetsche, for example, picks up Schöpf's theme of over-engineering: 'Mercedes-Benz was answering questions that customers never asked'. He continued: 'The brand was associated with arrogance, not customer orientation'. And 'the best or nothing' had come to be the driving force, for the engineers at least, of the brand's internal culture. But while the engineers fiddled, and the management politicked, sales stagnated and profits began to dip alarmingly.

Some, like Professor Hubbert, whom Breitschwerdt had asked to take over corporate planning in 1985, could see the looming danger. Despite the distractedness of his bosses, particularly Reuter's new strategy, Hubbert at least understood the problem. He joined the board in 1987 and told me: 'We had ten-year-old products. We had to refocus. Our image was weak — one survey had asked consumers to select a picture of an animal that they associated with our brand — they picked a nodding dog' (a rear-shelf icon from the 1980s that epitomised old, slow, traditional cars and their owners at that time).

This page: BMW 750il, 1988

Opposite: fall of the Berlin Wall, 1989

The customer must indeed have been confused, even bewildered, by what was going on with 'their' brand. Brands, as noted earlier, are the property of the customer too. And none is closer to the heart of most Germans than Mercedes-Benz.

Inactivity, if anything, was the principal characteristic of Mercedes-Benz in the late 1980s. New models were few and far between (the SL being the only launch of note in this period). The new S-Class, due to be introduced in 1989, was delayed for two years. More interesting cars were coming from Munich than Stuttgart: BMW's new 7 series was launched in 1987, aimed right at the heart of Mercedes-Benz 'big saloon' franchise. But in fact, the events that were really capturing the public's attention weren't in either of these cities, but nearly 400 miles away in Berlin.

In that city, at the very close of the decade, there was action galore. The fall of the Berlin Wall was a defining moment in post-war German history: symbolically and emotionally, politically and economically. At a stroke, it not only added 17 million people (27%) to the new German nation, it also opened up previously stunted markets to the east, most significantly Russia.

The company had had a presence in these markets before (from 1974 there had been a representative in Moscow servicing VIP cars), but the incomes of those living in the Warsaw Pact nations could seldom stretch to new cars, let alone new Mercedes-Benz. All of that, potentially at least, was about to change. For now, though, the celebration of the reconciliation of East and West Germany was the

main event — a new spirit was emerging, and with it, another change of values in that society.

Ostentation, conspicuous consumption, the image of the overpaid (and often overweight) businessman cruising at high speed down the *Autobahn* all seemed to run a bit counter to that new spirit. The West Germans knew that reunification would involve a price, at least short term, to achieve the integration of their Eastern neighbours. Now was the time to extend the hand of friendship and support, not for visible, even provocative, displays of wealth. This, then, was the world into which the delayed S-Class was launched in 1991.

The new S-Class (W140) was literally a giant of a car (it measured 5,113 x 1,886 x 1,486 millimetres) and polarised opinions from day one. In fact, even before day one, as one interviewee (preferring to remain anonymous on this point) observed: 'My boss took me to see the first pre-production, full-size model which had been such a secret until then. He was so proud of it, but I just looked and thought "my God, it's so big". He was disappointed, but by then it was too late anyway'.

In fact, according to Dr Reitzle (then at BMW), if anything the car grew in dimensions during the development phase. 'We were about to launch the 7 series,' he recalled, 'and I sent Niefer a pre-production car to look at. I think they were surprised by how good it looked. Niefer decided to change the specification of the S-Class even at this late stage to make it bigger. That's why they lost time and delayed the launch'. One can only speculate on what might have happened if the car had been of a smaller size and launched in 1989 — ahead of the attitude shift prompted by the fall of the Berlin Wall.

But on day one (7 March 1991) things didn't go well either. As Professor Hubbert recalls: 'We did everything wrong. At the launch to the motoring press in Geneva we hired a small room in a hotel — which made the car look even bigger — and then spent 120,000 marks decorating it, which made the whole thing seem ostentatious. I could tell from the body language what the journalists thought.' Dr Schmidt is even more critical: 'The S-Class was the incarnation of "the best or nothing": no compromise — weight doesn't count, cost doesn't count, dimensions don't count'. Big, it seemed, was beautiful.

And for some it was. To the ex-Chairman, Professor Breitschwerdt, it was 'a good car at a bad time'. Even to designer Bruno Sacco, of whom we'll hear more later, it was 'not such a bad car, perhaps a bit too severe'.

Customers were also polarised. Some, of course, lapped up this even bigger, bolder statement of power and prestige. Others, though, felt less comfortable. Horx and Wippermann sum up this dilemma sociologically: 'The S-Class became a symbol for an angry debate on values. [It] was a "dinosaur" and "splitter of society" before it even hit the market. The PR department, used to well-behaved journalists... was suddenly confronted by an angry mob hell bent on criticism.'[1] The effect of all of this on public opinion was devastating.

Horx and Wippermann spare no feelings in describing the popular reaction in Germany: 'Overnight Mercedes appeared overaged, heavy and sluggish. The S-Class was stigmatised, had a body odour that appeared hard to wash off. It was the smell of a dying target group, people who sit lethargically and ponderously in their mobile castles, people whose idea of comfort was... doors which, if not fully shut, are sucked in by 64 electric motors weighing half a ton.'

Scathing indeed, and probably a bit over-stated. But one gets the general drift: this was a car that raised hackles, that provoked, that polarised — more than any before. Above all, it was a car that looked backwards, not forwards. Backwards to the Benz-like tradition of solidity and durability, but now expressed with a vengeance: a final triumph of function over form, but one that was out of touch with the customer — and with the competition.

David E Davis summed up the mood from the US perspective: 'Mercedes-Benz used to produce cars that had a special, unique, enduring quality. But with the S-Class they reached a high water mark for over-engineered cars.'

Over at BMW in Munich, Reitzle was ecstatic: 'I thought when I saw the car "wow, now we have them". The design of the car... the fact there was not one innovative thing about it, that they had developed ridiculous solutions.' These ridiculous solutions included the addition (because the car was so big) of two small antennae that could be mechanically

extended from the rear wings to help the driver park. At the same time, BMW was developing electronic parking sensors — and the contrast between these two technologies is significant. Similarly, while the S-Class had a mechanical odometer, the BMW had an electronic one. When BMW made fun of these differences, Mercedes-Benz ran advertisements in the papers saying that such electronics were complex and unreliable.

How telling again. Benz (for this car surely was the epitome of that side of the brand) insisting to the world that its 'steel and mechanics' were right — and that the new electronics were wrong. At this point, Benzness was perhaps at its zenith, but *Mercedes*-Benz was at its nadir. Total volumes dropped further — to a low point in 1993 of 100,000 fewer cars than had been produced just six years earlier. And, unthinkably, profitability moved into the red.

But if being in the red was unthinkable for the company it was also unbearable for Werner Niefer. Even though he had only been Chairman of

Mercedes-Benz AG since 1989, he more than anyone had been associated with the S-Class. And he more than anyone symbolised the engineering-dominated culture that now permeated the whole company. One commentator even described the S-Class to me as being like 'Niefer on four wheels'.

According to Reitzle (who knew him well right up to his death), Niefer was 'the ultimate manufacturing guy, a hero in the factories'. Hilmar Kopper, Chairman of the supervisory board, confirms this: 'Niefer didn't look at the market, he didn't "feel" the market.' But the criticisms come from within too. Dr Zetsche, for example, described Niefer as being of the 'extreme old school, a total traditionalist', and in June 1993 Niefer retired and was succeeded by Helmut Werner as Chairman — now the sixth person responsible for Mercedes-Benz cars in the company's recent past.

Opposite: 'Faults in onboard electronics often end up this way'; Mercedes-Benz advertisement; 1991

Fehler in der Autoelektronik enden häufig so.

„Bitte, nehmen Sie mich mit!"

▶ Mit der Elektronik in Ihrem Auto ist es wie mit einem Computer in Ihrem Unternehmen: eine echte Hilfe, wenn er funktioniert – ein echter Alptraum, wenn nicht. Die Erfahrungen, die einige Fahrer von Oberklasse-Autos mit der Elektronik machen mußten, sind bekannt – und waren für die Betroffenen sehr ärgerlich. Besonders nachts am Straßenrand.

Mercedes-Benz stand der allgemeinen Elektronik-Begeisterung immer sehr reserviert gegenüber. Und viele ADAC-Straßenwachtfahrer haben diese Reserviertheit mit uns geteilt: Was nützt der schönste digitale Fortschritt unter der Haube, wenn schon eine leicht gelockerte Steckverbindung zusammen mit einem Spritzer Feuchtigkeit den König der Überholspur zum Tramper am Straßenrand macht?

▶ Bisher hat Mercedes deshalb zum Beispiel bevorzugt die KE-Jetronic eingebaut: eine mechanische Einspritzung, die mit elektronischer Unterstützung arbeitet. Bei einem Fehler in der Elektronik arbeitet sie immer noch rein mechanisch. Und so kann der Mercedes-Fahrer zumindest noch weiterfahren.

▶ Nun hat die Elektronik ein paar unbestreitbare Vorteile, weswegen kein fortschrittlicher Automobilhersteller darauf verzichten kann. Ohne Elektronik ist beispielsweise auch eine umweltschonendere Verbrennung des Benzins genausowenig zu erreichen wie eine spürbare Entlastung des Fahrers oder eine aktive Verhinderung von Unfällen durch Systeme wie ABS, ASR oder ADS. Die Frage ist nur: Wie geht ein Automobilhersteller mit dem elektronischen Fortschritt um? Eher vorschnell nach der Devise: Wir werden ja schon sehen, ob's funktioniert. Oder eher kritisch und mit geradezu konservativem Qualitätsbewußtsein.

▶ Immerhin benötigt ein Auto der Spitzenklasse heutzutage rund 3 Kilometer Kabel, ein gutes Dutzend Steuergeräte, 60 Relais und rund 3000 Steckverbindungen. Da muß man sich schon etwas einfallen lassen, wenn das alles funktionieren soll wie ein Mercedes. Schön wäre zum Beispiel, wenn man diese riesige Menge an möglichen Fehlerquellen drastisch reduzieren könnte – denn ein Stecker, den es nicht gibt, kann auch nicht abfallen.

Die neue S-Klasse geht hier in eine völlig neue Richtung: Sie wird mehr elektronische Funktionen bieten – mit weniger elektronischen Teilen. Womit wir uns, ganz nach Art des Hauses, auch bei der neuen S-Klasse wiedermal nur auf das Wesentliche beschränken. Gute Fahrt!

Freuen Sie sich auf die neue S-Klasse.

Mercedes-Benz

'We all knew the business environment had changed... We had a deep crisis'

In the end, it was probably the profit decline more than popular reaction to the S-Class that sealed Niefer's fate. The car, after all, did sell — and a lot of subsequent design effort, cosmetically at least, went into making it look smaller than it actually was. To Hilmar Kopper though, the two factors, commercial performance and product, are closely linked. As he explained: 'I often think that the shape of the product reflects the shape of a company. The old S-Class was symbolic of the state of the company. They were over-staffed, unproductive and making the wrong cars. The company that had no idea of loss started making losses. Yet success, *economic* success, is part of the image of the brand.'

In this single observation, Herr Kopper puts his finger right on the heart of the problem. It was the company that had overindulged, grown fat, got a bit lazy. The product that emerged was a symptom of that, not in itself the cause. The brand suffered because it was so inextricably linked to the fortunes of the company, and therefore to the company's latest and most visible symbol, the S-Class.

But if Niefer's departure brought the beginning of the end of the dominance of the engineers, it wasn't without a struggle. Certainly some of the key battles were already being fought (some of them are described in the next chapter), but organisational culture does not change overnight. As Professor Hubbert described it: 'This was a company that from the mid-1950s to the mid-1980s had never experienced a crisis. Thirty years of success destroys the character.'

'Crisis' isn't a word one hears often in the vocabulary of Mercedes-Benz. It feels somehow out of place in the cool, quiet corridors of the company's offices in Möhringen. Yet Dr Schöpf described the scene a decade ago even more pointedly: 'The engineers took the attitude "Could we be affected? No. Do we want to see the evidence? No." But we all knew the business environment had changed. So I asked myself, "Are we sure that we are robust enough to survive?" and my answer too was "no". We had a deep crisis.'

That the S-Class of 1991 sold at all in Germany might seem strange given all the negative publicity surrounding its launch. In fact, to begin with it sold reasonably well, perhaps paradoxically because of the economic situation immediately after the reunification. The economy had been hit hard by the costs of integration but, as Marsh and Collett point out: 'Cars act as economic barometers. When times are bad there are additional incentives to show off one's pecuniary powers because fewer people are able to do so... Driving a more expensive car is a sign that one has the power to withstand the difficult times.'[2] For some, this seemingly perverse logic clearly held good. For many others, though, the sense was that the S-Class was out of tune with the

S-Klasse: Wegen schwerer Extras können oft nur zwei oder drei Leute mitfahren

Super-Benz sperrt Dicke aus

Stuttgart – Vier gewichtige Manager öffnen die Verschläge des neuen S-Klasse-Mercedes. Drei lassen sich satt in die Ledersitze fallen. Doch für den vierten Mann heißt es: Ich muß leider draußen bleiben. Anderer Fall. Mama (80 Kilo) und Papa (100 Kilo) rüsten zur Ferienfahrt mit dem neuen Schlachtschiff. Dazu kommt standesgemäßes Gepäck. Schlecht für den Filius (90 Kilo): Er fährt Bahn. Alle haben dasselbe Problem: Die neue S-Klasse schleppt so viel Speck mit sich herum, daß schon zwei Personen mit Gepäck das zulässige Gesamtgewicht erreichen können.

In Tests von Fachblättern wurde das Gewichtsproblem aufgedeckt. Mal hatten die bis zu 200 000 Mark teuren Karossen nur noch 270 Kilo für Passagiere und Gepäck übrig, mal nur 262 Kilo. Grund ist die üppige Zusatzausstattung von der Klimaanlage bis zum Geruchsfilter, welche das Nacktgewicht der Autos über die Zwei-Tonnen-Marke treiben.

„Ist der Mercedes nicht etwas zu groß für einen Zweisitzer?", fragen Schadenfrohe. Das Unternehmen wiegelt ab. Mit der Fahrsicherheit gebe es keine Probleme. Und beim TÜV sei inzwischen ein höheres Gesamtgewicht beantragt.

Zwar wird die Polizei kaum ein unverdächtiges Auto auf die Waage stellen. Aber bei schweren Unfällen sucht jede Versicherung nach Wegen, aus der Regulierung herauszukommen – Gewichts-Überschreitungen werden gerne als mögliche Unfallursache vermutet.

Die neue S-Klasse von Mercedes (300 SE bis 600 SEL) hat Probleme mit dem zulässigen Gesamtgewicht.

Zeitgeist. With many cars of the new model now on the road, the problems if anything got worse.

The S-Class's shape and size had principally been determined by the need to accommodate an adult male of 1.9 metres in height comfortably in the back seat without his head touching the roof. The results of these overblown proportions soon started to be felt by German owners. Some noticed it on the day they took delivery, when the car wouldn't fit into their garages. Others discovered that when they took their car on holiday, using the German railways' 'motorrail' system to get to their destination, the S-Class was too wide to fit on the train.

Most humiliating of all for both customers and the company was the fact that German technical regulations required manufacturers to specify the gross weight of their cars so that equipment such as brakes and suspension could be shown to be appropriate to the size of car. Once loaded with options (and passengers), the S-Class was found to exceed its permitted specification. This led to the extraordinary sight of the German police stopping S-Class drivers and issuing tickets for their cars being overweight. What fun... and what a field day the press had: 'fat' and 'overweight' became the new language of the brand, in the newspapers at least.

This page: 'Super Benz locks out the overweight', **Abendzeitung München, 24 June 1991**

Mercedes 300 E.

Der typische Mercedes-Fahrer trägt Hut.

▶ Wenn Sie einmal darauf achten, wer einen Mercedes fährt, werden Sie feststellen, daß viele unserer Fahrer Fahrerinnen sind. Allein im letzten Jahr haben sich rund 22.700 Frauen einen neuen Mercedes gekauft. Was zeigt, daß Deutschlands Frauen nicht nur immer erfolgreicher werden, sondern auch immer mehr Freude daran haben, diesen Erfolg zu genießen. Die Automobile von Mercedes-Benz kommen dieser Freude besonders entgegen.

▶ Beispielsweise mit einem Fahrerplatz, der sich genau auf seine Fahrerin einstellt: Sitz und Sicherheitsgurt sind auch in der Höhe verstellbar. Und das natürlich serienmäßig und

grundsätzlich bei allen Modellen. Eine Servolenkung ist bei allen unseren Wagen genauso serienmäßig wie der elektrisch verstellbare Außenspiegel auf der rechten Seite. Und selbst das Anti-Blockier-System (ABS) ist bei fast allen Mercedes-Modellen serienmäßig.

▶ Sicher, ein Mercedes ist manchmal schon etwas teurer als andere Automobile. Dafür steckt er aber auch voll unsichtbarer Details, die Sie erst dann wahrnehmen, wenn Sie sie wirklich brauchen. Angefangen von den beheizbaren Düsen für die Scheibenwaschanlage im Winter bis zu dem Elektromotor, der die Heckklappe des Mercedes T-Modells selbständig zuzieht.

Damit Sie sie zum Schließen nur antippen müssen.

▶ Ein Mercedes stellt eben keine Ansprüche an seine Fahrerin. Sondern stellt sich lieber auf die Ansprüche seiner Fahrerin ein. Daß zu diesen Ansprüchen auch Stil, Eleganz und ein gewisser Luxus gehören, versteht sich eher von selbst. Wir betonen deshalb gerne die vernünftigen Seiten unserer Automobile. Denn unter einem schönen Hut steckt gewiß auch ein kluger Kopf.

Mercedes-Benz
Ihr guter Stern auf allen Straßen.

With high depreciation (up to 35% in year one), reported vandalism to one in four cars and fuel consumption of less than 15 miles to the gallon the market soon started to dry up. Unthinkably, Mercedes-Benz was forced to offer discounts of up to 15%, free hotel vouchers and no-cost optional extras. In Germany, waiting times plummeted and, more worryingly, BMW picked up trade-ins at a rate of knots. Non-European markets were less affected; sales in Asia in particular held up well. In the USA

though, where the car's size was a much lesser issue, volumes dropped sharply after the launch period despite heavy discounting.

Interestingly (and again giving a little glimpse of the attitude of its creators) even the US specification of the S-Class didn't feature a cupholder — so vital an accessory in that market's 'drive thru' culture. When queried about this, the company's response (as reported by Hubbert) was that 'people shouldn't really be eating and drinking in this car'.

This perhaps more than any other of the multitude of anecdotes about this model perfectly sums up the fundamental issue within the company that the car came to symbolise.

The S-Class's ongoing problems had, however, given added impetus to the debates that were by then raging within the company. Professor Hubbert, working to his original brief from Breitschwerdt but now on the board of the company, had commissioned the 1990 research that threw up the 'nodding dog' association. In the same year he had also briefed management consultants McKinsey to give the company its vision of the future for Mercedes-Benz. Not surprisingly, the latter had made three key observations: ageing product line, weak image and difficult future market conditions. At least all were agreed about the problem, or so it seemed.

It was Dr Schmidt (then responsible for corporate planning) who first drew the board's attention to just how badly the company was performing relative to its old and new competitors. In 1990, a five-year study by the Massachusetts Institute of Technology (MIT) of the underlying economics of the global automobile trade was published as *The Machine that Changed the World*.[3] In particular, it compared the performance of the Japanese companies (now including Lexus) and those of the 'European specialist producers', such as Mercedes-Benz.

The results are still revealing today, especially in the area of new product development. Whereas Japanese manufacturers took on average 1.7 million engineering hours to develop a new car, the

Unser
meistgebrauchtes
Ersatzteil.

► Wie gut, daß wir unser
Geld nicht mit dem Verkauf von
Ersatzteilen verdienen müssen.

Denn bei der sprich-
wörtlichen Langlebigkeit von Mer-
cedes-Bauteilen läuft der Absatz
von Ersatzteilen erfreulich schlep-
pend. Und wir tun alles, damit er in
Zukunft noch schleppender läuft:
Während eine Auspuffanlage vor
ein paar Jahren üblicherweise alle
40.000 km ausgetauscht werden
mußte, ist das Doppelte heute die
Norm. Ein Keilriemen muß bei
einem Mercedes in der Regel über-
haupt nicht mehr erneuert werden.

Jedes Jahr lassen sich
unsere Ingenieure wieder eine
Menge Neues einfallen, was sich
erfreulich bremsend auf unsere Ersatzteilverkäufe auswirkt.
Schließlich wollen wir nicht der
größte Ersatzteillieferant der Welt

werden, sondern das beste Auto
der Welt bauen. Für dieses Ziel for-
schen bei uns mehr Ingenieure als
bei jedem anderen Automobilhersteller der Welt. Trotz hoch-
moderner Fertigungsmethoden mit
Robotern und Computern kommt
bei uns nach guter Mercedes-Tra-
dition immer noch auf 10 Auto-
werker ein Mann, der nur für
Qualitätskontrollen zuständig ist.

► An einem Bauteil sind
unsere Bemühungen um Langlebigkeit jedoch spurlos vorbei-
gegangen: am Mercedes-Stern.
Obwohl wir ihn genauso sorgfältig
herstellen wie alles, wird er öfter
verlangt als jedes andere Ersatzteil. Das sagt viel über die Lebens-
dauer dieser Ersatzteile, aber
auch viel über unser Markenzei-
chen. Manche hängen an ihm mit
solcher Inbrunst, daß sie es als

Souvenir mitnehmen. Deshalb
mußten wir den Mercedes-Stern
allein in den letzten zwei Jahren
1.480.521mal erneuern. Womit er
tatsächlich unser meistgebrauchtes Ersatzteil ist.

► Gegen die Beliebtheit
des Mercedes-Sterns können wir
nichts tun. Wir möchten aber alle
seine Liebhaber darauf hinweisen,
daß man den Stern auch ohne grö-
ßeren Kraftaufwand bei jedem
Mercedes-Händler erwerben kann.

Dort finden Sie auch
das, was diesen Stern so berühmt
gemacht hat – den Mercedes.

Mercedes-Benz
Ihr guter Stern auf allen Straßen.

Ersatzteil Nr. 1248800086.

European specialist manufacturers took almost double that time (3.1 million hours). But perhaps most alarming was the amount of time it took the European specialist manufacturers to return to normal quality levels after beginning production of a new model. At this time Japanese producers experienced only a short interruption to delivered quality (1.4 months) while it took European specialist producers a full year to return to their original quality levels.

Schmidt's task was to get the attention of the board, which he achieved by presenting them with a written summary of the MIT study. His conclusions were given added weight by the fact that, according to Zetsche, 'though the figures for individual European manufacturers were disguised by amalgamation, we all could see that Mercedes-Benz was at the bottom of the productivity league'. Schöpf's warnings about costs — he told of how he'd even heaved a full gearbox on to his desk and challenged

his engineering colleagues to point out exactly what it was that made this transmission 40% more valuable to customers than a competitor's equivalent — were coming home to roost.

Debates about the brand too (though this word was still not common parlance on the board) were taking place at the highest levels. In 1989, the company had appointed as its advertising agency the young, Hamburg-based Springer & Jacoby. Known for their unconventional creativity and strategic skills, the appointment had been a brave one. Though the brief, according to Konstantin Jacoby (founding partner of Springer & Jacoby), had been for lifestyle advertising, the company had won the account on the strength of some more radical solutions. These were in response to the problems that the brand had at the time, though the company was uncomfortable about admitting to them. Indeed, Jacoby claims that the 'problems' weren't discussed in the pitch, but emerged during some honest conversations over lunch. Springer & Jacoby's key observations mirrored (and in fact preceded) some of those highlighted by McKinsey.

Opposite and this page, from left to right: early advertisements from Springer & Jacoby challenged preconceptions consumers held about the brand: 'The typical Mercedes driver wears a hat'; 'Our most frequently replaced part', 1990

'The brand needed to turn from being seen as a reward after a successful career to being a companion to a successful career'

They saw four issues for the brand. Firstly, the quality issues that were still surrounding the 200 series. Secondly, that the brand was losing touch with the mood of the times. Thirdly, a lack of innovation — and we've seen how the 1980s was a somewhat impoverished decade in this respect. Fourthly, sales were slowing as a result of competitive incursions. Their creative solutions to these were far more fundamental than the lifestyle campaign that the brief had called for. At the board meeting in August 1988, at which all of this was to be presented, things didn't go quite to plan. As Jacoby recalls: 'One of the marketing managers stood up in front of me as I was presenting and tried to reassure the board that what the agency were saying was more radical than they actually intended to recommend. This happened more than once.' Eventually it was Professor Hubbert who said: 'Let the agency speak — what they are suggesting

is not too bad'. To quell further protest it was the Chairman, Niefer — perhaps surprisingly — who said 'let's listen to them', and the presentation was successfully concluded.

The board's take-out from this presentation was that, as a company, they had underestimated their brand, and were under-selling its excellence. Springer & Jacoby stressed the brand's 'authenticity' and the potential that could exist if the company had more self-belief, and the brand more confidence. Their creative work reflected this bolder approach.

With hindsight, Jacoby sees Professor Hubbert and Dr Schmidt as the prime movers at least in getting these new ideas heard — particularly the conclusion which the agency reached that 'the brand needed to turn from being seen as a reward after a successful career to being a companion to a successful career'. The average age of buyers then

was 54 — this strategy suggested a younger audience for the future.

But if the board was listening, it wasn't yet acting — this after all was the year when Niefer was making the S-Class bigger. The new, bold advertisements started running in 1990 but the company still had some way to go to begin fulfilling this new vision for its brand. It was to the *internal* brand that attention now needed to turn, to address the cultural issues of which, in the end, the cars were but a symbol.

As early as 1960, Theodore Levitt (Professor of Business Administration at Harvard Business School) had coined the phrase 'marketing myopia' to describe the blinkered (or, more accurately, short-sighted) approach that some companies took to their businesses, specifically to what business they were in.

His observations, now famous, included examples of companies that had defined their business as 'buggy whip manufacturing' — not surprisingly (to all but the owners) left bankrupt by the advent of the car. The simple message of Levitt's work was: be clear about what business you're in; be aware of how the world and your market is changing around you. On both counts, Mercedes-Benz was in Levitt's terms an 'at risk' business. Clarity, as we saw in the previous chapter, had been compromised at the very top. And the company's myopic focus on 'the best or nothing' at the luxury end of the car market also made it dangerously narrow in its brand proposition.

But the company was also, seemingly, unaware of how the market was changing, particularly in respect of that key attribute: quality. We've already seen how some of the brand's quality was simply invisible — Dr Schöpf's gearbox story highlights that. More interesting still, though, is how quality itself was being redefined in those years.

The things that had in the past defined quality for customers and manufacturers alike were simply becoming less important. Cars didn't rust like they used to, cars didn't break down like they used to. Cars even lasted longer than they used to — that is, if you chose to hang on to them when falling real prices meant that a replacement car was more affordable than ever. These fundamental qualities (note their Benz-like character) were, if anything, becoming the concerns of the second-hand market, not of buyers of new cars. Of course the two are related through residual values and of course there were exceptions to the rule (notably from Italy), but for most people, most of the time, most cars were now of a pretty high standard in respect of their functional fitness-for-purpose.

Quality in cars was, therefore, being redefined. By the beginning of the 1990s it was more about electronic capabilities than mechanical features, more about performance than durability, more about styling than depth of engineering — for customers at least. Arguably, styling was the only visible characteristic of cars that belied their age. None of this is to say that the fundamentals of construction did not matter, rather that they were increasingly taken as read; believed to be a characteristic of most cars — allowing the customer to move on and consider new aspects of brand choice.

I've dwelt on this issue at some length because it is important in understanding what happened next at Mercedes-Benz. After 1992, the company reacted to this redefinition of quality in some significant respects. But it was to be a painful transition.

For *any* company, a fundamental change of direction such as this is a desperately difficult process. Particularly so when it is preceded by signs and omens that suggest that what has been done to date has been somehow wrong, or at least misguided.

The temptation to stick with the old ways is powerful, the fear of change (and with it the uncertainty as to whether things will really improve) is acute. Change begins with admission — the honest acceptance that things are not as they should be. But having such feelings is not the same as expressing them openly. To admit openly that one has been wrong is the vital precondition to putting things right: for people, companies and brands.

Helmut Werner, the man who replaced Niefer as Chairman in 1993, sadly died in February 2004. In an interview only a few weeks earlier, he had been disarmingly frank with me: 'The company had never given any consideration to what the customer wanted. In fact, up until the mid-1980s, the engineers would only show new cars to the board two or three weeks before the launch.' Werner too felt the cars were over-engineered, but his more immediate concern was the worsening financial situation: 'We

were making a deep, deep loss,' he told me, perhaps even greater than the published results revealed, 'we had to have a new company'.

The crisis which Mercedes-Benz faced in the early 1990s was as much as anything a 'crisis of admission', and it took bravery by some to bring that out into the open, and then to act on it. Dr Schöpf had hinted at it ('we all knew the business environment had changed'), but it was Dr Schmidt, the man who had brought the MIT research to the board, who described this process most poignantly: 'Sales were stagnating, profits were even negative in one year. This was a culture shock for the company. Questions were asked: "Should we stay as a high-end, luxury maker — or should we go the way of growth?" Our costs were too high — with this phrase "the best or nothing" you'd *never* reach a target cost. People were saying "if we design a new product, let's start with the customer" — it was clear the company had to change completely.' And then comes the key point: 'It was clear that there would have to be a paradigm change — the company had always done the same things, but now others had overtaken us. This admission was shocking. Even more shocking was the admission that the cost structure was too

high — up to that time the engineers would have said they were very cost-effective.'

But Dr Schmidt's summary of the *The Machine that Changed the World* had itself begun to change the company. Niefer, according to Schmidt, 'understood early the truth'. Subsequently the company sent some of its senior executives to Japan to see for themselves the way in which that country, in manufacturing terms at least, was overtaking them.

A key moment then — and Dr Schmidt's quote is the more remarkable because it touches on so many of the shibboleths within Mercedes-Benz at that time: engineering costs, the luxury market position, Daimler's mantra, the need for customer involvement early on in the design process. All of these were fundamental to what the brand was, what it stood for and how it had all been achieved. For the company, the key point was the admission that others had indeed overtaken them and that a paradigm shift was needed.

Professor Hubbert picks up the story of how the board began to get to grips with this new set of challenges. '1992, the crisis year, helped to make people understand. The market was customer-driven, we weren't. We still talked about "the best engineered cars in the world" — the attitude was "We know what's best for you", like the cupholder story. We had to change the mindset of 100,000 people.'

Fascinatingly, though, Hubbert (by then Director of Passenger Cars), with his power enhanced through Niefer's replacement by the more pliant Helmut Werner, went on to describe two key actions that show just how delicately balanced the politics of this strategic shift were.

First, ahead of these critical board discussions, he got the key individuals who were supportive of these changes onside. When I asked how this was achieved, he replied quite simply: 'We made a pact. We simply wrote out on a piece of paper "Now there is no way back" and I and my team all signed it. I still have it at home'. The original is reproduced here — perhaps the most significant single piece of paper in the company's recent history.

The second thing Hubbert did was less private, but equally significant for what it said about the culture change that would have to follow. At the end of one of the key board meetings, and by now very much having stamped his authority on the management of the company, Hubbert called the directors back to the table. 'There is one more thing, gentlemen. This expression "the best or nothing" —

we can't any longer move forward with this phrase, it will kill our company. From now on we must think about "the best for the customer".'

At the time, Schmidt recalls being 'shocked' at this rewriting of the mantra that, internally at least, had so defined the character of the company and therefore of its brand. But reflecting on this over the years he now acknowledges that 'at first it left me unsure, but now I believe he was right'.

And if it was shocking for Schmidt, imagine the tremors it sent through the engineers on the board and, probably within hours, through the company. Here, after all, were Gottlieb Daimler's words of over a century before being rescripted in response to what some still saw as a temporary blip in the fortunes of the company. This too was clearly a profoundly important moment, and the beginning of the change of mindset that Hubbert had predicted.

This page: 'Now there is no way back'. Professor Hubbert's informal pact signed by several board members in 1992

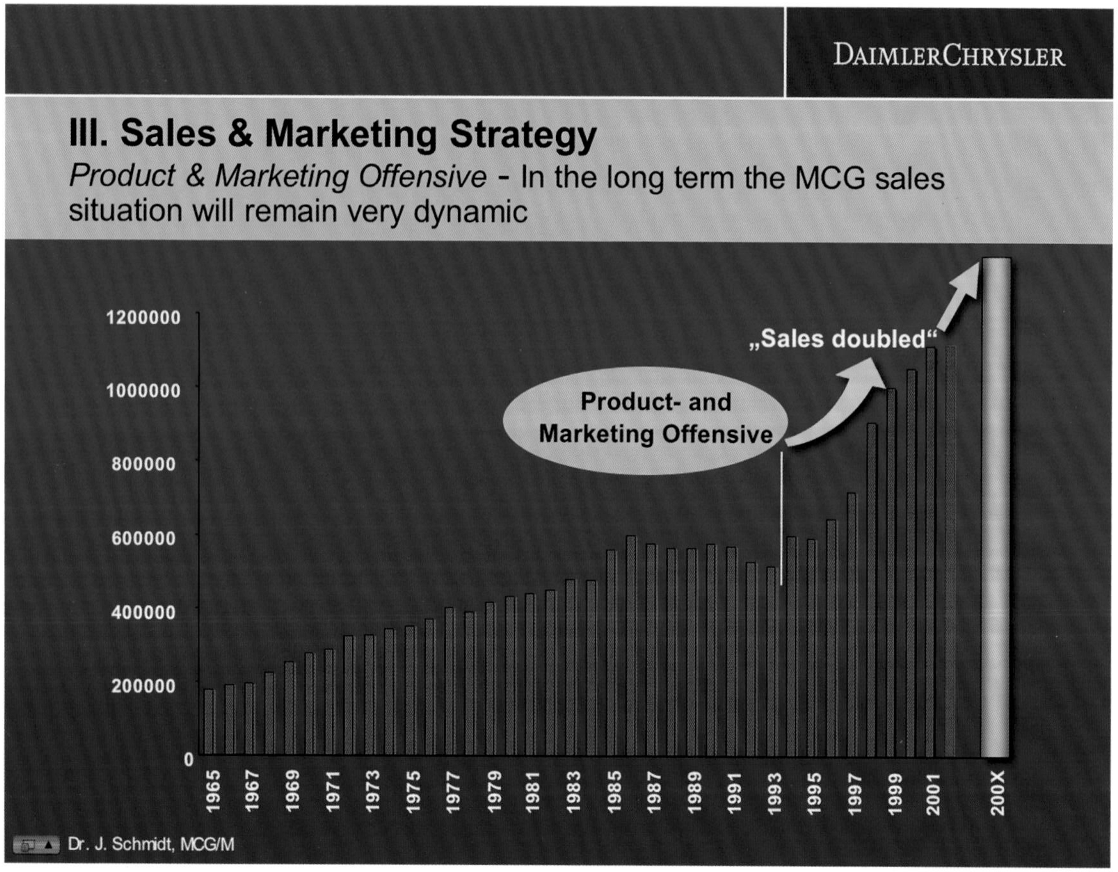

DaimlerChrysler
III. Sales & Marketing Strategy
Product & Marketing Offensive - In the long term the MCG sales situation will remain very dynamic
1200000
1000000
800000
600000
400000
200000
0
„Sales doubled"
Product- and Marketing Offensive
1965
1967
1969
1971
1973
1975
1977
1979
1981
1983
1985
1987
1989
1991
1993
1995
1997
1999
2001
200X
Dr. J. Schmidt, MCG/M

The implications for the external brand were clear. To the need for a new confidence in communications, a new awareness of the competition and a younger and broader appeal, was now added the need to redefine, right at the heart of the brand, what quality was in the consumer's eyes — and then respond to that in product terms.

Dr Dieter Zetsche, a key architect of these changes together with Hubbert, underlined these profound implications for the brand: 'Mercedes-Benz association with arrogance, not customer orientation, this move to "the best for the customer", the idea that the customer should define the product, not the engineers — we wrestled with all of these for years.' But by 1994, Zetsche observed: 'We started to take a more conscious look at the brand and the customer relationship. We designed a brand model that defined three areas: discipline (our traditional area), responsibility and emotion, or what we called "fascination". At this time discipline was 75% of what the brand stood for. The strategy was to keep this value as dominant, but enlarge the other two — responsibility and emotion — to 50%.'

If this all sounds too methodical or even mathematical, then its significance should not be underestimated. To rebalance a brand in this way is a major task — one that many brands struggle to achieve. The younger the brand, the easier it is. But for long-established, even 'institutionalised' brands like Mercedes-Benz, changing deeply held public attitudes is a major task. Achieving this goal, as all the key players now acknowledge, has brought problems of its own — it relied, of course, on changes from within (the internal brand), but equally on what was finally delivered to customers: the cars themselves.

In this context, Dr Schmidt likes to tell another 'story from the boardroom' from the early 1990s. He recounts the occasion when he said to his colleagues 'we are not forced to make boring cars', a statement that clearly articulates another 'admission' that the company would have to deal with. Schmidt follows up the story by producing a sales graph highlighting the point at which things began to change. A double line is drawn between the years 1993 and 1994, and labelled 'Product and Marketing Offensive'. From that point, the bars on the chart begin to rise again — regaining the pattern they had assumed from

1965 to 1986. Now often referred to as the 'first product offensive', its author Professor Hubbert is quick to point out that it was neither one nor two, but in fact four separate 'offensives' — product, productivity, learning and image.

We identified earlier the range of problems Mercedes-Benz faced in these years — here at last was the response. A four-pronged attack on the old ways of both thought and deed. A comprehensive (and aggressively phrased) set of strategies to put the company and the brand back on their feet. Schmidt highlights two of these 'offensives' in particular: 'The product needed good styling, good design. Image-wise our goal was for the press to talk about our styling and design, not just our *technik*.'

Professor Hubbert places emphasis on the other two also — productivity was clearly key for the reasons we've seen, 'learning' referred to thinking in new ways, and *un*learning some of the old ones.

From the brand point of view — and certainly for customers — it was product above all, though, that would demonstrate whether this new strategy was real. Perhaps that's why it is the label of 'product offensive' that has stuck. The reality of developing a

new car (as MIT had made painfully clear) was not a speedy process for the 'European specialist producers'.

For Mercedes-Benz it typically took 72 months in those days, 38 months today. So in 1992, what was to become the 'new' C-Class would clearly have been in development for some time; well past the time where the company's *Lastenheft*, its detailed product plan for every new model, would tell us that development was beyond the point of no return in respect of styling. Yet with the car due for launch the following year, Hubbert was under no illusions that the company's new direction would be judged by this product. Coming hot on the heels of the S-Class made this an important model too. Even though much more radical designs were by then in the pipeline, the new C-Class, aimed at replacing the 190 series at the lower end of the range, would be crucial to the brand's future — just as the 170 had been 50 years before.

Opposite: Dr Schmidt's sales graph, showing the impact of the first product and marketing offensive

Man muß kein typischer Mercedes-Fahrer sein, um einen typischen Mercedes zu fahren.

Die C-Klasse "Esprit".

▶ Den typischen Mercedes-Fahrer gibt es tatsächlich. Er lebt in den Köpfen einiger Leute, die keinen Mercedes fahren. Und es gibt auch den typischen Mercedes – zum Beispiel die C-Klasse „Esprit". Typisch daran ist unter anderem die Lackierung Lichtgelb (im obi-

gen Bild schön zu erkennen). Eine Farbe, die man genau wie die drei ungewöhnlichen Innenraumdekors in konservativen Kreisen als „na ja, recht erfrischend" bezeichnen würde.

Dazu kommt: Der „Esprit" liegt gut 2 cm tiefer auf der Straße. Und hat ein Fahrwerk, das – ganz

typisch für dieses Auto – wirklich Spaß macht. Ebenso typisch sind die weiteren Details, die diesen Mercedes umgeben. Zum Beispiel die Mercedes Sicherheit mit ABS und Airbag. Der Mercedes Komfort

mit mehr Platz als typische Autos dieser Klasse. Der Mercedes Antrieb mit 4 Ventilen pro Zylinder für deutlich mehr Durchzug und weniger Schadstoffe. Und selbstverständlich auch der sprichwört-

liche Mercedes Werterhalt für mehr Freude beim Wiederverkauf.

▶ Wie gesagt, ein ganz typisches Auto aus unserem Hause. Das einzig untypische ist vielleicht der Anschaffungspreis: Es kostet Sie keinen Pfennig extra, die C-Klasse in der „Esprit"-Version zu fahren.

Wir befürchten jedoch, daß es wieder ein paar Leute gibt, denen auch das nicht gefällt. Typisch.

Mercedes-Benz
Ihr guter Stern auf allen Straßen.

This page: 'No need to be a typical Mercedes driver to drive a typical Mercedes', 1993
Opposite: sketches for the original Smart car, 1995

'Outsiders,' Hubbert recalls, 'talked of the C-Class as a *Rettungswagen* (rescue vehicle) — a saviour for the company. If the C-Class hadn't worked, I wouldn't have been here. It was a *Rettungswagen* — and for the first time in ten years we had growth.'

The C-Class was hardly a dramatic new style statement, but it was a much fresher car than its predecessor and its lines were much smoother than many had expected — the press reaction was good.

The car was offered in standard format (later called Classic), but also in three other variants: Elegance, Esprit and Sport. The last, in particular, was clearly aimed at a younger audience and later an AMG version would up the performance stakes much further. To Hubbert's relief (and the rest of the board's) the car was well received by the public too,

and the C-Class contributed in no small part to the upward shift in the sales graph. But even though 1993/4 is hailed as the beginning of the 'product offensive', in truth it was the models still in development that would really begin to change the face of the cars, and of the brand. This was, after all, the period when the soon-to-arrive E-Class was having the final touches put to its design, and it was the debate about whether that car's slanted four-headlight arrangement was too radical that had prompted Schmidt's comment about 'boring cars'.

This was also the period when cars like the CLK, the replacement S-Class, the SLK, the radical A-Class concept and even initial ideas for the M-Class were being debated. It was these models that would really define the 'product offensive' and put down

bold new markers for where the brand stood, and where it was going.

But this was also the time when a much smaller project, a joint venture in fact, would be the one that brought the word 'brand' into the language of the boardroom. Professor Hubbert recollects that: 'Brand thinking and brand language really only started with Smart... the first conversations I remember were in about 1993. Before that... the attitude was "Why have marketing when you don't have competition?".'

To some it will appear astonishing that it was only as recently as 1993 that the company began to use the vocabulary that was, by then, part of the everyday language of just about every consumer goods manufacturer in the Western world. The fact

is, however, that many non-marketers (as Professor Breitschwerdt's interview illustrated) use the word 'brand' in its limited meaning of logo and packaging design. It is probably this narrow definition that permeated the board's view too, and hence 'company' became a better surrogate for 'brand', as most would define it, than the word itself. As we've seen, the company had had a brand (or rather two) since its earliest days — but the fact that the word wasn't in common parlance is significant nonetheless.

Dr Zetsche talks passionately about how the new Mercedes-Benz models would reshape both the brand and the internal culture. As he points out: 'We were moving from a world in which we had launched three cars in ten years, to one in which we would be launching ten cars in three years. It was a massive transformation — partly to persuade 9,000 engineers that sales and marketing had a role to play. All of it had to be linked to an understanding of the importance of brand and the direction of our brand.'

In a master-stroke of symbolism aimed at highlighting this new cross-disciplinary thinking, Zetsche assembled the 9,000 engineers in a hall and physically tore down a wall representing the barrier between production and marketing. Coming so soon after the events in Berlin and delivered so personally, the message couldn't have been clearer.

On the productivity front, there were painful messages to be delivered too — but here they took the form of redundancy notices. Few were compulsory, but through early retirement and non-replacement particularly, the company reduced its workforce by 20,000 in the years after 1993. But what the internal brand lost through job insecurity and the uncertainty of new ways of working, it gained from greater clarity and the sense of commercial success that was beginning to return.

Opposite: the AMG-5.5 litre engine
This page: the SLK55 AMG safety car

From a brand perspective, what is perhaps most interesting about these years is that, after 20 years of Benzness, the brand was beginning to rediscover the Mercedes side of its personality.

Referring back to the Benz brand model in chapter 4 might be interesting at this point — just to remind ourselves of how closely the brand in, say, 1990 resembled the Benz brand in 1914. It is uncannily similar. What we can see in the 'product offensive' (and its three sisters) is the re-emergence of the Mercedesness that was last in perfect harmony with Benz in the 1950s and 1960s. In the new brand being shaped by Professor Hubbert and his colleagues after 1992, values of innovation and a newly defined 'quality' were beginning to emerge. There was also a sea-change in customer focus — and, with the brand's re-entry into Formula One in 1994, the rebirth of some of the competitive spirit that had been so sorely missed in the 1980s. The products, when they arrived, would be more technically advanced, performance orientated and luxuriously equipped than their forerunners. And for customers the more 'Mercedes-like' associations would begin to flow from these.

As if to confirm this new direction yet further, this was also the period in which Daimler-Benz concluded an agreement with Aufrecht Melcher Grossaspach (better known by its initials, AMG) to offer another level of sporting enhancement to its cars. AMG quickly became the symbol of new standards of ride, handling and performance — delivered via hand-finished engine customising, tuning of brakes and suspension and distinctive additional bodywork design details.

Momentous decisions were being made. New models, new culture, new image, new definition of quality, new (and cheaper) ways of delivering it. But what had preceded all of these, and now underpinned each of them, had been the biggest decision of all: what *kind* of car business Mercedes-Benz wanted to be.

The choice was simple, but simple doesn't mean easy. Springer & Jacoby (Mercedes-Benz advertising agency) had alluded to it in its 1989 presentation: defining the strategic choice as being that between 'king of cars' and 'leader of the pack'. The former was about sticking to core competencies, focusing on the lower-volume but higher-margin luxury segment, and possibly even developing a

separate sub-brand for cheaper models. The latter involved recognising that the luxury segment was under attack and likely to shrink. This meant pursuit of the strategy of being a premium car in a number of different segments, including small cars.

This was strategy at the highest level: defining the shape of a worldwide brand for its worldwide markets for the next 30 years at least. But it was too big a decision for an agency to make (remember that at this stage Daimler-Benz was still a conglomerate, with other divisions to think of) — so the debate now moved back inside, to the board and its advisers. Most senior among these was Hilmar Kopper, Chairman of the supervisory board, and a true confidant of the directors for many years. In the late 1980s, Kopper had been 'scared that since Hubbert was Niefer's lieutenant, he would follow Niefer's lead, but he did not'. (Niefer undoubtedly would have pursued the 'king of cars' route had he still been in the hot seat.)

Kopper was in no doubt where the future lay. As he told me: 'We had to take the brand out of its niche, and allow for economies of scale. We couldn't restrict ourselves to some sort of Tiffany brand.'

The idea of new sectors appealed to Professor Hubbert. As he remembers it: 'Lexus was a wake-up call. The visit to Japan was a wake-up call.' The strategic decision for him was born out of a realisation that: 'Exclusivity is not just about price, it's about concept. Achieving a premium position in *each* sector is possible.'

The strategic decision was made. And Dr Zetsche, for one, approved. 'If we hadn't gone down this road, we'd now be on the way to being Rolls Royce,' he comments. The other decisions would follow. This though *was* the 'fork in the road'. The company had made its choice.

The outcome of these momentous decisions started to be seen quickly. The turnaround in 1994 (on the back of the new C-Class) was maintained, and sales rose rapidly over the next few years: back through the 600,000 mark in 1995, to 700,000 in 1997, approaching a million by the end of 1998. By the end of the decade (and of the millennium) the number of models in the brand's portfolio had risen from five to 13, and by then embraced A-Class, M-Class, CLK and SLK, together with relaunched C- and S-Classes.

But the car that really broke the mould, that literally changed the face of Mercedes-Benz, preceded all of these. It was the E-Class, launched in 1995, and its story takes us now into the world of brand design and the shaping of the physical product.

My interview with Bruno Sacco, Head of Design for Mercedes-Benz from 1974 to 1999, could have taken up a chapter in its own right. But the focus here is on the brand, and how Sacco's skills were deployed in shaping, and then reshaping, the cars that tangibly delivered the brand.

The first thing that strikes you about Bruno Sacco is that he's not German. He is from Italy — 'the land of singers and artists' as he calls it — and this Latin temperament clearly shows through in his words and his more recent designs. Sacco is deeply conscious of the Mercedes-Benz design traditions — and of his responsibility for evolving these thoughtfully. Along the way, he's clearly been frustrated on many occasions and he talks vigorously about the cultural hurdles, as well as the design challenges, that needed to be overcome.

'In the 1930s the company made some beautiful cars, like the SSK, but its "bread and butter"

cars, the 170 and the 240 were less so.' He describes the original 1952 SL as being driven by 'function' (as we saw earlier) and that it was only with its road-going version in 1954 that 'form' started to develop in parallel. 'Design followed engineering in those days,' he says. 'It took a long time to have its own place next to technology.' How was that achieved? 'We had to persuade the engineers to leave out some aspects of functionality — to give more freedom to designers. It was a hard job — we had to pick them off one by one.' Citing (and drawing) examples such as rain channels in the A-pillars, door-handle covers to protect drivers from getting their hands dirty and the 'double bumper' design of the early S-Classes, he says: 'We had to show them how the cars could look better without these things, if they were less Teutonic'.

Lack of resources didn't help Sacco in these endeavours. At the time he joined the company in 1958 there was only one stylist, plus a group of clay modellers: 'It was the engineers who drew up the plans, the carpenters simply made up models from these plans'.

'See Mercedes with new eyes'

By the time Sacco took over as Head of Design in 1974, though, things had changed significantly — the department now numbered around 150 people. But Sacco too had changed — by then, as he acknowledges, having very much embraced the 'best or nothing' philosophy of his employer. Perhaps more conscious now of his 'evolutionary' responsibility, the pace of design changes seemed to slow — we've already seen the paucity of new ideas in this area during the 1970s and 1980s.

Certainly the 'guidelines' were becoming more rigid — the *Karlsruhe* design philosophy of 1979 stipulated both 'horizontal' and 'vertical' integrity, namely continuity of design both across models at any one time, and between successor models over time. Arguably, in the 1980s Sacco paid too much attention to tradition (he's still proud of the 1991 S-Class) and he talks quite seriously about the need to maintain 'a clear design lineage' in aspects like the classic front grille design of the saloons, or the side air vents of the sports coupés. But to Sacco, the true nature of a Mercedes-Benz is a bigger concept than just the sum of these evolutionary details. 'A Mercedes must always look like a Mercedes,' he has been quoted as saying on many occasions, and when asked what exactly this means in design terms, he talks of much bigger 'propositions'.

Volume, proportion and details are what define the look. Proportion, as he says, 'visually, not just mathematically', big details — like the characteristic flowing line over the bonnet and into the A-pillar — and of course the grille, and the position of the star within it, on the coupés. These are the things, Sacco says, that make a Mercedes the car it is.

Something though must have changed during the late 1980s. Whether Sacco's philosophy became more liberated, or whether he simply became more cognisant of the 'wind of change' blowing through the company — design took big steps forward during these years, culminating in a whole new range of cars in the 1990s. By then he was clearly aware of the need for the brand itself to change, and the role that design could play in physically demonstrating this. The new C-Class in 1993, though critically important, was still conservative by contrast with the new E-Class that arrived in 1995. This car too would have been in development throughout the period of the boardroom struggles — and who knows what pressures Sacco came under to deliver a radical design. But radical it certainly was, particularly in respect of its wholly new front-end, embodying the characteristic, slanted twin-headlight design.

The company's website acknowledges this departure from the Karlsruhe philosophy: 'The formal difference between model series had become too small and it was seen that relaxing these strict rules would allow more innovations.' Sacco himself has said: 'The public demonstrated its acceptance of these themes (the twin headlights) as Mercedes elements but, more importantly, it had accepted them as *elements of a different Mercedes from the one that existed before*.'

This is the key point. The new E-Class marked a clear departure from some of those traditional themes. It spoke volumes for what the brand was trying to become: lighter, sleeker, more human, even more feminine in its look and in its persona. Suddenly, here was a car that had the values (and even the gender) of Mercedes, not instead of, but as well as, the build quality of a Benz.

The launch advertising highlighted the new look, but also hinted at the bigger changes taking place at the heart of the brand. It asked potential customers to 'See Mercedes with new eyes' — and that is exactly what was beginning to happen.

Opposite: the radical new E-Class, launched in 1995

n 1995, plans were in hand for designs that would be even more radical than the new E-Class. CLK would bring a sleeker, coupé look to the mid-range models; SLK would reinvent some of the classic features from the 'Silver Arrows'; the 1998 S-Class would be an altogether more elegant (and smaller) car than its predecessor. But for the design teams the really serious challenges would be to craft cars that would be key to the future success of the brand — and in categories that were entirely new to the company: A-Class in the small-car market, and M-Class in the off-road category.

These innovations, as much as the saloons and coupés, would define the brand in the approaching new millennium, and they would prove to be a significant challenge for the designers. After all, Sacco had said that even though he had little time for design research ('it's not an issue on which to question customers'), it was from research among non-owners that he had learnt about the 'integrity' of the Mercedes look. 'We showed them photos of new models, but blurred — so that all you could really see was the profile of the car — then we showed clearer and clearer ones. Even with the first blurred photos, the majority recognised that the car, which they had never seen before, was a Mercedes.'

For any brand, but particularly one whose shape has to change over time, this ability to recognise a core characteristic, an essential 'look' to the product is fundamentally important. Coca-Cola and a multitude of other brands are instantly recognisable simply through their iconic shape. For car brands such consistency is impossible — they rely on a 'family look' to retain recognition and integrity. How well Mercedes-Benz would deal with this issue as the very different models of the late 1990s hit the market would be crucial.

In the previous chapter I talked at length about the 'fork in the road' that the brand faced in the late 1980s and early 1990s. That is because I believe this was one of the most critical periods in the brand's life since 1926. The management decisions made at the time, though protracted and painful, were absolutely fundamental to the current direction of the company.

There have been tales of politics and pacts, pressures from within and without — and hopefully some fascinating insights into how a company can admit to its mistakes, but also have the strength of character to correct them. The intention is not to parade before the reader all the intricate machinations of a company in crisis, but rather to illustrate that

there was, throughout, still something powerful at the heart of the company that held it together. In this chapter, I will argue that this 'something' was indeed the Mercedes-Benz brand; internally, it united a core group of people behind a common set of beliefs. Externally, it held the product together, even at a time when the customer's patience was being sorely tried.

The 'product offensive', and its three parallel initiatives, did succeed in pulling the brand back from the brink. Could the company really have failed in these years? Opinions differ. Kopper, perhaps best placed to give an objective view, believes it was a possibility: 'The company feels much safer today,' he observes. What is without doubt is that Professor Hubbert's initiatives, supported by Dr Zetsche and Dr Schmidt, did represent a clear strategic decision about the kind of company Mercedes-Benz was to be.

Internally, that meant the end of the dominance of the engineer and the emergence of a new spirit of team working. Externally, it meant a refreshed brand with a new sense of purpose and with new markets to explore. That journey would have its own difficulties, but at least for now the corporate future had been clarified and secured.

It was this new sense of purpose that characterised the company in the closing years of the 20th

'The brand is what holds it all together now, not design'

century. There was a revived spirit within, and a different kind of 'body language' for the brand in the market: brighter, sexier, more vibrant, more 'fleet of foot'. Here was a brand behaving in new ways in new markets, with more exciting cars opening up precisely the segments that Hubbert and his colleagues had identified — now to considerable press and public acclaim. The 'product offensive' had worked, the company had made its strategic choice, the 'fork in the road' was behind it — a clear path lay ahead. The brand was inexorably moving (in the language of marketing) from a 'luxury' positioning (that is exclusivity at the peak of the market in total) to a 'premium' positioning — seeking to occupy the top slot in each segment within which it was competing.

And these segments were multiplying: large, medium and small saloons (with S, E and C), compacts (with A), off-road SUV (with M and the ageing but still classic G-wagen), coupés (with CL and CLK), estates (with E and C again), sports convertibles (with SL and SLK). Plus, albeit coming from the commercial vehicle division, there was V-Class as an MPV, and Smart (micro-segment), widely known to be from its Mercedes-Benz parent. Ten segments, 13 model ranges with prices ranging from €17,000 for an A140 to €135,000 for a CL600 in

the domestic market. A huge range in other words, bigger even than Ford, bigger by a mile than BMW's core 3/5/7 series line-up. While the market took to these models enthusiastically — production by 1999 was touching the 1.1 million mark, with 62% being exported — the very success of this strategy was beginning to create issues of its own back in Stuttgart.

Of these, the most visible was that of design consistency. Clearly, it was impossible across a range such as this to have a singular Mercedes-Benz look, so the thinking in this area had to move on. Professor Peter Pfeiffer, Senior Vice-President of Design (and Sacco's successor from 1999) explained how the new design philosophy (beginning with E-Class and then A-Class) had been forced to move to a family concept, 'within which each line has its individual character'. But, he claimed, 'customers don't see this as a break with the past because when we enter new niches, the first question we always asked was, "Is it a Mercedes?" even at first glance'. Here, clearly, is an echo of Sacco's approach. Pfeiffer went on to explain: 'That means it's both intuitive and literal — evolution of design of the radiators for example, but also an interpretation of quality in that niche'.

Pfeiffer is careful and precise with his language — and a very different character to Bruno Sacco.

Stressing how radically different the company was now from the time when 'design was completely technically driven', he nevertheless found it hard to speak with great emotion. What he did stress was that, despite the pressure of all these new models, the key word for him in the design area and for the brand as a whole was 'continuity'.

Returning to the theme of design philosophy, and now contrasting Mercedes-Benz with BMW, he suddenly produced a real insight: 'It's as though we're swapping roles with BMW — the old 7 series says "please drive me", the new one is more like "take a seat, be driven" — whilst our brand is moving the other way, becoming more sporty, dynamic, active.' Pfeiffer, I felt, captured an important new thought with this observation. And despite his earlier description of how the designers might cope with model proliferation, he was speaking frankly when, towards the end of the interview, he said: 'Our brand is the most important thing we have. *The brand is what holds it all together now, not design*.'

Opposite: during the mid-to late 1990s, Mercedes-Benz launched a number of cars in new sectors, including the M-Class

Pfeiffer is right. It is impossible to have total design consistency across so many ranges. Of course there can be a family look externally, but the company probably has to face the fact that the strategy it chose will lead to a diffusion of the image that people hold in their mind's eye of a Mercedes-Benz. For most, even now, that image is still of the classic three-box outline (the E-Class probably defining the typical size and proportion) — but already the picture is blurred by cars like the A-Class. The next generation of buyers may have a very different shape in mind when they think of the brand a decade from now.

The Mercedes-Benz commercial vehicle division has probably accentuated this issue with the launch of V-Class and, more recently, Vaneo. These are cars that Bruno Sacco could hardly bring himself to speak about — but for the consumer they're still, like them or not, part of the Mercedes-Benz brand. Perhaps, as suggested in chapter 1, people will continue to be able to selectively perceive 'their' bit of the Mercedes-Benz brand, but the absolute *volumes* of these new models might militate against this. So if exterior design is not going to hold the models together, what is?

Pfeiffer has already referred to the crucial role of the brand. But perhaps it is also to the *interior* of the cars that we should turn for consistency of look and feel. Owners, after all, spend more time looking at the interior of their cars than the exterior. For this book I commissioned Ros Elwes, an expert in social and semiotic meaning, to look at Mercedes-Benz and the role of cars in society today. One of Elwes' conclusions was that the 'cocooning' role of the car in today's cities will become ever more important and that the whole concept of personal space is one that could be elevated to a higher level within the future design of car interiors.

Stefan Sielaff is one of the new breed of designers at Sindelfingen, responsible for interiors, and only recently joined from Audi. He too has strong views about continuity: 'Every time I sit in a Mercedes-Benz, it doesn't matter if it's an A- or an S-Class, it should feel the same.' A Mercedes-Benz interior should look timeless, not too fashionable, a classic statement, he believes. Then the insight: 'It's essential for a quality product to have the continued genetic code of a family — our cars can have their own character, but they also have to be similar'.

This DNA reference is fascinating. It is close to the concept of brand essence described earlier — an inherited, recognisable trait of the brand that is at the heart of all that it does and stands for. Now Sielaff was saying that this same concept held good for design too. I asked him to identify that code on the outside. 'A Mercedes-Benz should never look childish, should never have "big eyes" for example. It needs a certain brutality to exude power.'

The bottom line is that today and in the future Mercedes-Benz will have to manage its way through this proliferation of new models — seeking consistencies where it can, retaining the look and feel of the brand where possible. But sometimes, perhaps, Mercedes-Benz will need to be brave enough to say 'no' to new models (or even new segments) if it feels that design integrity is being stretched too far. Sacrifice, after all, is a key characteristic of strong brands.

Opposite: consumers seek ever greater comfort and 'cocooning' from the interiors of their cars

Of all the new models introduced in the 1990s, none was more radical than the A-Class. Embodying Béla Barényi's early thinking about running the engine and transmission under the floor for safety reasons, the A-Class was a major departure for Mercedes-Benz. The company wanted to stress its difference from all other models and hated the car being called (as the 190 had been in the 1980s) a 'Baby Benz'. Soon, though, it would be glad of that lifeline.

Opinions about the A-Class design vary, but the car was fundamental to Professor Hubbert's ambitions, and today outsells all other models bar C- and E-Class. It has fulfilled a significant volume ambition for the company — and supports a whole community in Rastatt where the car is built. But

it was a problem child — and the 'Elk test' was another defining moment in our story of the brand. Regardless of the debate about the technicalities of that test, suffice it to say that when the A-Class rolled over (and the pictures of it doing so flashed around the world), the company wobbled with it. Here was the unthinkable happening — in real time — just days after the car's official launch.

Some are of the view (especially in the US market) that the A-Class dilutes the core values of the brand and compromises its exclusivity. Just by virtue of being high and short the car will never look good to such commentators. Others make points about targeting — one interviewee talked about the A-Class as 'a car for housewives and

pensioners' or how, these days, 'the people who used to clean my Mercedes now own one'.

Dr Reitzle (at BMW at the time) questions the whole logic behind A-Class. On the specific point about the Elk test he makes a more profound observation: 'On that day, Mercedes-Benz lost forever the mantle of infallibility'. This is probably a harsh judgement: the Elk test was serious but not potentially as disastrous as Reitzle suggests. What would matter most would be how the company reacted and how strong the brand would be in covering for its new offspring.

By contrast with what might have happened ten years before, the company (after initially hesitating) responded well. Hilmar Kopper remembers that the board's reaction was: 'Stop production. Remedy the problem. Do it fast. Keep spirits up'. This, to him, was as important as the technical solution of fitting ESP to every car. The fact that all of this was done openly and honestly was also massively to the brand's benefit in the eyes of the public. And the brand itself helped the A-Class to ride out the storm. Suddenly it was the virtues of being a Mercedes-Benz (not being 'different') that were vital. In other words, people had given the brand the benefit of the doubt. Contrasting the company's reaction to the Elk test with that towards the problems of the 200 series a decade earlier shows just how far the culture had changed in the intervening years.

In military terms, the A-Class episode was a kind of rapid, commando-like attack on the brand — and one that was swiftly repulsed. Much more significant, most believe, is the long-term 'war of attrition' that the company is fighting on the quality front. This is a more severe, and much more significant challenge. And it is important to this

„Ich habe aus
meinen Rückschlägen
oft mehr gelernt als
aus meinen Erfolgen.“

Boris Becker

Die A-Klasse ist wieder da.

► Wer im Sport erfolgreich sein will, darf nie aufhören, an sich selbst zu arbeiten. Und muß bereit sein, aus seinen Fehlern zu lernen. Viele Sportler wären heute nicht an der Spitze, wenn sie diese Fähigkeit nicht besäßen. Aber auch in anderen Lebensbereichen wären viele außergewöhnliche Leistungen nie erbracht worden, wenn es nicht immer wieder Menschen gegeben hätte, die mit Ehrgeiz und Herzblut konsequent an ihrem Ziel festhielten. Nur durch ständiges Hinterfragen und Optimieren können neue, ungewöhnliche Lösungen entstehen. Wie bei der A-Klasse von Mercedes-Benz.

► Viele Jahre Entwicklungszeit und viel Liebe zum Detail haben dafür gesorgt, daß die A-Klasse voller Innovationen steckt, die das Autofahren angenehmer und sicherer machen. Anfgrund der Ereignisse der letzten Monate haben wir sie zusätzlich mit ein paar technischen Errungenschaften ausgestattet, die sonst nur in unseren Oberklasse-Limousinen zum Einsatz kommen. Z.B. ist die A-Klasse jetzt serienmäßig mit ESP** ausgestattet. Ein System, das u.a. die drei zur Zeit wirksamsten Fahrhilfen beinhaltet: das Antiblockiersystem ABS, die Antriebsschlupfregelung ASR und den Bremsassistenten BAS. Daneben sorgen eine andere Fahrwerksabstimmung und neue Niederquerschnittsreifen zusätzlich für eine verbesserte Straßenlage.

ESP (Elektronisches Stabilitätsprogramm) ist eine eingetragene Marke der Daimler-Benz AG.

► Die A-Klasse ist heute nicht nur ein Optimum an Platz, Komfort und Sicherheit: In der A-Klasse stecken viele Erfahrungen, die kommenden Autogenerationen helfen können, einen neuen Standard zu erreichen.

► Mehr über die A-Klasse und ihre Neuerungen erfahren Sie kostenlos unter Tel. 0130/0140 und im Internet: http://www.mercedes-benz.com. Oder direkt vor Ort bei einer Probefahrt. Ihr Mercedes-Benz Vertriebspartner freut sich auf Ihren Besuch. Wir glauben an die nächste Generation.

Mercedes-Benz
Die Zukunft des Automobils.

story because product quality still sits at the heart of the brand's core values today.

There is no need to list all the various pieces of evidence that illustrate this issue — since the late 1990s there have been innumerable comments, research reports, quality surveys and the like that clearly demonstrate that there is a problem here. And most, but not all, of the executives I spoke to acknowledge this. Part of the 'problem', of course, is that Mercedes-Benz reputation in this area has historically been so strong that *any* slippage attracts undue attention. As one interviewee said, 'it's like the school swot who everyone wants to see fail in an exam.'

When I talked to Professor Hubbert, he like others acknowledged the issue — and was particularly concerned about the latest JD Power survey that placed Mercedes-Benz only at number 12 in terms of overall customer satisfaction in the UK (behind Lexus, BMW and Jaguar) and at number eight in Germany (behind BMW and Audi). He was admiring of Lexus which, he said, 'did a great job in meeting these demands'.

But he was also proud of the fact that in the recent German ADAC-AutoMarxX survey (June 2004) Mercedes-Benz was still rated number one brand overall, and on product quality was only beaten by Porsche. Referring back to an earlier time, Hubbert talked about how in qualitative research the days when people characterised the brand as a 'nodding dog' had been left behind — in recent research the

brand has been likened more to a dolphin: sleek, fast, elegant, effortlessly powerful... and intelligent.

It is these dimensions of image that he felt most characterised the brand today. In fact, there's some evidence to suggest that the 'humanity' of the brand has improved over the years. The A-Class episode, because it showed that this stalwart of German industry could make a mistake, but that it could also have the humility to apologise, may paradoxically have made people feel warmer towards the brand. 'Dented, but not broken' is the general view of the effect of this shortfall in quality on the brand's image. That is not an excuse for complacency — merely to say that, because it has a strong brand, the company has at least a window of opportunity to improve matters.

More generally, interviews with Rainer Valentin and Mathias Töpel in the Mercedes-Benz market research department paint a picture of brand image around the world that is surprisingly consistent and generally quite positive. Though the company was a latecomer to research, its bank of quantitative and qualitative studies is now considerable. Judgementally, Valentin suggests that close to 80% of the purchase decision for a Mercedes-Benz is based on image, the remainder on rational considerations. He also points to the fact that brand images for cars are often created in childhood and take a long time to shift substantially. Power and leadership are key components of the Mercedes-Benz brand personality, often translating into status and prestige in more image-conscious countries.

Opposite: after the A-Class rolled over in the Elk test, images of the damaged car appeared in the media all over the world
This page: 'I have learnt more from my failings than from my successes'; A-Class advertisement, 1997

Women, unsurprisingly, have quite different perceptions and, though changing as a result of cars like the A-Class, this is a market area to which the company increasingly needs to address itself. Overall, the sense is that this is a brand that commands respect rather than affection — a brand you'd shake hands with rather than kiss on both cheeks. But, of course, that slight air of formality has always been a characteristic of Mercedes-Benz — to be too 'warm and cuddly' would be somehow out of kilter with what the brand stands for. A little respect, a sense of this being a brand you look up to, is probably a virtue.

Two interviews lent texture to this conclusion. In conversation with Beverly Rae Kimes, she ventured the opinion that part of the reason why Mercedes-Benz had been so successful in the USA in the post-war years was because it played well to what she called the American attitude of 'entitlement'. This, she said, was the product of the indigenous work ethic of that country — people felt they earned the right to ownership. In a similar vein, Helmut Werner contrasted Mercedes-Benz with BMW. The latter brand, he felt, was 'a seducer, and easily conquered'. Mercedes-Benz was 'not so easily conquered — it's almost a brand that needs to be convinced of you, whether you'll be a good match'. As a result, Werner argued, the ensuing relationship is likely to be longer — and loyalty levels higher.

It was the need to understand and then address these kinds of subtleties of image that had led to the development of the brand model that Dr Zetsche described in chapter 9. And its development does illustrate that, from the mid-1990s, the company was beginning to take a more structured and thoughtful approach to its brand. Gone were the days of 'the brand is the company, the company is the brand' (with engineers effectively defining both). Gone too was the era when, as Dr Schmidt had recalled, he was directed towards engineering rather than marketing for the best career opportunities. Marketing was now in the ascendancy — and this was to be no passing fad. From being the 'new kid on the block' in 1990, marketing had, rightly, grown in influence within the company over the subsequent years. Dr Schöpf (unthinkably by the standards of the past) now says: 'We work as a team. We won't make decisions without having the marketing people in the room.' Dr Schmidt took over the marketing directorship in that year and was himself responsible for implementing a product management system within the company. He talked passionately about how 'it was a dream to work for Mercedes-Benz', but also about how at that time 'people never spoke about brand, it was not a marketing company, their passion was for technology'. He, and the team that supported him both from above and below, did win through though, and succeeded in securing a top-table position for the marketing function.

With marketing, of course, came all the necessary paraphernalia of brand management — the day-to-day tools that ensure the consistency that Interbrand had defined as being one of the three key criteria for successful brands. The brand model to give structure to briefs for new cars, guidelines for use of the brand's logo in all situations, agreed advertising formats and typefaces worldwide — all of these brought a new discipline to the company's thinking as well as to the literal presentation of its brand.

The management structures to support these also started to be put in place. National and international forums and committees for developing and implementing marketing strategy began to appear, though typically for Mercedes-Benz these were described with baffling sets of initials like GCF, COC, GCC, AK-M etc. At the customer interface too, greater consistency was the order of the day: a common look and feel for dealer showrooms, consistent brochure materials, a strategy for exhibitions and events — again, all necessary and for many a new and tighter way of thinking about 'brand'. Though the logo itself didn't change, the way it was used also started to become more considered and managed.

Opposite: Autohaus Roth Mercedes-Benz dealership, Alsfeld, Germany

'The Future of the Automobile' seemed an optimistic and confident statement of the brand's new focus

For 40 years, the star in its chrome circle had sat alone on the rear of all cars. On the front, though, there had been two variations: the star emerging upright from the centre of the blue Mercedes-Benz logo, with its laurel leaves around the base, on saloon cars; and on sports models (including coupés) the much larger star placed centrally in the grille.

Today the usage is more varied. The SL, SLK and M-Class, for instance, use the large central star format (with the full badge flat on the top of the bonnet), as do the coupé variants of C- and S-Classes, and Vaneo. The saloons still use the logo upright in its circle with the badge around its base. Perhaps tellingly, the original A-Class was the only model not to carry the name 'Mercedes-Benz' anywhere on its exterior, using only the star in its grille.

Finally, in 1997, attention turned to a company 'slogan' or 'endline' to be used consistently around the world. Historically, Mercedes-Benz advertising had employed a number of different lines, usually on engineering themes or based on puns around the star. Now, though, after a series of candidates had been discussed and researched, the company chose a new, single statement: *Die Zukunft des Automobils*, 'The Future of the Automobile', as its public mantra. In tone and direction a far cry from the internal motto of 'the best or nothing', this seemed an optimistic and confident statement of the brand's new focus, its heritage of innovation and, implicitly, its authenticity.

Andre Kemper, Creative Director of Springer & Jacoby at the time, and now co-owner of his own agency Kemper Trautmann, picks up the story: 'Originally Mercedes-Benz briefed us for a new "mission statement" for the brand — not an endline — and I think we wrote nearly a thousand! The predecessor was "*Ihr guter Stern auf alle Strassen*" [your good star on every street]. The more lines we wrote, the more we always came back to the fact that Mercedes-Benz invented the car; they were the benchmark, always ahead of the industry.' Hence the line, although with hindsight Kemper concedes that today it seems 'a bit stiff, not very emotional' given the way the cars have evolved in the last seven years. More significantly, for Kemper the line represented a goal, a target rather than in any way hinting at the journey towards that destination. For that insight, the company would have to wait a few more years.

Opposite: usage of the star across the model ranges is varied. From top to bottom: C-Class, M-Class, and the SLR

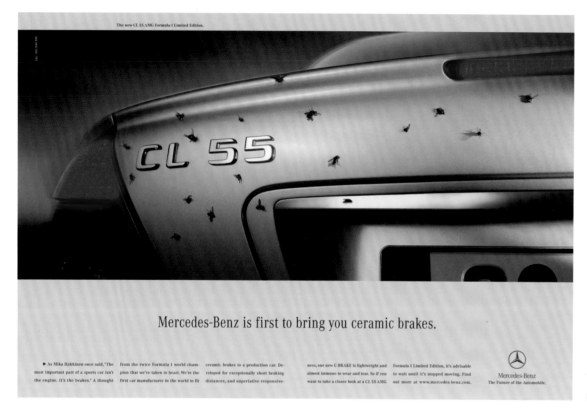

The new CL 55 AMG Formula 1 Limited Edition.

CL 55

Mercedes-Benz is first to bring you ceramic brakes.

▶ As Mika Hakkinen once said, "The | from the twice Formula 1 world cham- | ceramic brakes to a production car. De- | ness, our new C-BRAKE is lightweight and | Formula 1 Limited Edition, it's advisable
most important part of a sports car isn't | pion that we've taken to heart. We're the | veloped for exceptionally short braking | almost immune to wear and tear. So if you | to wait until it's stopped moving. Find
the engine. It's the brakes." A thought | first car manufacturer in the world to fit | distances, and superlative responsive- | want to take a closer look at a CL 55 AMG | out more at www.mercedes-benz.com.

Mercedes-Benz
The Future of the Automobile.

This page and opposite: Springer & Jacoby advertisements from 2000 and 2001

There are others too who feel that the line is a little cold — not expressive enough of the new humanity of the Mercedes-Benz brand. I have sympathy with this, but for its time it was an important statement for a brand that in some ways was trying to reorient itself, shake off some of its past, and truly look to the future.

The advertising that carried this line, created for the German market and some overseas territories by Springer & Jacoby, was also a breath of fresh air for the brand. The images were brighter, younger and more confident than what had gone before — the tone of voice had a wit and humour that was new for the brand but enjoyed by the customer. The advertisements expressed pride in the cars' heritage,

but also sought to portray a sharper, more dynamic, sexier image for the new models. Consistency has been achieved, even across markets not using Springer & Jacoby's work, again to the credit of the marketers in Stuttgart.

But all of these aspects of the brand — logo, advertising, endlines, guidelines for typefaces, dealerships and the rest — are the visible tip of the iceberg. Beneath lie bigger and deeper issues that go right to the heart of the brand. These too began to receive attention in the late 1990s.

In a way, what prompted these discussions was the fact that the company was now in possession of not one brand but two: Smart was to be launched

under that name in 1998. Even then, the first thoughts about what was to become the Maybach brand were also being formulated. And within a year of Smart's launch, the company made the momentous announcement that it was to merge with the Chrysler Corporation of America, itself the owner of the Chrysler, Dodge and Jeep brands. Now, more than ever, it was becoming essential to really get to the roots of what the Mercedes-Benz brand was — and then succinctly define it.

This is not an easy task and, again, a whole chapter could be spent on the tortuous processes that companies go through to define the essence of their brands. For Mercedes-Benz, the whole exercise was made more complex by the plethora of vehicles

Sigh.

Longing.

The C-Class Sportcoupé. Let your feelings go.

▶ Lorem dolor sit amet, conse   no nono sum ommy nibuh euismod   ma gna ali quam eretur ore meat   minertas weim venit am, quis no   Infos unter 0180/5 46 67 und im   Mercedes-Benz
ctetuer adipiscing elit, sed di am no   tinci dunte ut laoreet Lito in dolore   volut pattiom. Uto wisi enim. Adnan   strud ex Berci tation laloc quisal.   Internet www.mercedes-benz.com   The Future of the Automobile.

that carried its three-pointed star and the variety of ways in which the brand interfaced with the customer. Customers, as we've seen, seemed to have an almost innate ability to self-select. Even though they knew and could see the brand on trucks, buses, vans, sports cars, saloons and taxis, they seemed, with great agility, to be able to pick, and then hold in their heads, that bit of the range that was 'their' Mercedes-Benz. But the company couldn't count on that forever. As more models and new generations of buyers arrived in the market, the brand needed a more permanent touchstone from which all aspects of presentation and delivery could stem.

The marketing department's attention turned to this issue in earnest in the late 1990s, and driving

it was the central question of 'what is it that holds the whole thing together?' — or, in our terms, 'what is the *essence* of the brand?'

Much of the work done at that time underpins the thinking behind this book. But in truth, the whole concept of this being 'the tale of two brands' only emerged later. What is gratifying (and exciting) is that that later observation served to bolster confidence in the original work. 'Mercedesness' and 'Benzness' may not have been part of the thinking in 1999, but this later theory marries up perfectly with those earlier endeavours.

Even though the 'official' brand model that Dr Zetsche had originally described to me was made available, my own view is that the version developed

here is a simpler and more useful construct for the purposes of this book. Principally, that is because it serves as both a helpful way of showing how the two 'sides' of the Mercedes-Benz brand arose — and of explaining how they evolved to become one.

This book has defined both the Benz and Mercedes brands as they stood in 1914, and has charted their course before and after the merger in 1926. Above all, it has sought to describe the way in which one can see aspects of the Benz brand and the Mercedes brand coming to the fore at different times in the company's life.

The balance moved from harmony in the 1930s, to the necessity for Benzness to predominate in the post-war years, to Mercedesness again

Two words perfectly sum up what is at the heart of the brand... Enduring Passion

arguably ahead in the late 1950s and 1960s. From 1968, though, we identified how Benzness dominated for over 20 years and the problems this created. It was the 'product offensive' of the 1990s that restored Mercedesness to its rightful place and produced the balanced relationship that carried the brand in its entirety to new heights by the turn of the millennium. So, still using that same model, what does the amalgamated Mercedes-Benz brand look like today?

Looking firstly at product, we can see how the characteristics have evolved (and grown) as the company and its model range have expanded. Some of the more basic Benz qualities have gone, to be replaced by a new focus on safety. Benz 'durability', though, is retained — but now sits alongside an array of former Mercedes virtues that are still by and large intact: advanced, luxurious and high-performance.

In terms of values, Benz 'authenticity' is still centrally important, but its simplicity and consistency have clearly been lost. Mercedes values of 'innovation', and a newly defined sense of 'leader-

ship' are there; as is quality, the one value that the two originally separate brands shared.

Associations (less within the control of the brand owner) have changed too over time. The 'trustedness' of Benz now sits alongside the more dynamic, 'special' image of Mercedes. On the negative side, while the brand has by now shaken off its Benz image of 'heavy' and 'dull', this has been replaced by a kind of serious, traditional halo; and Mercedes associations of exclusivity (and expense) still linger, creating an image, for some, of ostentation.

The flip side of product and values (the unintended negative outcomes of being the brand you are) — are today's concerns about complexity, inconsistency (particularly of model ranges) and, though not the doggedness of Benz, still a hint of complacency that one senses sometimes in the internal culture of the company.

At the centre is the brand's essence. Two words that perfectly sum up what is at the heart of the brand, what holds it all together. Working with J Justus Schneider (Director of Global

Marketing Communications for Mercedes-Benz), and the marketing group at DaimlerChrysler, it was this essence that the team had sought to define.

For the original Benz brand, the essence was identified as being 'fitness-for-purpose' — the bullet proof reliability and longevity of its cars. Combining that with the word that, as Peter Pfeiffer had pointed out, was the one that more than any other had defined the brand over its history — continuity — provided the first half of the Mercedes-Benz brand essence: 'enduring'.

Leadership, the constant quest to be ahead of the field, was the essence of the Mercedes brand of old — in innovation, racing, against market competitors. This word went right to the heart of that brand. But today's Mercedes-Benz is driven not just by that will to win, but also by a deeper set of beliefs about what the company holds dear. Both from its history and its cars, but above all from where it sees itself going in the future, the second defining characteristic (and hence word in the brand essence) is: 'passion'.

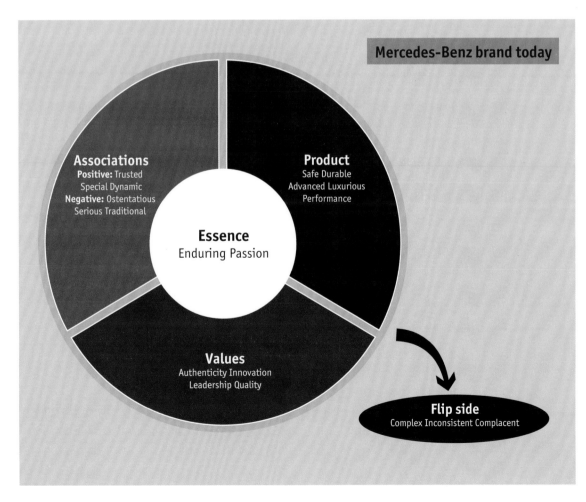

Mercedes-Benz brand today

Associations
Positive: Trusted
Special Dynamic
Negative: Ostentatious
Serious Traditional

Product
Safe Durable
Advanced Luxurious
Performance

Essence
Enduring Passion

Values
Authenticity Innovation
Leadership Quality

Flip side
Complex Inconsistent Complacent

Enduring Passion. A unique, succinct and unexpected pairing. The first word suggests tenacity, commitment — and hints at the brand's status as an 'original' as well as its build quality. The second word: more fiery, suggestive of the inner drive to lead the market as well as the spirit of competition and performance within the cars. But as one reads it, one realises there is also a kind of inbuilt tension within the combination.

We're familiar, in relationships for example, with passion — but it seldom endures. On the other hand, we're used to enduring relationships — but recognise that it is usually love, not passion, that characterises these.

It is intentionally a duality. The two words are drawn from the two sides of the brand: Benzness and Mercedesness. They sit, though, as equals alongside each other — each poorer in the absence of the other, each strengthened by the other's proximity. Head and heart, left brain and right brain, male and female — the metaphors are endless. Duality is after all a universal truth but here, rather than acting as opposites, the two words complement each other. And that's why they are potentially valuable as a management tool, because they can be steered.

Highly visionary companies liberate themselves with the 'genius of the and'

Like the bass and treble controls on an amplifier, the two can be fine-tuned and adjusted — for individual models or for the brand as a whole — to literally bring out the best in the brand. They are not about volume, they are about harmony.

'Enduring Passion' suggests a set of beliefs that drives the hearts and minds of those associated with the brand. Not every car, customer or employee exhibits it all the time. But it unites the brand at its core and it points the way forward by defining the character and culture of the brand for the future.

Andre Kemper applauds this step forward. 'It was a great help, more emotional, it explained "*Die Zukunft des Automobils*". "Enduring Passion" is the way, "*Die Zukunft*" is the goal.' Such distinctions might seem like complex semantics — but the shape they give to how the brand thinks about itself and communicates with the outside world is crucial. Even more importantly, Kemper confirmed the view that '"Enduring Passion" is key to *steering* the brand — it's a brilliant combination'.

But what gives the Mercedes-Benz brand the right to own such powerful territory? How is it to command these heights and manage the tension within these two words? The answer to this lies in a recent study of what it is that defines great companies, not just great brands.

In 1994, James Collins and Jerry Porras of Stanford Business School reported on their conclusions from an examination of 18 of the world's most visionary companies, and compared them with others in their category.[1] Importantly, visionary companies were defined not just in terms of market share

(this wasn't just a comparison of 'winners versus losers'), but as companies that had significantly outperformed others in the category — usually the number two brand.

One of the key conclusions of the study is worth reporting in full, because of its relevance to Mercedes-Benz: 'Highly visionary companies do not oppress themselves with the "tyranny of the *or*", — the rational view that cannot easily accept paradox, that cannot live with two seemingly contradictory forces or ideas at the same time. The "tyranny of the *or*" pushes people to believe that things must be either A *or* B, but not both. Instead of being oppressed in this way, highly visionary companies liberate themselves with "the genius of the *and*" — the ability to embrace both extremes of a number of dimensions at the same time. Instead of choosing between A *or* B, they figure out a way to have both A *and* B.' Crucially, as Collins and Porras point out, this is not just about 'balance', with its implication of 50/50 compromises. The companies they are describing want to do two things well, 'both at the same time, all of the time'.

This concept of the 'genius of *and*' is fundamentally important. Mercedes-Benz has been a successful company for most of its life — but it has only been a visionary company in the last ten years. As such, though, it is now much better placed to manage the duality of its brand. It can have

This page: Jürgen Schrempp, Chairman of
Daimler-Benz AG, 1995-8, and Chairman of
DaimlerChrysler AG since 1998

Mercedesness *and* Benzness. Its brand can be
'enduring' *and* 'passionate'.

Suddenly too, this thought of 'the genius of
and' begins to lift the fog of how to deal with issues
such as apparently conflicting model strategies, or
even the more general disconnect between cars and
commercial vehicles. The answer is to do both, but
do both excellently. Have as the goal for the brand
the ability (already demonstrated) to be able to
'live with two seemingly contradictory forces'. Few
brands have the inherent strength to achieve this.
Mercedes-Benz does.

'Enduring Passion' and with it (through 'the
genius of *and*') the idea of actively managing the
two sides of Mercedes-Benz, is also important to
the *internal* brand. In May 1995, Jürgen Schrempp
replaced Edzard Reuter as Chairman of Daimler-Benz
AG. What followed, according to business historian
David Lewis, was 'unprecedented in the culture
of German management'.

As well as swiftly refocusing the company on
its core automotive businesses, Schrempp cut staff
both in the factories and at the company's head
office. He instituted a much stricter regime on
productivity and bonuses — all of which had the
effect of fundamentally shaking up the company.
The impact of Schrempp's positive actions was
profound — not so much on the culture of the

organisation, as in destroying any remaining sense
of complacency within the workforce.

Unsettled and less secure, Mercedes-Benz
employees needed to unite around a common cause,
and Dr Schöpf has already highlighted the key role of
the brand in this respect. The Schwabianness of the
workforce (at least in the southern German factories)
probably helped too. Their stoic demeanour meant
that they perhaps redoubled their efforts to ensure
the future success of the company.

Certainly, recent staff research (now conducted
regularly by NFO Infratest) shows that 'employee
commitment to Mercedes-Benz is significantly stronger
than the average of German employees'. Crucially,
the research concludes, unlike other conglomerates,
'the commitment of employees with the "mother"
company (Mercedes-Benz) is as strong as their commitment to their site, plant, business unit or department'.

This is a key positive measure of the strength
of the internal brand, but the research also highlights how the two (internal and external) can be
negatively related too: 'For employees the quality
claim is one of the most crucial elements of the
Mercedes-Benz brand. Thus, negative press reports
on quality are experienced almost as damage to
their personal identity.'

What better example can there be of the intricate, but absolute, interconnectedness of the internal

brand and the external brand? For me, one of the impressive things about the internal culture (especially at management levels) is the loyalty and longevity that seem to exist. Unlike many other companies that I've worked with, there isn't the endless turnover of staff and general disaffection that are normally a feature of so many large organisations. From the brand point of view, this continuity and positive attitude have to be virtues.

What is striking at the company's Möhringen head office is how polite everyone is (they still address each other by their surnames even when they've known one another for years). It is not uncommon for two generations of the same family to work there, certainly for husbands and wives to do so. And though there are irritating formalities (like the hierarchical secretarial system), the general sense is of a generous employer and an appreciative workforce. Both are the result of a shared confidence in a common cause: the Mercedes-Benz brand. To reinforce this, I was told almost as an aside that, since the merger with Chrysler, most people here had reverted back from using the previous name, Daimler-Benz, to saying 'I work for Mercedes-Benz'. Some just say 'I work for the star'.

But despite the positive findings from the NFO staff research and the confident culture in Stuttgart, a visit to the company's factories in Mannheim gives

a different perspective. Here, in the heartland of the former Benz & Cie, I found a quieter, more purposeful mood — proud and industrious certainly, but tinged with a slight sense of sadness. One's first impressions of these factories, especially the bus and coach works, is of an altogether different era of German industry. The facades date from the early 20th century, and proclaim their Benz brand origins in bold letters. The production lines are massively labour-intensive — there is little of the high-tech robotics of Sindelfingen to be seen.

The difference is understandable. Buses are, after all, produced to a high level of individual customer specification, and for widely varying purposes. Each in its way is a 'one-off'. The result, though, is that the plants here represent manufacturing in the true sense of the word: hard manual labour... and the noise of hammering and welding is deafening. Mannheim has a strong industrial and labour tradition — and the sense of history in the factories is palpable. But there is sorrow too.

My host for the day, Wolfgang Presinger (Executive Managing Director, Mercedes-Benz Buses and Coaches), painted a vivid picture of this very different part of the DaimlerChrysler empire. He began in German: *'Benz erscheint gar nicht mehr'* (Benz doesn't feature any more) — a reference to the Benz name having been dropped after the merger with Chrysler. 'Everyone here was very sad when that happened. After all, our most valuable brand is Mercedes-Benz — but Mercedes is Jellinek, Benz is Benz.' But, said Presinger, history is not just about nostalgia. For him, it is the reason why customers are able to hold the disparate images of the Mercedes-Benz range in their heads. 'The elasticity of the brand is unbelievable,' he said, 'it could not be created from scratch.'

When questioned about the economics of the bus and coach factory (given that it turns out only around 14 units a day), Presinger concedes that 'for decades it's been a loss-making business — it's only in the last five years that it's been in the black'. 'Our pride,' he said, 'has been diluted through commercial crisis, through hire and fire, through new workplace practices — but we are still strong. This is more than a company, it's an institution.' (In fact, the man most responsible for the profit recovery within this side of the business was Dr Eckhard Cordes — subsequently rewarded in November 2004 with the top job at Mercedes Car Group.)

Opposite: DaimlerChrysler's Möhringen head office, Stuttgart, Germany
This page: Mercedes-Benz bus and coach works, Mannheim, Germany

Stuttgart
Mannheim
(Home of the automobile)

Basel
Karlsruhe
Heidelberg

Nevertheless, the feeling I was left with was that the Mannheim operation is something of a commercial backwater for the company, albeit one with a powerful ethos and tradition. In a sense this makes the Benz influence within today's brand even more remarkable. Clearly it is not a function of sheer corporate power — rather it is a product of the immense pride that one can almost feel emanating from these plants.

Fortunately, though, some of the deep-rooted strengths of the Benz tradition still make their presence felt in Stuttgart. Before I left, Presinger took me on a short tour of the area — taking in Karl Benz's home, the Karl Benz museum and the original factory of Carl Benz Söhne, which still exists (and provides components to DaimlerChrysler) to this day. I left feeling enriched by the history, but also inspired by the pride of today's managers in their unique contribution to the Mercedes-Benz brand.

Few are better placed to round off this historic perspective than Dr Harry Niemann (Manager of Corporate History and Archives and biographer of both Wilhelm Maybach and Béla Barényi) and Max-Gerrit von Pein (Director, Classic — the division with responsibility for building the new Mercedes-Benz Museum). Both men pointed to the very different origins and attitudes of the founders and of how this came to equip the company with a range of skills rather than a narrow focus. Both too highlighted the differences between the companies at the time of the merger, and how this complementarity became a strength. Niemann, in particular, talked about how the company had not only invented the car but had become, in the 1930s, the 'home' of the automobile — attracting key individuals like Porsche, Horch, Barényi *et al*, and continues to do so to this day. This 'legacy of excellence', he believed, was a key reason for the brand's success.

Von Pein identified pride as a defining characteristic of the organisation — but wished it could translate into more of a sense of passion. Interestingly, given Stefan Sielaff's earlier comment, von Pein also talked about the DNA of the brands and — though he didn't refer to the idea of Benz and Mercedes perhaps being that double helix — revealed that this concept would shape the physical building in which the Mercedes-Benz Museum is due to be rehoused in 2006.

But the biggest lessons from history relate back to the three criteria for great brands explored in chapter 1. When the brand lost its clarity, as it did in the 1980s with the diversification into entities like Fokker and AEG (both incidentally closed down by Schrempp in 1996), it suffered. When the brand (perhaps through the imbalance of its two sides) behaved inconsistently, as in the 1970s, it suffered. When the brand somehow lost its 'leadership', its ability to 'exceed expectations', as it did in both of those decades, it suffered. These, then, are the lessons for the future. This trio: clarity, consistency, leadership (together with authenticity — being an original) are the things that the company must keep in mind as it plots its brand's destiny. So what of the future? What are the principal challenges the brand faces in the years ahead?

CHAPTER ELEVEN

'DIE ZUKUNFT DER MARKE'
(THE FUTURE OF THE BRAND)

At a corporate level, one of the most signifi-cant challenges the company faces today is sorting out the relationship between the Mercedes-Benz brand and its Chrysler portfolio in the USA.

Commercially, the Chrysler business has been pulled back from the brink of the profit abyss it faced in 2003 — and hopefully those improvements can be sustained. New products like the Chrysler 300 range are selling well — better than rival models from GM and Ford. But the issue of brand differentia-tion, even separation, from Mercedes-Benz won't be resolved as quickly. The USA, after all, is the biggest market for Mercedes-Benz after Germany, and the increasingly integrated strategies of the two divi-sions of DaimlerChrysler in that territory are receiving close scrutiny from a number of directions.

As I left the interview with Professor Hubbert, he handed me an article that had appeared in the US press that week which talked about the 'sheer marketing folly' of moving Chrysler upmarket, and Mercedes-Benz down (largely through the then planned addition of the B-Class compact to the US model range). The author, Paul Lienert, was even more critical of cross-platform sharing of compo-nents and 'the impact on Mercedes once the word gets out'.[1] Hubbert was obviously concerned, and

rightly so. Increasingly, the challenge as he saw it was for the teams in Stuttgart and Auburn Hills (DaimlerChrysler's US headquarters) to balance doing what is sensible economically with what is right for the brand.

Mercedes-Benz is now but one brand in a portfolio, but Dr Zetsche, the man charged with running the Chrysler operation in the USA, is clear about the strategy: 'We're looking at greater separa-tion between each of the Chrysler brands — and between all three and Mercedes-Benz.' Good news in theory, but the reality of more and more overlaps in price points as well as components may make this a tough task.

An interview with Alex Gellert of Merkley Newman Harty (the agency responsible for advertising Mercedes-Benz in the USA) threw more light on this vexed subject — and also on the competitive threat from Lexus in that market. To Gellert, Mercedes-Benz position in the US is clear: 'We are *the* premium luxury brand. We don't do taxis. We don't do cloth interiors — only leather. It's luxury.' But within this, heritage has a role to play: 'Owners like to know that they have bought something that has a little history — it's not the number one reason to buy, but it's powerful stuff and Lexus don't have that. Heritage becomes the tie-breaker, if it is a tie.'

Gellert is quick to acknowledge the threat from Lexus, particularly in terms of service, but his bigger concern (echoing Lienert) is the maintenance of a clear differentiation of Mercedes-Benz from the three Chrysler brands — Jeep, Dodge and Chrysler itself. As he puts it: 'The day someone reads that the engine in a Dodge truck is the same as the engine in a C-Class, we'll have a problem.'

This is not an issue that's going to go away. The simple economics of global car manufacturing mean that cross-platform sharing will continue — the appearance of the Chrysler ME Four Twelve, powered by a Mercedes-Benz V12 engine, at the Detroit Motor Show in January 2004 highlighted the issue once again.

Furthermore, these potential threats to brand differentiation are arriving just at the moment when the need for such distinctions is becoming more urgent. As Gellert says: 'The time for technological or styling leads is reducing. Luxury cars are still not a commodity, but one of the challenges is how you can continue to differentiate other than through product.' Helmut Werner, the former Chairman, was more abrupt in his views: 'Right strategy, wrong time' was his verdict on the merger. Now that it is a reality, however, Werner's opinion was that 'the company should make sure that the Mercedes-Benz brand isn't mixed up with the Chrysler brand'.

Stemming the tide of red ink at Chrysler of course only serves to switch the spotlight back on to the problems facing the Mercedes Car Group in Stuttgart.

While quality is an issue in its own right, stagnating sales and profits for Mercedes-Benz in 2004 and 2005 have other deep-rooted causes. Of these, perhaps the most significant is the ageing product portfolio. Any car manufacturer needs a carefully planned product-renewal strategy, so that the timing of new models is phased in such a way that as one car begins to reach the end of its lifecycle (the 'run-out' phase as it is called in the industry), another new model is being introduced in a separate category. This is a complex planning process, particularly given the lead times for developing a new car. The aim should be a managed and staggered sequence of introductions, overlapping one another — rather than, say, four new models in one year, then none in the subsequent two years.

The problems for Mercedes-Benz in that area are manifold. Because of the rash of new cars in the mid-1990s, many models were coming up for replacement in the period 2003 to 2005. Key products like S-, M- and A-Class, were all in 'run-out' mode at the same time — the period in which promotional support is most necessary, and hence profitability is at its lowest.

Compounding this problem has been the fact that not only are model lifecycles themselves getting shorter (driven by consumer demand), but also that the competition in every one of these sectors is getting fiercer. BMW's current 7 series and Audi's A8 are both younger and, arguably, sexier than the S-Class. M-Class, having originally effectively defined the category of road-friendly Sports Utility Vehicles (SUVs), has subsequently faced an army of imitators — from Lexus, VW, Porsche and BMW to name but a few.

So portfolio renewal is a major issue for Mercedes-Benz — albeit one that will come right as the desired strategy works its way through the range. Right now, though, it is merely exacerbating the much more visible issues of quality that the company is grappling with.

As recently as October 2004, the business press was reporting falling profits as a result of 'persistent poor quality'.[2] Acknowledging that Mercedes Car Group had 'admitted its luxury cars... were prone to breakdown', the UK's *Financial Times* carried a front-page graph of the brand's JD Power rating in the USA over the past 15 years, charting the steady decline from the number one spot on reliability, to its 2004 position at number 28. One quote, from Maria Bissinger, motor analyst at Standard & Poor's, gave particular cause for concern: 'Mercedes has been beset by product quality problems,' she said, 'necessitating costly actions to prevent further harm to its brand image.'

In the same week, Wolfgang König, writing in the UK's *Autocar* magazine about the arrival of Dr Eckhard Cordes (to replace Jürgen Hubbert) as CEO of Mercedes Car Group, commented on the same issue: 'For Mercedes, to make things cheaper by reducing quality has to be taboo. Past experience with this strategy severely damaged the brand's reputation as the core values of quality and reliability dwindled. To restore the image of offering tank-like quality and utmost peace of mind has been given the number one priority, and Cordes is the man who will have to see this through.'[3]

Cordes himself acknowledges this responsibility for making product quality a priority. In one of his earliest public statements, at the Detroit Motor Show in January 2005, he told journalists: 'Only satisfied customers can keep alive the future of the brand. I will hold myself accountable for this.'

Opposite: the Chrysler 300C — the new face of Chrysler

This page and opposite: the Mercedes-Benz SLR McLaren. McLaren is a key partner of Mercedes-Benz on and off the race track

The *reality* of product quality is that the faults in absolute numbers are small, but the constant retelling of anecdotes (particularly over the internet) and the excessive press interest inflate the true scale of the problem. The company acknowledges that it will take more than small annual improvements in quality statistics to fundamentally shift public perceptions. And generally, the key people don't make excuses, because they recognise that they built this reputation and now have to maintain and defend it.

Dr Schmidt and Dr Schöpf point the finger at suppliers, but acknowledge that the management of these was their responsibility too. Erich Klemm (Chairman of the Workers' Council of DaimlerChrysler AG) agrees, but also says that the policy of out-sourcing has led to deskilling of the workforce both in the development centre and on the production line. Moreover, he claims, the key problem is the complexity of the electronics. Add to these the other explanations often ventured (pressure to keep costs down, pressure to get cars to market more quickly) and one has a heady mix of reasons for quality slippage. The answer, says Schöpf, lies in better

management of suppliers (and of the supplier's supplier), greater in-house R & D expertise and investment in people. He disagrees with Klemm's point about deskilling.

Others that I have spoken to, though, believe the problem is more fundamental — and goes much deeper. When researching this book, I interviewed Ron Dennis, Chief Executive of McLaren — a key partner to Mercedes-Benz not just in Formula One, but also in the development of new cars like the SLR. Dennis' ambition is clearly for a yet-closer alliance between his company and Mercedes-Benz, so he is acutely aware of the quality issues affecting the organisation. When asked about the Mercedes-Benz brand, he draws a distinction between the brand five years ago — 'excellent engineering, safe, long-lasting, longevity of styling' — and the brand today. Expanding on this, Dennis continues: 'The company has become great through passion — it's full of passionate people working in a passionate environment. But when you marry that up to a focus on quarterly returns and more volumes it increases the challenge of maintaining quality. That makes building a brand even more difficult.'

Many of the people I spoke to share the view that part of the problem lies with the increasing dependence on outside suppliers. Some go as far as to suggest that whereas, say, ten years ago well over 50% of a Mercedes-Benz was made by Mercedes-Benz, today that figure would only be around 30% — the balance coming in the form of bought-in (and often fully assembled) parts and componentry.

Others go a step further and point out that (despite Schöpf's reassurances) the supplier network is now so complex that it is impossible to control (or even know) who the suppliers are at the very bottom of this 'food chain'. This intricate outsourced network — essential to the economic production of cars in today's market — represents a very real management challenge if quality is truly to improve.

Compounding this issue is the fact that the Mercedes-Benz tradition of constant innovation means that for a new model (like the 2002 E-Class, for example), as much as 90% of the components will themselves be new. This contrasts with a figure of only around 30% for a new Lexus model, where much more use is made of tried and tested components from its predecessor. The implication of this —

the lack of what is called 'ripe product' — particularly in the early years of a new model's life, is a further headache for Stuttgart's senior managers.

Innovation, it seems, may in some senses be contributing to the problem. New technologies, particularly electronic ones, too complex now to be developed in-house, are bought in from multi-tiered suppliers and fitted to new models, themselves being developed ever faster to meet changing customer demands in various niches. All of this is a recipe for quality problems and may well mean that insufficient allowance is made for eradicating the 'gremlins' that so often accompany these technologies. It is a problem for managers — not least in disentangling these various potentially contributory factors — but is it really to the benefit of the customer?

It is interesting to observe how customers *actually* judge quality in dealerships or at motor shows. The majority still employ tactile or sensual measures, not analytical skills. They touch the interior materials, feel the gearstick, open glove boxes, run their hands around the steering wheel, open and close doors. While they will frequently flick the switches and turn the knobs, in these purchase environments the cars usually have their ignitions turned off — so there is no opportunity to interact fully with the electronic systems.

I would argue that just as with, say, mobile phones or DVD players, most will never use more than a fraction of the various features and functions available. The majority of buyers never read their car's instruction manual — and, for most, the available technology is now so far ahead of their personal skill-set that they are not even able to judge its applicability or value. The implications of this are important. Perhaps the focus on electronic innovation, and with it increasing levels of complexity, needs to be rebalanced against an equivalent focus on relevant, visible, customer-focused features that can be identifiably linked to the quality judgements that consumers actually make.

In this regard, there may again be lessons to learn from brands like Lexus. Generally, Lexus is not a state-of-the-art innovator, but rather what is sometimes called a 'fast follower', just behind the leading edge. And when the company does innovate it *is* relevant, visible and customer-focused — like the automatic parallel-parking technology on its latest models; truly a benefit to anyone with a large car, particularly one full of children and with restricted rear visibility. This debate goes back to the fundamental question posed in chapter 9 — what kind of car business does Mercedes-Benz want to be?

Ten years or more ago, as a small player, perhaps 'leading-edge technology and innovation' was the place to be. But as a producer of over a million cars a year, spread across so many segments, is it still as appropriate today? Would the company, and hence the brand, not be better served by focusing once again on some of its more 'Benz-like' qualities of durability, reliability and fitness-for-purpose? Innovation itself may not be the enemy of quality, provided it is focused and planned. Complexity almost certainly is. Dr Schmidt recognised the problem — that complexity as an area needs particular attention. He even bemoaned the fact that the electronic engineers 'still try to improve the cars on a daily basis'. In truth, these engineers probably get bored long before the customer. Even leaving aside the expense of innovation (research and development costs Mercedes-Benz around €5,000 a minute, over €2.5billion a year), one has to question whether this obsession with change is always relevant to the customer or valuable to the brand.

Opposite: the B-Class was launched at the Geneva Motor Show, 2005

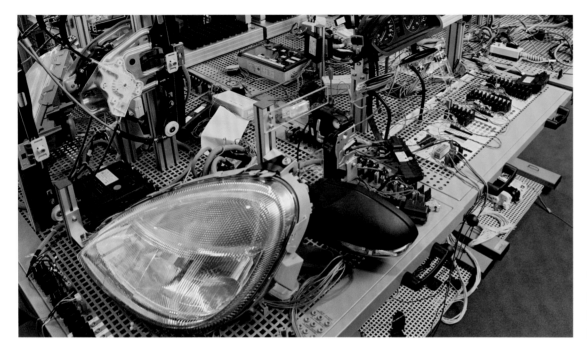

This page: technical complexity may be the root cause of many of the quality issues facing Mercedes-Benz
Opposite: The new A-Class. Its predecessor sought to attract younger people, and more women, to the brand

Complexity may be the Achilles heel of the brand today, just as over-engineering was in the 1980s. Schmidt was optimistic that the problems could be solved. Significant programmes, he says, were in place to address a number of aspects of quality: for example, cross-functional management teams, a major review of supplier standards, a system of quality 'gates' both in the development phase and on the production line.

All are laudable, though none addresses the attitudinal, perhaps even philosophical, issue beneath the surface. Senior managers point hopefully at charts that list all the practical things that need doing — but while there is recognition of the problem, and a commitment to act at this practical level, one is left wondering whether the company's admission truly embraces the depth and fundamental nature of some of the issues debated here.

In this context, Dr Schöpf at least gave an insight into the contribution of the internal brand: 'The only thing that guarantees quality is individual pride in what you are doing.' The attitude he sought to instil as Director of the Sindelfingen plant was one in which each and every worker thought, 'I'm the last person to touch this part, no one may ever see it, but I know it's mine.' This, said Schöpf, was the 'spirit of Sindelfingen' — one in which people 'feel attacked if something doesn't work'. I asked where that spirit came from. 'From the brand, from the star, from Mercedes-Benz' was the answer.

Just about everyone I spoke to acknowledged that product quality, pure and simple, was a challenge in its own right, independent of the brand's volume ambition. For Hilmar Kopper, a friend of the company for so long, 'the truth is quality did come down three or four years ago, but what we learnt is that nothing

is more expensive than warranties. In the last two years things have improved a lot.' To Kopper, quality is ultimately more important even than absolute dollar-for-dollar price competitiveness: 'When you buy a Mercedes-Benz it's only the first one that's expensive.'

Think about that comment for a second and you can see the original logic for the A-Class. In Kopper's view, and that of many others, the A-Class exists primarily to bring people into the brand at an earlier age and life-stage. It becomes the new entry point to the brand — priced at perhaps two-thirds the level of the C-Class — and hopefully begins a lifetime relationship with Mercedes-Benz that starts in one's thirties, not one's fifties. Product quality, strong residual values and favourable trade-in terms (so the logic goes) will encourage A-Class owners to trade up within the brand rather than look outside.

The truth is that the success which the original

A-Class enjoyed (it did sell over a million units after all), has been a lot more patchy than Kopper's strategic logic might have suggested. Yes, it attracted new, younger customers — especially women — in important markets like France and Italy. And yes, this did have a positive impact on the image of the 'masterbrand'. But in other markets, notably Germany, it sold mainly as a second car within existing Mercedes-Benz-owning households, rather than gaining the true 'conquest' business originally planned. The net result is that, in markets like this, the average age of an A-Class owner is still over 50.

From being a truly innovative car at the time of its launch, the A-Class now has a bigger part to play as a fully fledged member of the brand's model family. For the strategic logic to really work, the new A-Class has to exhibit all that is best about the more *traditional* Mercedes-Benz virtues: durability, luxury,

authenticity and, above all, quality. In doing so, the A-Class will fulfil its original promise, and confirm its role as the crucially important gateway to the Mercedes-Benz brand.

The issues surrounding the A-Class, important though they are, are still only a part of the bigger challenge facing the company in this area over the coming years: the continued and successful implementation of the original product strategy. It is here, above all, that Mercedes-Benz will need to manage its brand most carefully. Already the company is concentrating on a 'second product offensive' that has seen and will see a whole raft of new models being launched between 2004 and 2006. How, as a management team, are they going to do that while still (to paraphrase the Interbrand criteria) retaining strategic clarity, brand consistency and the hard-won reputation for leadership?

In terms of strategic clarity, the shift from 'luxury segment' to 'premium positioning' is one to which the company is clearly committed. Dr Schmidt even had a phrase for how this strategy would work: '*Spitzenklasse in jeder Klasse*'. First-class in every class. What 'first-class in every class' means is that, unlike the earlier strategy of only operating in the top half of the total car market, the brand today is represented in a number of segments.

But the key point is that *whichever* segment the brand is in, it seeks to be at the top of that segment: the best (however that is defined) in that class. Theoretically, this gives the brand permission to enter any segment it chooses, as long as it is always 'the best'. In practice, once again, it is less simple. Firstly, defining (and then designing) what 'best' is and means in any segment requires not only a totally honest assessment of what the competition

This page: Smart fortwo, 2005
Opposite: Maybach 57 S, 2005

is doing, but also the ability to anticipate how this might change over a product's lifecycle. No mean feat, as we've seen. Secondly, the whole concept of segments is itself becoming blurred as more and more 'crossover' models are launched that sit between conventional segments.

But if Dr Schmidt's logic at least brought clarity of a kind, the question now is about brand consistency. Many share a persistent concern that this is the real challenge. How to pursue the premium positioning in so many segments yet not dilute the brand through the consequent array of models.

'The secret is consistency,' said one eminent commentator, 'all these new models — A-Class, M-Class, C-Class coupé — they are all diluting the core values of the brand.' Andre Kemper, too, berates this dilution at the margin: 'There are so many new models, it's hard to keep a *typical* Mercedes-Benz look and feel. Models like V-Class and Vaneo are not liked as cars or as Mercedes-Benz. The company disowns them

— they say they come from the truck side — but the customers don't see that. They don't inspire passion, let alone enduring passion.' Strong stuff — but many have sympathy with these views and in fact production of Vaneo ceased in mid-2005. Encouragingly, though, I sensed from some people that I spoke to that there was not only a recognition of the short-comings of some of these models, but also an element of conscience, a feeling that lessons could be learnt from these experiences. The new A-Class indeed may be a case in point.

Dr Schmidt's response was more emphatic: 'Dilution of image doesn't concern me so long as people still see the brand as high quality, innovative and fascinating… but then we have to deliver this.' Professor Hubbert agreed: 'The counter argument to dilution,' he says, 'is to keep fighting for the same values: safety, comfort, innovation, quality.' But in the last ten years the brand's situation has become more complex.

Mercedes-Benz now sits at the centre of a small constellation of brands — and these at least set the parameters of what Mercedes-Benz as a brand *won't* do. Strategically, this is an important concept. Whereas corporate growth strategies may well be about knowing what to do (and when), brand strategy is often about knowing what *not* to do.

In terms of product, these 'sacrifice' decisions will be crucial in the future. The company will need to make tough choices about whether to merely have representation within a segment, or whether it can truly offer the *best* product within that segment. The temptation to be opportunistic will be huge, but the strategy should dictate that unless the brand can genuinely succeed at the *top* of any given segment, then the company should not enter it. That is what sacrifice means.

Within the portfolio, Smart sets the lower limit. For Mercedes-Benz, Professor Hubbert asserted, there will be nothing 'below' the A-Class. At the other

end of the scale, he was equally adamant that there'll be nothing 'above' the S-Class. Beyond that point, the brand role falls to Maybach. Separately there's now also AMG to consider — since 1999 wholly owned by DaimlerChrysler. It sets the limit in terms of specialist, custom-built variants, offering a level of performance models that sit at the top end of each segment.

Jean-Noël Kapferer is Professor of Marketing at the HEC School of Management in Paris, and one of the leading contemporary writers on brands. His view (and he cites Mercedes-Benz on occasion within his books) is that there is a paradox between the need for consistency and the irresistible pressure for change. Citing Collins and Porras (he's obviously a fan too) he refers to this being 'the time for *and*' — specifically to combine consistency at the core of a brand with progress around the edges. He thinks the risk of alienating current customers (part of what I mean by dilution) is often overstated, believing that

younger audiences in particular are receptive to change, and that current users of a brand can even be flattered by it. To Kapferer, the key is to maintain 'icon' products at the heart of the brand — a bit like Nivea's famous blue tin — that then allow other variants room for manoeuvre.

Perhaps Kapferer's thinking about 'icon models' points the way forward. It is a view shared by the author of the study I commissioned to look at the implications of social attitudes on car brands, specifically on Mercedes-Benz. As well as highlighting the role of icon products, Roz Elwes' report also identifies two further trends that the brand could potentially tap into, both of which the company is already well placed to deliver. Creating 'crossover' models that bridge gaps between existing categories to better reflect people's lifestyle needs is one, and the company is actively developing precisely these kinds of cars as part of its 'second product offensive'. The other, the 'need for personal-

isation', is one that the company could quickly capitalise on. Dr Schöpf, after all, had described the company's business model as being to produce 'tailor-made cars'. But either of these might undermine exactly what needs to be preserved: the consistency of the brand. Exciting opportunities they may be — but there's still the issue of how to unite, while all around are pressures that might divide.

My own thinking about a response to the challenge of brand consistency also began with 'icon models' — flagship cars that are promoted disproportionately to their absolute volumes, because of what they say and symbolise about the brand as a whole. Quickly, though, I hit two potential stumbling blocks. Firstly, that over time these models will become less and less representative of the range as a whole and that therefore this approach might even exacerbate the divisions between the top of the range and the volume models. Secondly, and more serious, is the concern that adopting such a strategy might

If icon models weren't sufficient to unite the brand, then maybe icon values could be

in a sense give permission for laziness about how to solve the consistency issue right across the range. It was a discussion with J Justus Schneider about this issue, and Kapferer's perspective on it, that took the thinking to an altogether more interesting place. Schneider's view was that if icon models weren't sufficient to unite the brand, then maybe icon values could — specifically one icon value that acts as a unifying characteristic across all cars.

But what should this icon value be? We know what the candidates are from the brand model: authenticity, innovation, leadership and quality. Authenticity in a sense is a given. It's a fact; Mercedes-Benz owns it. But it's hard to express as an icon value in a continuously fresh way as part of a contemporary brand message. Innovation too has its limitations. I've outlined the double-edged sword that it can represent: how in product terms it can potentially work against the goal of quality.

Leadership, the third potential icon value, makes a strong case for itself, but ultimately it is also too narrow to deliver the consistency the brand needs. Almost by definition, it pushes one towards

the edges of the brand rather than working at the centre. Clearly related to innovation, it would steer the brand towards stories about performance or exceptional experiences, rather than send out messages that intrinsically unite across the range.

Quality, the final candidate, is the one that united Mercedes and Benz in their earliest days, has been a central part of the internal culture ever since, and has been true of most of the company's cars for most of the company's life. It is the most fundamental of the brand's core values, the one the company still most wishes to own and the one customers most want to buy. For quality to assume this position of pre-eminence means that resolving some of the product issues discussed earlier becomes even more important, and more urgent. But this definition of quality goes further. For quality to be an 'icon value' for the whole brand, not just the cars, it needs to embrace much more than just fault-free product.

Of course, quality product is fundamental to any such 'iconic' ambition — and the initiatives which Hubbert, Schmidt and Schöpf described are all vital to that goal. But quality product, across the

entire range, is in some sense the least the company should aim for. Beyond that lies a much bigger prize.

No other brand is better placed than Mercedes-Benz to offer quality in all areas of the market in all sorts of ways. For example, building on Schöpf's observation, the brand can offer quality in the form of cars that are even more tailor-made — cars specified and personalised to suit the wishes of the buyer. In so doing, the brand could increasingly 'own' discerning customers — the quality end of each model segment.

But it is in the area of service and brand experience that the greatest opportunity exists for Mercedes-Benz to develop the icon value of quality as a means of delivering consistency. While customers are making more and more assumptions about product performance in the car market, their experience from other markets (especially sectors like hotels, airlines, even retailers) means that *service* expectations continue to rise.

Opposite: Designo interior in a 2004 SL

Today it is this complete experience that needs to be taken into account, because that, not just the car, is what people are buying. How they are handled at first enquiry, the purchase process, the dealership environment, the servicing cycle, how they are treated if they have a complaint, what happens at trade-in — all of these contribute to the 'total brand experience' of Mercedes-Benz.

The challenge for the company is to meet these new quality expectations in *all* aspects of its delivery – at every point of customer contact — right across the range. Again, it's a tall order — but who better than Mercedes-Benz to deliver against it? Others, notably Lexus, are putting more and more emphasis on this area, but the field is still open and it is these service aspects of quality that will increasingly mark out the winning brands from the 'also-rans' in the world's car markets.

But the suggestion of the pursuit of quality as an icon value is not driven by the desire just to do good things for the brand. While what it can contribute to consistency is very powerful, the 'bigger prize' is a commercial one.

The attainment of this redefined quality standard would be immensely valuable to Mercedes-Benz as a business. If Mercedes-Benz can make product quality a more prominent virtue *within* its cars, people will pay more for them. If Mercedes-Benz can epitomise quality across its range, in every segment — and for the entire customer journey — this will be the strongest possible justification for the brand's price premium.

If the company could do both, and as a result improve its margins and profitability, maybe this would also take some of the heat out of the chase for volume that it is currently engaged in. Schneider calls this alternative approach 'qualitative growth': the pursuit of improvement in quality in its widest sense, rather than increases in quantity. The quest for profit, not just volume – but still across all sectors. He sees qualitative growth shifting the management emphasis from concerns about the economics of cross-platform sharing and finite production capacity, to a focus on customer loyalty and the maintenance of margins. Qualitative growth would resolve some of the questions around the

kind of car business Mercedes-Benz wants to be. And it could even help to clarify the relationship with Chrysler.

Schneider's view is that qualitative growth might be a powerful solution to the issue of brand consistency — and a new way of channelling future Mercedes-Benz business strategy.

But can the company afford to pursue such a route? One thing that's for sure is that the current strategy of constantly striving to be *better* through product innovation is massively expensive — Mercedes-Benz R & D costs reflect this, as we've seen. Perhaps some of that money might be more effectively spent on being *different*: innovating across the entire customer experience, improving service at each and every stage of the customer journey. Creating, in other words, a genuine and unifying quality difference across all market segments, not just in individual cars.

If icon values are powerful at delivering consistency for the customer, then they are potentially equally powerful at delivering consistency internally. Quality is a 'natural' in this respect.

This page: interior of the original 1997 A-Class
Opposite: interior of the 2004 A-Class

Without doubt, in today's world clarity and consistency around the issue of the internal brand are vital. More and more organisations are making the quest for coherence between the internal and the external brand a priority. Why? Because of the need for directing and unifying the effort of all concerned if a business is to succeed competitively. As employee numbers grow (today DaimlerChrysler employs nearly 400,000 people worldwide), the need for that direction and unity is more important than ever.

So now there is a degree of clarity about strategic direction: first-class in every class. And a view, among some at least, about the sources of brand consistency: clear portfolio strategy, quality as an 'icon value' that infuses all parts of the offer, the goal, perhaps, of qualitative growth and a tightly defined internal culture. An organisation, in other

words, that in all senses puts brand, not just product, at the centre of its operations.

But what of the third criterion: the retention of Mercedes-Benz reputation for leadership? Leadership as a brand value may not have 'icon' status. Leadership in this more general sense, as a brand and business goal, is a crucial priority. Mercedes-Benz has led the way in so many respects over its history. To forsake this position now would be tragic. But again, it is a goal that needs redefining.

We've seen how definitions of product quality are changing — and questioned whether consumers are able fully to judge leading edge features of a car. So if leadership is about more than just product innovation, how else might Mercedes-Benz as a brand stay ahead of the field?

One route is to revisit some of the consumer expectations about 'what makes a Mercedes a Mercedes'

— and the 2004 A-Class certainly demonstrates a focus back on some of the traditional virtues of the marque. Bright interior trims, coloured plastics and patterned fabrics have all been eschewed in favour of a more classic interior design and level of finish. The emphasis once again is on quality, functionality and fitness-for-purpose, not just fashion — reintroducing some of the expected Mercedes-Benz touches, just as Stefan Sielaff had promised us. Leadership, in other words, by being a standard setter, not just a style statement.

But to deliver a leading customer experience as well as leadership products again means that the company needs to ask itself: 'What kind of car business do we want to be?' This question takes us right back to Levitt's observations about 'myopia'. Unless Mercedes-Benz has complete clarity about the answer, the company will stumble. At the moment, some of the answers around this question are conflicting.

Ron Dennis has observed that there is a potential clash between stock-market returns and quality. Dr Schmidt identified complexity as a by-product of innovation. I have pointed out the conflict between both of these and quality — and so the circle goes round. The answer to all of these potential conflicts lies not with the customer but within the organisation.

How does the senior management define leadership? Which markets do they want to be leaders in? How is that leadership to be demonstrated and communicated? Which 'expectations' do they want to exceed – and for which customers? These are the fundamental questions that now need answering. And those answers will define the future of the brand.

The job here is not to answer each of these questions on behalf of the company, but it was interesting that Ron Dennis identified a book that

perhaps points the way to some of the solutions. *Good to Great*[4] is in fact the follow-up to *Built to Last*. In it, author Jim Collins identifies ways in which companies can excel, and Dennis is obviously a fan. Collins' central conclusion is that greatness lies at the intersection between three fundamental decisions: what it is that the company is deeply passionate about; which specific economic ratio or indicator does the company wish to excel at; and, perhaps most crucially of all, a clear view about what the company can be the best in the world at doing. Expanding on this last measure, Collins explains that the wording here is vital: 'It is not about a goal to be the best, a strategy to be the best, an intention to be the best, a plan to be the best. It is an understanding of *what you can be the best at*. The distinction is absolutely crucial.' The implications for Mercedes-Benz are clear: the company needs to look

within itself for what it is that it is *already* doing that makes it the best — and then do more of that — and nothing else. Therein, Collins believes, lies potential greatness, and hence leadership.

Mercedes-Benz, after all, is a brand that has a unique claim to leadership: it invented the car. What that means today is that the company knows and can lay claim to some fundamental areas of excellence that are just as relevant now as they were over a hundred years ago. The temptation is to list three, four or even a dozen of these potential areas of excellence: reliability, safety, longevity, engineering, catering for discerning customers — all might be candidates.

The tougher task, though, is to identify precisely *which* of these is the one that most powerfully qualifies the brand for being the best in the world today. The leadership credentials are there — it is a question now of identifying which one to

amplify. Once identified, that defined area of excellence can also provide the brand with the continuity that Pfeiffer spoke of in chapter 10 — the link to the past, the 'groundedness' that all great brands need.

As this book nears its end, it is clear that some of these conclusions could have significant implications for the future of the company and of its brand. I have not shied away from being critical (though hopefully constructively critical) of some aspects of the business. But these observations are driven by good intent, and by a belief that Mercedes-Benz is strong enough as a company to respond positively. As Helmut Werner, the former Chairman, pointed out: 'Mercedes-Benz has never been a company to overlook its mistakes.' Nor has it ever been afraid to learn from them.

Nothing that has happened in over a hundred years of the brand's life has not happened to other brands at some point in their histories. The challenge for Mercedes-Benz is how it responds to the lessons of that experience.

This story has been of a brand (once two, now one) that has been tremendously resilient. It has withstood pressures and obstacles that would have demolished many another car brand. And, though we've not had time to discuss these, the road behind us is littered with the casualties of past struggles. In Germany, Adler, Horch and Borgward have gone; in the UK, Morris, Triumph, Austin and a host of others. In the USA, Packard, Studebaker and (most recently) Oldsmobile have all left the stage.

By contrast, the Mercedes-Benz brand has endured, and maintained the necessary continuity to be a survivor of all this mayhem. But it has also grown and prospered through its ability to harness an inner strength, one that has allowed it to address and conquer these historic threats.

Unless the company responds equally positively to today's challenges, it won't truly be Mercedes-Benz. The company has always been confident and honest in recognising both its strengths

and its weaknesses. Arguably, the only times when its brand have suffered is when management has turned a blind eye to problems they knew in their hearts needed addressing.

Exploring the issues raised here, being frank about mistakes as well as victories, having the strength to admit, and then to learn — all of these are essential if the brand is to survive and forge ahead in the next hundred years. The continuity and leadership that the brand has shown historically almost guarantee that future. Courage from today's new management can make it a certainty.

This page: extinct automobile brands from left to right: Horch, Studebaker, Morris, Borgward
Opposite: Cadillac Ranch art installation, Amarillo, Texas, USA

The brand in 2005 faces challenges every bit as great as those it faced when Hubbert made his pact with his colleagues in 1992. Another watershed has been reached, and the decisions made now by Dr Eckhard Cordes and his team will be equally formative of the Mercedes-Benz brand in the future. Since his appointment in November 2004, Cordes has certainly not been slow to act in tackling some of these challenges. Perhaps prompted by the worsening financial position, even within his first six months in post, he appointed a new Chief Operating Officer, Rainer Schmückle, and a new Head of Sales, Dr Klaus Maier — to replace Dr Joachim Schmidt from April 2005.

An immediate priority for Cordes has been to address the loss-making Smart division where, despite pressure to close it down, he's taken the view that the range needs trimming, and the brand needs to be 'presented anew'.

Cost cutting too is in the 'urgent' folder on Cordes' desk — in the first instance he's announced plans to shave around €700 million from the company's overheads. 'Whether this is enough,' says Cordes, 'remains to be seen'. His assumption, though, is that more pruning will be needed. But it is in Cordes' view of the brand, and the relationship with the customer, that the greatest hope lies.

Shortly after taking office, he announced a four-part programme — called the four Cs — that seeks not only to address cost, but also complexity, culture and, slightly awkwardly, 'cuality' (quality). Given the prominence of these last three to the debate unfolding in this chapter, it's reassuring to know that Cordes is intent on facing up to what are arguably the *most* fundamental threats facing the brand today.

The refocusing on quality is very significant. It suggests a shift towards qualitative growth and a renewed emphasis on getting the basics right. Cordes is outspoken on this subject. 'We are now producing the best quality product ever,' he says 'and our aim is to ensure that those vehicles in the hands of customers which are the cause of complaints achieve a standard of quality that reflects our highest expectations.'

This is a laudable ambition — and it was backed up with an immediate decision to recall over a million cars, from several model ranges, to put right some of the electronic and other problems that have proved such a headache for owners over recent years.

Words *and* actions. Precisely what is needed at this time to reassure current drivers, as well as potential purchasers of the marque. Expensive but necessary, if the brand is to reclaim the quality highground it has held for so long.

The commitment of Cordes is encouraging. To hammer home the message, he has publicly pledged to take 'personal responsibility for bringing Mercedes' quality back to the highest levels again'. Only time will tell whether that refocusing will find favour in both the world's car markets and the world's stock markets.

What is clear immediately upon meeting Dr Eckhard Cordes, however, is that here is a very different type of CEO from what has gone before. When I interviewed him in May 2005, I was struck by both his vigour and his candour — Cordes was

'When you look at the competitive environment, I would say the situation today is even more critical than in 1992'

outspoken about the company's recent history, and its recent management. And he is in no doubt either about this being a watershed moment: 'When you look at the competitive environment, I would say the situation today is even more critical than in 1992.'

Referring to the brand, he continues: 'The most valuable asset we have has already been damaged. We have to get a handle on the quality issue — that's clear. But that's not sufficient. There is also the issue of dilution. Take A-Class, for example — it looks completely different to the rest of the line-up. I'm the new kid on the block — but I'm not sure these kinds of issues were ever discussed: "Do we want A-Class or don't we?" My feeling is that some-one just gave birth to A-Class... and then it was there!' This is clearly not a decision that Cordes approves of and, even after eight years in the market, he believes 'that A-Class so far has not contributed value to the company or the brand'.

Citing handling, looks and the internal feel of the car, Cordes says none of these is truly 'Mercedes-like'. His use of the single brand 'Mercedes' is significant, and it's clear that Cordes' ambition is to reinstate more 'real' Mercedes characteristics in the A-Class, or at least in its successor.

Illustrating, though, how interconnected these issues are, he continues: 'We need these smaller cars because in Europe I think we'll see more downsizing. If that were *not* the case, I think we could have a port-folio without A-Class.' At this point, however, Cordes reveals how the agenda at Mercedes-Benz is beginning to change: 'There was a dream here — in fact a target — that said "we need 1.5 million cars". To make that, the portfolio was broadened and we changed from a clear pull strategy to a brutal push strategy.' By 'push', Cordes means a strategy that places emphasis on directly stimulating demand through pumping more product (and with it promotion) into the marketplace.

He is clearly opposed to this approach: 'If we change the product line up, it will not be to broaden, but to gain greater focus. With the current portfolio, I would feel comfortable with a volume of one to 1.1 million, but definitely not aiming for 1.5 million.' This seems to hint at a move back to more of a luxury positioning aimed at supporting the brand's premium price.

To develop this thought further, I asked Dr Cordes to talk about what kind of future he saw for the brand. 'If Mercedes were a watch,' he replied, 'I'd love to create a brand that was close to Patek Phillipe; distinctive, valuable, not old, not young. An image of high quality and high value — but not old-fashioned.' When I probed him on whether this was not too focused, Cordes' response was that this is the brand's position in the USA and China — the two markets from which he sees most future growth coming. By contrast, he's relaxed about lower

This page: the CLS Coupé launched in 2004

volumes coming out of Germany — and derides the 'numbers competition' with BMW in that market: 'If our brand image is higher than BMW, then our volume may be lower — that's not a problem,' he says.

Towards the end of the interview we returned to a familiar theme: innovation. Once again Cordes was outspoken: 'Some of my predecessors believed in differentiation by innovation — it just doesn't work. You have to assess innovation as to whether it's relevant from the customer perspective.'

Finally we come to what Cordes believes is perhaps the most fundamental issue: the internal culture and management's goal for the future: 'I have a feeling that people inside the company have lost orientation — what it is that they stand for... our vision. Fifteen years ago it was clear; today we have lost track a bit. But we need this to provide internal and external guidance.' For Cordes, developing such

a vision is a priority if he is to get the new management team to pull in the same direction. But that vision, that direction will itself be a new one. Cordes is clearly less prepared to accept some of the compromises of the past. His goal is to reclaim for Mercedes-Benz the territory of 'best cars in the world'. This will mean greater focus within the product portfolio, lower volume targets, prioritising quality over quantity, putting customer experience and the brand in total ahead of pure innovation, and reinstating luxury as a core Mercedes-Benz value. Each of these will stand in sharp contrast to what went before, and not that long before.

One gets a real sense of a new wind of change blowing through the organisation since Cordes' arrival. And it's not just the priorities that are changing, it's the culture too — becoming leaner, sharper, more questioning. All of which is probably good for the company and certainly good for the brand.

Brands are resilient, but like all organisms they have to adapt to survive and Mercedes-Benz is going through just such an evolutionary stage at this time.

One of the last interviews I conducted for this book was with a life-long fan of the Mercedes-Benz brand and someone who is an expert in the area of balancing continuity on the one hand with change on the other: Giorgio Armani. His company plays this tricky game day in, day out, seeking to achieve 'a harmonious balance between modern and traditional'. He too has strong views about the potential of Mercedes-Benz in this area — its ability to unite these two seeming opposites: 'Mercedes-Benz has known how to maintain its identity over the years but also how to evolve with the times and with changing needs.'

Enduring passion... can be the 'cri de cœur' for the brand in the future

The brand, he says, has 'a style that has been very coherent over time but with a clear idea of solidity. The cars have continued to evolve, but they still have a glamour element, one that has been able to be updated.' Interestingly, when Armani talks about his own brand, he points out the dangers of 'inflating or overexposing' it. 'It's a question,' he says, 'of knowing what people want at any particular time, and this means sometimes having to sacrifice certain things that I might have personally wanted to do.' Again, the language of this interview is highly significant for Mercedes-Benz, particularly Armani's stress on responsiveness to changing wants and needs, even if it means sacrifice.

Above all, Armani returned time and again to the issue of continuity: the way Mercedes-Benz had evolved, its coherence over the years, clear ideas about solidity and glamour — but with the ability to update these. 'Restless about self-renewal', as Interbrand would call it.

Herein, I believe, lie the clues to greatness: the ability to weld together authenticity and continuity from the brand's history, with single-minded leadership credentials for the future – and a preparedness to sacrifice along the way.

Hence the truth and power of the brand essence defined in chapter 10: Enduring Passion. It expresses continuity *and* leadership. It can be the *cri de cœur* for the brand — not as a slogan, but as an inner belief. It also expresses the duality that has been a key part of the brand's story since Mercedes and Benz came together in 1926.

There have been times when the tensions within that duality have nearly brought the brand to its knees — 1992 is still for many a defining moment. But we've also seen how that same duality has been a source of strength. Most brands don't have it — they make a virtue out of being singular. Mercedes-Benz, though, can go a step further. By leveraging and managing the two 'halves' of its character, this brand can succeed where others have failed.

Two words are what have held Mercedes and Benz together — and are what sets Mercedes-Benz apart from every other car in the world: Enduring Passion.

1883 Benz & Cie founded by Karl Benz.

1886 Benz Patent Motor Car unveiled. Gottlieb Daimler and Wilhelm Maybach's engine in pre-made carriage becomes first four-wheeled vehicle.

1888 Benz's wife Bertha drives the first long-distance trip in a motorcar (over 60 miles).

1890 Gottlieb Daimler establishes Daimler-Motoren-Gesellschaft (DMG).

1893 DMG exhibits the only car at Chicago World Fair.

1894 Benz Velo becomes first large-scale production car. First car race (Paris to Rouen). Nine of the 21 vehicles carry Daimler engines, and one a Benz.

1900 Death of Gottlieb Daimler. Jellinek orders 36 cars, tied to exclusive sales rights in key markets and renaming cars 'Mercedes' after his daughter.

1901 New 'Mercedes' wins debut race (Nice–Salon–Nice).

1902 Trademark 'Mercedes' officially registered.

1903 Mercedes wins Gordon Bennett race. Karl Benz leaves Benz & Cie, but is appointed to the supervisory board.

1909 Three-pointed star registered as DMG's trademark.

1914 Outbreak of First World War. Benz plants switch to production of military and transport vehicles, submarines and aircraft engines. DMG produces aero-engines and aircraft.

1926 Benz & Cie merges with DMG to form Daimler-Benz AG.

1929 Deaths of Karl Benz and Wilhelm Maybach. Wall Street Stock Market crash, followed by the Great Depression.

1931 Type 170 launched: a smaller, more affordable Mercedes-Benz.

1934 Rear-engined Type 130 showcased (arguably design forerunner of the Volkswagen). 'Silver Arrows' era begins.

1936 First diesel car presented by Daimler-Benz AG at Berlin Motor Show (260D).

1937 Seven out of 13 Grand Prix are won by Mercedes-Benz 'Silver Arrows'.

1939-1945 Daimler-Benz AG converted to wartime production; factories suffer extensive damage as result of Allied bombing.

1947 Type 170V series production resumes.

1951 Béla Barényi's safety cell granted patent. Chancellor Adenauer selects a Type 300 as his official car.

1954 Launch of Type 300SL, the famous 'Gullwing'.

1959 Launch of Types 220, 220S and 220SE (first production cars to have safety cells).

1963 Launch of prestigious Type 600 and 600 Pullman.

1973 Fuel crisis, prompted by the Arab–Israeli war. Consumers look for more economical cars.

1982 190 series launched, the company's first compact car for over 40 years.

1989 Fall of the Berlin Wall. Daimler-Benz AG changes its corporate structure, and becomes the holding company for four independent divisions: Mercedes-Benz AG; AEG AG; Deutsche Aerospace AG and debis. Advertising agency Springer & Jacoby appointed.

1992 The 'fork in the road'. Daimler-Benz AG acknowledges need for a more customer-focused approach.

1993 Start of first 'product offensive'. Launch of C-Class (190 successor) heralds change in model names.

1995 Managerial stability secured with Jürgen Schrempp as Chairman. Launch of E-Class – advertising invites people to 'See Mercedes with new eyes'.

1997 Debut of the M-Class, a luxury 4X4, and launch of the beautiful CLK coupé. A-Class rolls over only a few days after its launch, during Elk test.

1998 Daimler-Benz AG merges with Chrysler Corporation. Smart city-coupé launched under own brand name.

2003 Launch of Mercedes-Benz SLR McLaren.

2004 Start of second 'product offensive'. Launch of seductively shaped CLS.

2005 Launch of B-Class (Compact Sports Tourer) and R-Class (Grand Sports Tourer).

Prof Werner Breitschwerdt

Werner Breitschwerdt studied electro-technology at Stuttgart University of Applied Science and joined Daimler-Benz AG in April 1953. He took on various responsibilities in the field of research and development for Mercedes-Benz passenger cars, before being appointed to the board for development and research in 1977. During his time as head of this division, great progress was made in improving passenger safety as well as in enhancing the economic and energy efficiency of Mercedes-Benz vehicles.

From 1983 to 1987, Werner Breitschwerdt was Chairman of the board of Daimler-Benz AG. Afterwards, he moved to the corporate supervisory board and remained a member until 1993. He is still active as a consultant for DaimlerChrysler.

Dr Eckhard Cordes

Eckhard Cordes joined Daimler-Benz AG as a management trainee in 1976, after graduating in business studies at the University of Hamburg and gaining a PhD in business administration. He has been a member of the DaimlerChrysler AG board of management since 1998, holding various positions, such as responsibility for corporate development, IT/management, MTU/diesel engines and TEMIC, before becoming responsible for the commercial vehicle division in 2000. Since October 2004, he has been Head of the Mercedes Car Group.

Eckhard Cordes' main achievements have been the successful restructuring and development of DaimlerChrysler AG's commercial vehicle division under his stewardship, and his contribution to the merger of Daimler-Benz AG and the Chrysler Corporation.

Prof Jürgen Hubbert

Jürgen Hubbert began his career at Daimler-Benz AG after completing an engineering degree in 1965. Key roles included being in charge of production scheduling at Sindelfingen, being involved in the establishment of the Bremen plant and managing the operations planning division. In 1985, he was made Director of Corporate Planning. Two years later, he became a deputy board member for the passenger car division. Until 2004, he held board-level responsibility for the Mercedes-Benz passenger car division as well as Maybach and Smart.

Jürgen Hubbert's main achievements include two product campaigns, the internationalisation of production, and the formulation and implementation of marketing strategies which doubled sales and profits. The success of the Mercedes-Benz brand at the turn of the millennium can to a great extent be cred-

Hilmar Kopper

Hilmar Kopper started as a bank trainee with the Rheinisch-Westfälische Bank, later known as Deutsche Bank, which sent him to New York for training with the J Henry Schroder Banking Corp. On his return to Germany, he worked in Deutsche Bank's international division in Düsseldorf, then held a position in Leverkusen prior to becoming a board member of the German-Asiatic Bank AG in Hamburg. In 1975, he became CEO of Deutsche Bank and was appointed to the board in 1977. In 1989 he was elected CEO of Deutsche Bank's board of management and deserves much credit for the international expansion which helped turn Deutsche Bank into the most important bank in Europe. He chaired the supervisory board from 1997 to 2002.

Since 1990, Hilmar Kopper has been Chairman of the supervisory board at Daimler-Benz AG. He played a decisive role in the merger between Daimler-Benz AG and the Chrysler Corporation, which formed DaimlerChrysler AG.

Helmut Petri

Helmut Petri began his career in engineering at the Hanomag-Henschel Vehicle Works in Hanover, remaining there after the company was integrated into Daimler-Benz AG. In 1982, he was appointed to the position of technical manager for the Berlin-Marienfelde plant. In 1990, he became technical manager at the Sindlefingen plant, and in 1994 he took on business management of the plant as well.

Helmut Petri was appointed deputy board member responsible for passenger car development in 1985. From 1999 to 2003, he was on the board of the Mercedes Car Group as the Executive Vice President responsible for production. Helmut Petri's particular contributions were optimising development and production processes.

Prof Peter Pfeiffer

Peter Pfeiffer started his career in 1963 as a designer with Ford Works AG. In 1968, he moved to Daimler-Benz AG. After various managerial positions, he was appointed Divisional Manager for Design of Passenger Cars and Commercial Vehicles. Vehicles such as the S-, E-, C-, A- and M-Classes, the SLR and the CLS are examples of the models which have been created under his leadership. He has also been responsible for many projects involving commercial vehicles.

In 1999, Peter Pfeiffer succeeded Bruno Sacco as head of the design division at DaimlerChrysler AG, where since July 2000, he has held the position of Senior Vice President of Design.

Bruno Sacco

Bruno Sacco joined Daimler-Benz AG in 1958 as a stylist and construction engineer and contributed to projects such as the Mercedes-Benz 600 and the Roadster 230SL. He was in charge of styling from 1975 until his appointment as Director of Design, Mercedes-Benz passenger cars in 1987. From 1993 until his retirement in 1999, he was also involved in the design of Mercedes-Benz commercial vehicles.

For over 20 years, Bruno Sacco left his mark on the design of Mercedes-Benz cars. The main focus of his work, in addition to the formal integration of innovation and tradition, was the creation of balance between design and technological requirements.

Dr Joachim Schmidt

After gaining a doctorate in mathematics, Joachim Schmidt became a production manager at Procter & Gamble. In 1979, he joined the passenger car division of Daimler-Benz AG. After a brief stint at Brose, he returned to Daimler-Benz AG in 1988. He later became Director of Corporate Planning and Director of Sales and Marketing Planning. In 1995, he was appointed Head of Sales and Marketing for passenger cars. From 1995 to 2005 he was a member of the board for the business segment of Mercedes Car Group, responsible for sales and marketing worldwide.

Significant achievements included identifying new vehicle segments, building up product management and communication systems and ensuring continual brand development.

J Justus Schneider

J Justus Schneider gained a masters degree in economics from the University of Hamburg and started his career as a trainee at Lintas Hamburg before becoming a product manager at Unilever in Hamburg. He then moved into marketing and communications, initially as Client Service Director at the advertising agency Springer & Jacoby, then as Head of Communications, Minolta Deutschland, and also as Head of Advertising at Adam Opel. From 1995 to 1999 he lived in Singapore, covering a region spanning India, China, South- and North-East Asia, and from Japan to Asia-Pacific, initially heading marketing communications for Opel, later as regional brand manager for that company.

Since March 1999, J Justus Schneider has been Director of Global Marketing Communications for

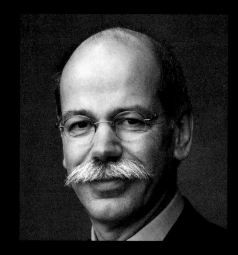

Dr Hans-Joachim Schöpf

After gaining his degree in mechanical engineering in 1969, Hans-Joachim Schöpf began his career with Daimler-Benz AG. Following various managerial positions in the research and development section of Mercedes-Benz passenger cars, he was appointed director of the A- and C-Classes in 1994. He was in charge of the Sindelfingen plant from 1995 to 1998. From 1999 to 2004, he was a member of the Mercedes Car Group board, responsible for product development.

During his time with Mercedes-Benz passenger cars, Hans-Joachim Schöpf played a significant role in introducing technical innovations such as the 7-gear automatic transmission, ESP and common rail diesel technology. He had particular influence on the CLS and Mercedes-Benz SLR McLaren.

Dr Dieter Zetsche

Dieter Zetsche received a masters degree in electrical engineering in 1976 and a doctorate in mechanical engineering in 1982. He joined Daimler-Benz AG in 1976. During his career he has held a number of leading management positions, including President of Mercedes-Benz Argentina, President of Freightliner Corporation USA, Head of Engineering and Design for Mercedes-Benz passenger cars, Head of Sales and Marketing for Mercedes-Benz worldwide and Head of the DaimlerChrysler commercial vehicle division.

Dieter Zetsche became President and CEO of the Chrysler Group in November 2000. In this capacity, he is responsible for the worldwide operations of Chrysler, Jeep and Dodge. He was elected to the Daimler-Benz AG board of management in 1992 and has been a member of the DaimlerChrysler AG board of manage-

1992

C-Class saloon

E-Class saloon

E-Class estate

S-Class

2005

A-Class (3 door)

A-Class (5 door)

B-Class

C-Class saloon

CLK-Class cabriolet

E-Class saloon

E-Class estate

CLS-Class

R-Class

M-Class

G-Class

Vaneo

MODEL RANGES 1992 AND 2005

S-Class coupé

SL-Class

G-Class

C-Class estate

C-Class sports coupé

SLK-Class

CLK-Class coupé

S-Class

CL-Class

SL-Class

SLR-Class

Viano

NOTES

Chapter 1

1. International Olympic Committee survey into symbol recognition. Sample of 7,000 people questioned in the UK, US, Germany, Australia, India, Japan. Details published in *Today*, 20 July 1995.

2. Interbrand's annual analysis of leading brands is published in *Business Week*. Last published 2 August 2004.

3. Prices are from the UK *Autocar* magazine, October 2004.

4. Research conducted by Butterfield8, 2002.

Chapter 2

1. *Chambers 20th Century Dictionary* (Chambers, 1980).

2. Marcel Knobil (ed), *Cool Brandleaders* (Superbrands, 2003).

3. Karl Benz, *Lebensfahrt Eines Deutschen Erfinders: Meine Erinnerungen* (Koehler & Amelang, 2001).

4. *Maybach Moments 01* (DaimlerChrysler AG, 2001).

Chapter 3

1. Sir Hector Laing, then Group Chief Executive Officer of United Biscuits plc.

2. Constantinos C Markides, *All the Right Moves: a Guide to Crafting Breakthrough Strategy* (Harvard Business School Press, 1999).

3. Quote, from Nike's website (www.nike.com/nikebiz). Last accessed on 30 May 2005.

Chapter 4

1. Karl Benz, *Lebensfahrt Eines Deutschen Erfinders: Meine Erinnerungen* (Koehler & Amelang, 2001).

2. Karl Benz, *Allgemeine Automobil Zeitung* (1915). Quoted in Harry Niemann, *Wilhelm Maybach: The Father of Mercedes* (Mercedes-Benz AG, 1996).

3. Beverley Rae Kimes, *The Star and the Laurel - The Centennial History of Daimler, Mercedes and Benz, 1886–1986* (Mercedes-Benz of North America, 1986).

4. David Scott-Moncrieff, St John Nixon and Clarence Paget, *The Three-Pointed Star — The Story of Mercedes-Benz* (Cassell, 1955).

5. David Scott-Moncrieff, *Veteran and Edwardian Motor Cars* (BT Batsford, 1955)

6. Quoted in Kimes, *The Star and the Laurel*, p 92.

7. St John C Nixon, *The Invention of the Automobile* (Country Life, 1936).

Chapter 5

1. Quoted in Harry Niemann, *Gottlieb Daimler — Fabriken, Banken und Motoren* (Delius Klasing, 2000).

2. Beverley Rae Kimes, *The Star and the Laurel — The Centennial History of Daimler, Mercedes and Benz, 1886–1986* (Mercedes-Benz of North America, 1986).

3. David Scott-Moncrieff, St John Nixon and Clarence Paget, *Three-Pointed Star — the Story of Mercedes Benz* (Cassell, 1955).

4. Frederick Simms, quoted in Kimes, *The Star and the Laurel*, p 78.

5. Harry Niemann, *Wilhelm Maybach: The Father of Mercedes* (Mercedes-Benz AG, 1996).

6. Guy Jellinek-Mercedes, *My Father Mr Mercedes* (G T Foulis, 1966).

7. Quoted in ibid, p 100.

8. Quoted in Niemann, *Wilhelm Maybach*, p 170.

9. Quoted in ibid, p 168.

10. Quoted in Jellinek-Mercedes, *My Father Mr Mercedes*, p 213.

11. June 1904, letter, Maybach to Lorenz. Quoted in Niemann, *Wilhelm Maybach*, p 154.

12. Quoted in Jellinek-Mercedes, *My Father Mr Mercedes*, p 210.

13. Quoted in ibid, p 79.

14. Friedrich Sass, quoted in Niemann, *Wilhelm Maybach*, p 196.

Chapter 6

1. W F Bradley, November 1920, quoted in Beverley Rae Kimes, *The Star and the Laurel — The Centennial History of Daimler, Mercedes and Benz, 1886–1986* (Mercedes-Benz of North America, 1986), p 168.

2. Richard Langworth, *Mercedes-Benz — The First Hundred Years* (Beekman House, 1984).

3. ibid.

Chapter 7

1. Barbara Hopmann, Mark Spoerer, Birgit Weitz, Beate Brüninghaus, *Zwangsarbeit bei Daimler-Benz* (Franz Steiner Verlag, 1994).

2. In 1999, DaimlerChrysler was one of the founding members of the German Economy Foundation Initiative 'Remembrance, Responsibility and the Future'. The Foundation Initiative and the German Federal Government jointly contributed DM 10.1 billion. While the main purpose of the Foundation is to provide humanitarian help to former forced labourers and to compensate other victims of National Socialism, a Future Fund was also established to foster projects that promote better understanding and highlight the dangers of totalitarian regimes.

3. Neil Gregor, *Daimler-Benz in the Third Reich* (Yale University Press, 1998), p 249.

4. Dr Friedrich Schildberger, *The Annals of Mercedes-Benz Motor Vehicles and Engines* (Daimler-Benz AG, 1961)

5. Dennis Adler, *Mercedes-Benz, Silver Star Century* (Motorbooks International, 2001).

6. Volker Steinmaier, *DaimlerChrysler: spurring economic prosperity in Baden-Württemberg, in 50 Years of Baden-Württemberg* (Baden-Württemberg regional statistics, Stuttgart, 2002)

Chapter 8

1. Matthias Horx and Peter Wippermann, *Markenkult-Kultmarken* (Econ Verlag).

2. David Lewis, 'Jürgen Schrempp: Rambo in Pinstripes of Global Pioneer?', copyright FT, 2001.

Chapter 9

1. Matthias Horx and Peter Wippermann, *Markenkult-Kultmarken* (Econ Verlag).

2. P Marsh and P Collett, *Driving Passion, The Psychology of the Car* (Jonathan Cape, 1986).

3. James P Womack, Daniel T Jones, Daniel Roos, Donna Sammons Carpenter, *The Machine that Changed the World* (Rawson Associates/Simon & Schuster, 1990).

Chapter 10

1. James Collins and Jerry Porras, *Built to Last* (Random House, 1994).

Chapter 11

1 Paul Lienert, 'Chrysler Up/Mercedes down move may backfire on DCX' (*The Detroit News Autos Insider*, 23 July 2003).

2 UK *Financial Times*; 29 October 2004.

3 UK *Autocar*; 26 October 2004.

4. Jim Collins, *Good to Great* (Random House, 2001).

PHOTO CREDITS

Key
b = bottom; c = centre; l = left; lc = left column; r = right ; rc = right column; s = second; t = top; th = third

Cover image and all other images reproduced by permission of DaimlerChrysler AG except the following:

pp 6–7 © Leslie Butterfield; p 8 (lc t) Hiroshi Takahashi/Photonica; p 8 (lc th) reproduced by permission of John Adrian; p 8 (lc b) Kari-Roland Schröter/Photonica; p 8 (rc b) Photodisc Collection /Getty Images; p 9 (lc t) Alan R Moller/The Image Bank/Getty Images; p 9 (lc s) Panoramic Images /Getty Images; p 9 (lc b) E Jane Armstrong /Botanica/Getty Images; p 10 Hiroshi Takahashi /Photonica; p 12 reproduced by permission of Giorgio Armani; p 14 © 2005 Andy Warhol Foundation for the visual Arts/Artists Rights Society (ARS), New York; p 22 *American Gigolo* © Paramount Pictures. All Rights Reserved/Richard Gere; p 23 (l) the Coca-Cola logo is a registered trademark of the Coca-Cola Company; p 23 (sl) the Gillette logo is a registered trademark of The Gillette Company; p 23 (th l) used with permission from McDonald's Corporation; p 23 (r) reproduced by permission of SONY; p 26 (r) © Royalty-Free/Corbis; p 27 (r) reproduced by permission of John Eden; p 30 (l) reproduced by permission of N Harris; p 30 (sl, th l, r) reproduced by permission of the car owners; p 33 reproduced by permission of Morgan Freeman/Selah Media; pp 34–35 and p 36 reproduced by permission of John Adrian; p 38 © the Coca-Cola Company; Original illustration by Haddon Sundblom; p 44 Getty Images; p 48 (l) and (c) reproduced by permission of Schlegelmilch; pp 52–53 Karl-Roland Schröter /Photonica; p 57 reproduced by permission of Livio De Marchi/DaimlerChrysler AG; p 58 (l + r) reproduced by permission of John Adrian; p 59 reproduced by permission of *Auto Bild*; p 60 David Gray, Images Brighton; p 61 EMPICS/PA; p 64 reproduced by permission of VW AG; p 65 reproduced by permission of Volvo Car UK/AMV BBDO; p 66 © Leslie Butterfield; p 72 INTERFOTO/Archiv Friedrich; p 87 © Leslie Butterfield; p 106 reproduced by permission of Schlegelmilch; p 109 © Leslie Butterfield; p 114 PE Reed/Photonica; p 117 reproduced by permission of Leslie Butterfield; p 118 reproduced by permission of Deutsche Bank; p 133 Manuela Hoefer/Stone /Getty Images; pp 134–135 Photodisc Collection /Getty Images; p 136 © Popperfoto.com; p 140 Walter Sanders/Time & Life Pictures/Getty Images; p 148 (t) and (br) © Corbis; p 148 (bl) ™& © HLC Properties, Ltd. All Rights Reserved. Licensed by Global Icons/ArtMM AG; p 152 reproduced by permission of Adam Opel AG; Thanks also to car brochure collector Edwin Storm; p 154 reproduced by permission of DPA/Frankfurt; pp 156–157 Alan R Moller/The Image Bank/Getty Images; p 160 INTERFOTO/Archiv Friedrich; p 161 © John Vachon/Getty Images; p 162 (l) reproduced by permission of Haymarket Publishing Services Ltd; p 162 (r) and p 163 (l) MPL - National Motor Museum; p 163 (r) reproduced by permission of Volvo Car UK; p 165 Masaaki Toyoura/Taxi/Getty Images; p 167 reproduced by permission of BMW AG; p 172 © Duane Rieder/Getty Images; p 176 MPL - National Motor Museum; p 177 EMPICS/PA; pp 178–179 Panoramic Images/Getty Images; p 185 reproduced by permission of Abendzeitung; p 189 reproduced by permission of Warren Dean Bonett; p 210 The Associated Press GMBH, Frankfurt/Main; p 211 reproduced by permission of Boris Becker/Gabo Trivellini/Iver Hansen/DaimlerChrysler AG; p 216 reproduced by permission of Daniel Hartz/DaimlerChrysler AG; p 217 reproduced by permission of Peter Gehrke /DaimlerChrysler AG; p 219 © Leslie Butterfield; p 220 Ralph Morse/Time & Life Pictures/Getty Images; p 224 Thinkstock/Getty Images; pp 226–227 E Jane Armstrong/Botanica/Getty Images; p 232 reproduced by permission of Schlegelmilch; p 239 reproduced by permission of René Staud Studios; p 242 reproduced by permission of Schlegelmilch/DaimlerChrysler AG; p 247 © 1974 Chip Lord, Hudson Marquez, Doug Michels; p 248 reproduced by permission of Warren Dean Bonett/DaimlerChrysler AG; p 251 reproduced by permission of Emir Haveric/DaimlerChrysler AG; p 272 reproduced by permission of René Staud Studios

100 Jahre Daimler-Motoren-Gesellschaft 1890–1990 (Mercedes-Benz AG, 1990)

100 Jahre Mercedes (HEEL Verlag GmbH, 2001)

Adler, Dennis, *Mercedes-Benz: Silver Star Century* (MBI Publishing, 2001)

Automobile Leidenschaft: Mercedes-Benz und Springer & Jacoby (Stern, 2002)

Benz & Cie, Zum 150 Geburtstag von Karl Benz (Motorbuch Verlag, 1994)

Benz, Karl, *Lebensfahrt Eines Deutschen Erfinders: Meine Erinnerungen* (Koehler & Amelang, 2001)

Bols, Udo, *Mercedes PKW: Eine Chronik von 1886 bis 1996*, (Verlag Walter Podszun, 1996)

Bolsinger, Markus and Becker, Clauspeter, *Mercedes-Benz Silver Arrows* (Delius, Klasing, 2002)

Chronik 1883–1998 (DaimlerChrysler AG, 2000)

Engelen, Günter and Riedner, Mike, *Mercedes-Benz 300 SL — Vom Rennsport zur Legende* (Motorbuch Verlag, 1999)

Frostick, Michael, *The Mighty Mercedes* (Dalton Watson, 1971)

Gregor, Neil, *Daimler-Benz in the Third Reich* (Yale University Press, 1998)

Harmsworth, Alfred C, *Motors and Motor Driving* (Longmans, Green, 1902)

Henry, Alan, *Mercedes in Motorsport — Pioneers in Perfection* (Haynes, 2001)

Jellinek-Mercedes, Guy, *My Father Mr Mercedes* (GT Foulis, 1966)

Kimes, Beverly Rae, *The Star and the Laurel — The Centennial History of Daimler, Mercedes and Benz, 1886–1986* (Mercedes-Benz of North America, 1986)

Kruk, Max and Lingnau, Gerold, *100 Jahre Daimler-Benz: Das Unternehmen* (Hase & Koehler Verlag, 1986)

Langworth, Richard, *Mercedes-Benz — The First Hundred Years* (Beekman House, 1984)

Ludvigsen, Karl Eric, *Mercedes-Benz Quicksilver Century* (Transport Bookman Publications, 1995)

Ludvigsen, Karl Eric, *Mercedes-Benz Renn- und Sportwagen* (Motorbuch Verlag, 1999)

Marsh, Peter and Collett, Peter, Driving Passion, *The Psychology of the Car* (Faber and Faber, 1987)

Mercedes-Benz in Japan: The Shining Star in the Land of the Rising Sun (DaimlerChrysler Japan Co., Ltd, 2002)

Niemann, Harry, *Gottlieb Daimler: Fabriken, Banken und Motoren* (Delius Klasing, 2000)

BIBLIOGRAPHY

Niemann, Harry, *Béla Barényi: The Father of Passive Safety* (Mercedes-Benz AG, 1994)

Niemann, Harry, *Wilhelm Maybach: The Father of Mercedes* (Mercedes-Benz AG, 1996)

Nixon, St John C, *The Invention of the Automobile* (Country Life, 1936)

Oswald, Werner, *Mercedes-Benz Personenwagen 1886–1986* (Motorbuch Verlag, 1987)

Peters, Wolfgang and Zöllter, Jürgen, *Die Herausforderung: Die Beschleunigung der Marke Mercedes-Benz* (Delius, Klasing, 2004)

Robson, Graham, *Magnificent Mercedes: The Complete History of the Marque* (Foulis, 1981)

Rosengarten Philipp G, and Stürmer, Christoph B, *Premium Power, Das Geheimnis des Erfolgs von Mercedes-Benz, BMW, Porsche und Audi* (Wiley, 2004)

Schildberger, Dr Friedrich, *The Annals of Mercedes-Benz Motor Vehicles and Engines* (Daimler-Benz AG, 1961)

Schlegelmilch, Rainer and Lehbrink, Hartmut, *Mercedes Volume 1* (Konemann Verlagsgesellschaft, 1997)

Schlegelmilch, Rainer and Lehbrink, Hartmut, *Mercedes Volume 2* (Konemann Verlagsgesellschaft, 1997)

Scott-Moncrieff, David, St John Nixon and Clarence Paget, *The Three-Pointed Star — The Story of Mercedes-Benz* (Cassell, 1955)

Scott-Moncrieff, David, *Veteran and Edwardian Motor Cars* (BT Batsford, 1955)

Simsa, Paul and Lewandowski, Jurgen, *Sterne Stars und Majestäten — Prominenz auf Mercedes-Benz* (Verlag Stadler, 1997)

Simsa, Paul, Spross, Hans Jürgen and Wendt, Horst I (with introduction by Helmut Werner), *Der Stern Ihrer Sehnucht: Plakate und Anzeigen von Mercedes-Benz 1900–1960* (Cantz, 1995)

Vlasic, Bill and Sterz, Bradley A, *Taken for a Ride — How Mercedes-Benz Drove off with Chrysler* (Wiley, 2002)

Wright, Nicky, *Mercedes: The Enduring Legend* (Tiger Books International, 1991)

The new S-Class, launched at the Frankfurt Motorshow, 2005